The World and Richard Nixon

By C. L. Sulzberger

Such a Peace: The Roots and Ashes of Yalta (1982)
How I Committed Suicide (1982)
Marina (1978)
The Tallest Liar (1977)
Seven Continents and Forty Years (1977)
The Fall of Eagles (1977)
Go Gentle into the Night (1976)
The Coldest War: Russia's Game in China (1974)
Postscript with a Chinese Accent (1974)
An Age of Mediocrity (1973)
Unconquered Souls: The Resistentialists (1973)
The Tooth Merchant (1973)
The Last of the Giants (1970)
A Long Row of Candles (1969)
American Heritage History of World War II (1966)
Unfinished Revolution: American and the Third World (1965)
The Test: De Gaulle and Algeria (1962)
My Brother Death (1961)
What's Wrong with U.S. Foreign Policy (1959)
The Big Thaw (1956)
Sit-Down with John L. Lewis (1938)

The World and Richard Nixon

C. L. Sulzberger

Prentice Hall Press • New York

Published by Prentice Hall Press
A Division of Simon & Schuster, Inc.
Gulf + Western Building
One Gulf + Western Plaza
New York, NY 10023

Library of Congress Cataloging-in-Publication Data

Sulzberger, C. L. (Cyrus Leo), 1912–
The World and Richard Nixon.

Bibliography: p.
1. Nixon, Richard M. (Richard Milhous),
1913– . 2. United States—Foreign relations—
1969–1974. I. Title.
E856.S85 1987 327.73'0092'4 86-25535
ISBN 0-13-622994-8

Text Design by Barbara Bert

Manufactured in the United States of America

10 9 8 7 6 5 4 3 2 1

First Edition

This book is for
Jessica Berry and
Jonathan Berry.

With all my thanks to Eda Pallier and Fiona Terris for their great job in editing and typing.

Contents

Preface

Having lived abroad for almost fifty years, I have perforce lost considerable contact with my native land despite frequent visits, and on a recent trip to the New York and Washington areas, I was astonished at the emotional dislike for Richard Nixon I discovered among all kinds of people—old and young, rich and poor, Democrat and Republican. It was not just political disagreement but vituperative personal hatred, words deliberately chosen by me to describe the feeling of the majority of those with whom I spoke. I had no intention of taking an informal poll on the former president, but after my first two exposures to this unexpected phenomenon, I resolved to keep sounding out those I encountered to ascertain how accurate my first impressions had been.

To my surprise, despite the passage of time since the Watergate scandal, the fevered detestation seemed to continue unabated. There was anger at the law-breaking activity of the CIA under presidential orders, at the actual criminal break-in at Democratic offices, at the ridiculous taping of all conversations, and even at the pardon obtained from Gerald Ford after Nixon's associates were arrested and ultimately sent to prison. This anger was, I found, astonishingly personal, not in the least abstract. It was the same kind of personal hatred that survivors of Hitler and Stalin in Germany and Russia felt toward their persecutors.

I cannot explain this extraordinarily venomous sentiment, this blind rage that focused its attention entirely on one man and displayed not the faintest sign of forgiveness. Few among those who indignantly protested my lack of comprehension were willing to concede that there was anything in the least bit good about the former U.S. chief of state. Among those few were some who grudgingly admitted that Nixon had shown statesmanlike qualities in dealing with world affairs. But, for the most part, when I objected that at least it must be conceded by even the most carping critics that Nixon had displayed great knowledge and talent in his successful handling of foreign policy, the most frequent comment was, "So what!"

I acknowledge that absence from one's native land can often produce a gap in knowledge of all its problems. But I simply cannot acknowledge that this alone is the reason for such a blind division of analysis. I firmly believe that Nixon will be adjudged a better president by future historians than his contemporaries now seem willing to allow. Moreover, I fear that for some years to come, the bias will, if anything, become more prejudiced and more venomous as inquiring investigators work their way through the vast body of Nixon tapes (some five years' worth) that have been accumulated in the National Archives.

Thanks to his idiotic habit of recording all remarks (including his own) made either in person or on the telephone by those in the presidential ken near enough to a microphone or receiver to be heard and registered, an enormous body of valueless observations, magnetically capable of attracting distortion, is available for tomorrow's researchers. It is well known that Nixon often spoke loosely when he was fatigued and especially when he had had a drink, and many of his associates who were aware of this weakness scrupulously avoided comment on such petulance when it occurred. But such moderation or understanding will not be the trend among researchers of the future, above all those worn out by incessant shuffling through dusty pages of nasty taped comments by a man whose thoughts were certainly not always pure.

Much evidence is already available to the public in the White House tapes held by the National Archives that Nixon, especially under stress, often used bad, even coarse and obscene, language. This foible is certainly undignified and distressing when viewed or heard by history. Moreover, it is especially peculiar that Nixon, who of course knew that all his words were being taped as he spoke, should have ignored this embarrassing fact.

Nevertheless, this book is not intended to analyze Nixon's

behavior in its totality or to explain his singular unpopularity from the days of his start in political life. This book is intended as an examination of the foreign policy of a man who showed himself a remarkably adept and far-sighted statesman—as he was and still is perceived overseas, even if this positive fact is obscured at home by the frayed tempers of so many of his countrymen. At best—as demonstrated by his behavior on internal matters and by the enraged popular reaction it stimulated—Nixon's was a flawed personality. But he was also a man of quality, and on those diplomatic affairs he understood better than any American president this century, his value to his country merits praise and gratitude.

C.L.S.

I

Janus

Richard Nixon proved to be a paradox as president. In internal affairs his record as chief of state was disastrous. With respect to these, he chose several bad and corruptible advisers and behaved in an injudicious, immoral way himself. This contrasted sharply with his oft-pronounced respect for morality, learned from his devoutly Quaker mother. Watergate was the consequence of this ethical lapse. History will judge him harshly for his own role in that dirty affair and also for that of the advisers he chose and in whom he placed his confidence. Only thanks to the blanket pardon Nixon was issued by Gerald Ford—successor to the office from which he was forced to resign—did he escape probable criminal charges.

In external affairs, however, Nixon's record shows a remarkable divergence from his behavior in the scandal that will always be associated with his name. Nixon's foreign policy was, on the whole, a glowing success with important long-term results, despite the Vietnam cancer inherited from his predecessors. His positive achievements with respect to the Soviet Union and the People's Republic of China were accomplished with singular skill.

He had already prepared himself arduously for a statesman's role by foreign travel and frequent consultations with statesmen from other lands. And—from 1968, when he first entered the White House, until 1974, when he was driven out—he appointed distinguished aides to help him in perceiving and influencing the course of world history.

Because an American president's internal power and prestige are closely involved in his ability to influence events abroad, Nixon's foreign policy was adversely affected by the weakening of his position. I have no doubt that he would have striven more successfully to ward off the Vietnam disaster had he not been inhibited by the rapidly mounting Watergate cover-up, which cost him support at home and prestige abroad. And I suspect he might have reacted more vigorously and successfully than he did when Turkey invaded Cyprus in August 1974, at the very instant of his political collapse.

Thus, I think it is a good conjecture that Nixon might have staved off or mitigated the final Vietnam disaster in 1973, and also avoided the Cyprus crisis and its consequences in 1974, had there been no Watergate and the ensuing storm of criticism that crippled his political position and reduced his popular support for many months before he was forced out of office.

But this is a guess. The Vietnam War had been passed on by Presidents Kennedy, who sent the first 16,000 U.S. troops there, and Johnson, who enormously multiplied their strength. Yet it is dubious that America could have avoided defeat in the end no matter how prestigious Nixon's position. After all, in addition to the dogged and courageous Vietnamese Communists, both Russia and China, despite their own quarrel, joined in helping the valorous, skillful, and remarkably persistent Vietcong.

Nixon's direct involvement of the United States in the Southeast Asian war was an inheritance from the two Democratic administrations preceding his, just as Gorbachev, in Moscow, inherited the Afghanistan mess from his predecessors. Nixon had his Kennedy and Johnson; Gorbachev his Brezhnev, Andropov, and Chernenko. Yet there is little possibility of a "Kremlingate" to frustrate Gorbachev's search for a solution to his Asian war.

In Cyprus, likewise, Nixon inherited a historical hatred between Greek and Turk that would almost surely have erupted again even had there been no 1974 Turkish invasion of Cyprus.

Vietnam and Cyprus may be classed as the two blazing failures of Nixon's foreign policy, but in each case he inherited situations and did not create them. Nor was it likely that any American president could have done anything significantly different to avoid ensuing strains. Nixon took refuge from the Vietnam disaster by blaming Congress.

On the whole, Nixon's foreign policy was successful and cleverly conceived. A man reared on Quaker morals, he failed on Watergate's internal moral issues; but, a man who had deliberately educated himself on foreign policy, he accomplished great things —above all with the two Communist powers, Russia and China. Russia and China each helped the Vietnamese Communists defeat the United States yet negotiated substantial improvements in their relations with Nixon's administration. This situation may be compared with that of Gorbachev, who seems to want better relations with Washington while the United States helps Afghan guerrillas fight Soviet troops in their country.

Nixon determined from the start to elaborate and supervise the enactment of his own policy conceptions on a country-by-country global basis. Other nations were regarded with particular attention to their role vis-à-vis the Soviet Union. Nixon's was the most complete conception of an overall policy for a great-power America that had been produced by any U.S. president since Woodrow Wilson. And, to a large extent, it had evolved from the Wilsonian dream, although the latter ignored most of Asia, all of Africa, and even much of Latin America.

To denigrate Nixon's foreign policy because it was flawed by the Vietnam inheritance and overshadowed by the dirty Watergate mess is to misread Nixon's historical importance. It would be like dismissing General and President Ulysses S. Grant as only an alcoholic, or Richard Wagner as a composer because he was a boastful anti-Semite, or ignoring Oscar Wilde the artist because he was a homosexual.

Janus, the Roman god of gates and doorways, of all beginnings, is traditionally symbolized by a head bearing two faces—one bearded, one shaven—wholly different from each other. Better than any other ancient deity he symbolizes Richard Nixon, the bifocal president seen through such contrasting optics by the American people who felt deceived by him and by a large body of foreigners, aware of the helpful impact on their own fates of his policy. One face—truculent, dark, glowering, frequently saturnine—gazes across Watergate at America's convulsive political scene. The other—smiling, open, confident—looks overseas toward China, Russia, and the Middle East.

To Americans, whose curiously moral indignation is a powerful factor in national emotions, Nixon's behavior in the Watergate affair was so scandalous and offensive to their concepts of legal propriety and proclaimed rectitude that its stain on the country's honor blotted out the other accomplishments of his White House career.

To foreigners, above all Europeans and Chinese, what Americans saw as a blot eclipsing their moral reputation, was merely a foolish lapse of propriety on the part of a man who had manifested great distinction in his diplomatic accomplishments.

At the height of the scandal that marred Nixon's presidential image, cynical Frenchmen were shrugging their shoulders and commenting, "*Eh! Nous avons été Watergaté tant de fois* [We've been Watergated so many times]," referring to the private antics of some of their own past leaders.

They could not understand the puritanical horror that rose up across the Atlantic. Nor, for their part, could most Americans—used to occasional presidential sex play—comprehend the earlier fury of the British at the Profumo affair. They imagined that their English cousins were being stuffy about the dalliance of a cabinet minister with a call girl, whom he indiscreetly shared with a Soviet attaché, not that it was a shocking constitutional case in which a member of the government lied to the House of Commons.

I am writing this in an effort to indicate that Nixon will be less remembered by history for his dismal role in Watergate and his defeat in Vietnam than for his visionary view and steady hand in defining and implementing the role of the United States at a critical time in world affairs, and to explain why.

The contrast between the two Nixons, the one as seen at home and the other as seen abroad, is striking. A large number of Americans think of their former president as no more than a crafty and deceitful politician who violated the ethics of his office by ordering a break-in at the private preserves of the Democratic party, his political opponents, and who then, after his helots had accomplished these aims, sacrificed them on the altar of justice without even taking the precaution of destroying self-incriminating evidence in his possession.

But, in the fundamental view of a majority of foreigners qualified to follow the diplomatic travails of a complex and uneasy world, Nixon was the image of a subtle American chief of state with a global vision able clearly to perceive the basic elements of world confusion—one who elaborated a strategy of steering mistrustful powers away from the looming chasm of nuclear war. For the allied nations of the West, and for China and Japan, the face of Nixon is that of a shrewd statesman endowed with a diplomatic wisdom unusual in American presidents.

Throughout my adult life I have kept a diary. By glancing through its innumerable pages I find that Nixon's overseas reputation was already high before he won the presidency.

It has been my destiny to travel all seven continents and to encounter many leaders, both friendly and hostile, with whom our government had to deal. And during the Eisenhower years Nixon's international importance was steadily increasing. His name cropped up in conversations with those who guided the affairs of other nations, particularly in Europe and Asia.

To give at least a slight idea of the opposition between the face of Nixon that was seen to smile abroad and the one that frowned at home, I quote various examples from my diaries.

In August 1956 I dined in New York with Randolph Churchill, son of Britain's great prime minister and himself a widely traveled and observant journalist. The moment was during the U.S. presidential campaign. Eisenhower was the candidate of a relatively conservative Republican party for reelection against the liberal Democratic spokesman, Adlai Stevenson. I noted: "It was the first time Randolph had ever met Nixon and he thinks N. is a very fine fellow. 'Quite grown up.' He was so impressed that he says: 'I'm the only man in the world who supports a Stevenson-Nixon ticket.'"

In October 1959 I had a long talk in Djakarta with President Sukarno of Indonesia. Sukarno was considered a left-winger, which meant only that he favored the Soviet Union, not that his internal politics were remotely "liberal." I recalled of our talk: "Sukarno liked Nixon a lot. He considered him a good, direct man to do business with. He didn't care much for Adlai Stevenson (despite the theory among liberals that Adlai appeals to Asia). Sukarno thought him too vague and 'philosophical.' He didn't think Adlai really understood things. He preferred Nixon."

In October 1968 I visited Bucharest and talked with the Rumanian chief of state, Nicolae Ceauçescu, a relatively independent (of Moscow) Communist and certainly not to be considered an automatic supporter of any American conservative.

I asked what he thought of Nixon, whom he'd met two years earlier. "He was diffident. 'I don't want to seem to interfere in your affairs,' he kept saying. But, we had a very good talk. He impressed me. He showed a real understanding of international problems and of our own situation. I found that we agreed very substantially on China. We both thought there could be no solid basis for world peace until China was brought into it. We also agreed on disarmament. He impressed me as being an experienced and knowledgeable man."

The following year I lunched in Paris with André Malraux, the splendid French writer and resistance hero, a member of de Gaulle's cabinet and the closest to the general of any of the ministers. Nixon had visited Paris during his first year in the White House. Malraux recalled: "The visit here had been extraordinarily successful. Malraux himself had talked at length with Nixon and Kissinger (who accompanied Nixon). Both he and the General had found that Nixon had grown enormously in stature and was well informed. De Gaulle had an odd personal sympathy for Nixon, which was probably based on the fact that Nixon also had had his 'period of exile' [eight years, after losing to Kennedy in 1960], and de Gaulle knew what he had suffered. He had made a point of keeping in touch with him occasionally during this period and undoubtedly Nixon was deeply grateful." (De Gaulle's political "exile" lasted twelve years in France.)

In 1969 de Gaulle sent a message to Nixon saying: "I have for you...with good reason...esteem, confidence and friendship as great and as sincere as it is possible to have."

In May 1970 French foreign minister Maurice Schumann told me: "After Nixon's announcement of the dispatch of American troops into Cambodia to strike at Vietcong sanctuaries, there was no prospect in the near future of the overall Indochina peace conference France had been working for. But France won't forget it and will continue to repeat the suggestion.... The official reaction we announced was moderate. But in fact we feel much more strongly. However, we respect President Nixon and we wish to do no more to embarrass him."

On July 16, 1971, I saw President Giuseppe Saragat of Italy. Nixon had just announced he intended to visit Peking within ten months. Saragat asked rhetorically: "Why all this melodrama about China? Why did Nixon have to announce this thing and plan his trip in such a melodramatic way? We [Italy] are a country of melodrama, but even we were startled. Of course, we agree with what Nixon is doing. Months ago we recognized China ourselves. We think this is a good thing, as long as it is not taken as a move directed against Russia."

On March 31, 1972, the skillful Soviet ambassador in Washington, Anatoly Dobrynin, admitted to me that Nixon's project of a Peking trip had initially excited suspicion in Moscow. But this had since vanished; Moscow knew there had been no secret U.S.–Chinese alliance. Furthermore, Moscow knew that Russia was more important to the Nixon administration than was China. Russia and the United States remained *the* superpowers and there was no escaping this: "They can destroy each other and no one else can destroy them."

My friend Malraux, who knew China and China's leaders well, observed (Paris, April 21, 1972):

> Nixon is a strong, serious, tough man who learned a great deal from adversity after his defeat in 1960. He has a more profound sense of honesty than Kennedy. Kennedy was like a young boxer. He was nothing but reflexes—jabs and reactions. But Nixon thinks along deliberate patterns.
>
> Nixon had very wisely decided that it wasn't important to visit China on the basis of equality with Mao Tse-tung. Mao received Nixon for only one hour, and that probably meant less than thirty minutes of exchange if one allows for interpretation and trivialities....But Nixon did not care. He wanted to show the Russians. This was the biggest purpose of the trip, and it was very successful. Nixon was setting the stage for the much more important meeting with Brezhnev.

Three weeks later, in Paris, I lunched with Colonel General Koča Popović, until recently foreign minister of Yugoslavia and a practiced Marxist, Tito-style. He said: "The Nixon trip [a few months earlier] to Yugoslavia was a great success. Nixon had made a clever and correct move in ordering the blockade of North Vietnam, but nobody believed he could ultimately achieve a real military victory."

In Belgrade, Tito's capital, Milovan Djilas, a former Politburo chief who had dissented from the regime, said (August 5, 1972) that Nixon's trips to Moscow and Peking together constituted:

> a very impressive, historical event, as important as a war. This showed that Nixon understood what communism is. President Johnson played on the conflict between the Russians and the Chinese. That is a classical kind of policy. But Nixon saw it would be better to have good relations with both of them—while at the same time remaining strong. He knows you can't afford to be weak, but this has nothing to do with the Russian-Chinese question....
>
> The United States won the cold war because of the internal disintegration of communism; because you remained strong you were able to accelerate this inevitable process. Nixon's Peking and Moscow trips were a result of this cold war victory. But the United States should neither overestimate nor underestimate that victory. You won because you are nonideological and thus were able to avoid a stalemate like that which prevailed between Christianity and Islam after their wars, a victory for neither side.

Michel Jobert, an astute Frenchman who served as executive officer of the Elysée Palace (France's White House) and then as Georges Pompidou's foreign minister, considered (Paris, October 18, 1972) that the "three rocks" of great importance in the political world were Nixon, President Pompidou, and British prime minister Edward Heath. Their importance, in the order named, was that each had the "ability to make decisions and stick with them."

Shah Reza Pahlevi (Teheran, April 14, 1973) confided: "Fortunately I have always had good relations with U.S. leaders: Eisenhower, Johnson, and above all Nixon, whom I have known since 1953."

The dark shadow of Watergate at last had become so long that foreign leaders realized that it was not just a minor political squabble among American politicians but could destroy a government on which they depended heavily. I had lunch in Paris with Jean Monnet, father of the Common Market and European Community (May 18, 1973) and asked him if he thought that Nixon's diminished authority because of the Watergate scandal would delay or frustrate negotiations between the United States and Europe. He said: "Everything could be affected unless Nixon wins his battle. It would be catastrophic if he were stripped of his power. But I don't think this will happen."

That June I had a drink with Hervé Alphand, formerly de Gaulle's ambassador in Washington and a distinguished diplomat. He believed that "Nixon learned his foreign policy from de Gaulle. It is a policy which in essence is that nations have a national interest and ideologies must be ignored in favor of this national interest. Nixon learned this from us."

In 1973, as the Watergate crisis rumbled along, Harold Macmillan wrote to Nixon: "I trust that these clouds may soon roll away and that you may be able to take up with enthusiasm the task of promoting the Peace and Prosperity of the world to which you have already made such a notable contribution."

At the same time Japan's prime minister Eisaku Sato wrote: "As an old personal friend of yours, I have firm and quiet confidence...that you, as the great leader of this hope, will succeed in reestablishing the greater authority and integrity of your own office."

On October 26, 1973, I had a lengthy interview in Peking with Chou En-lai, the Chinese prime minister and foreign minister, one of this century's shrewdest and wisest statesmen. I asked him whether he thought the Watergate scandal had had any effect on Sino-American relations. "None," he replied.

> And we never use the word "scandal" when discussing this. Since it is entirely your own internal affair, we have never published anything about it in our press. It doesn't affect the overall situation. Only our Reference News Ser-

> vice [the unpublished reports put out by the official news agency, Hsinhua] mentions it and issues American commentaries....
>
> President Nixon and Mr. Kissinger opened up a new channel, and the joint Shanghai communiqué shows that there are common grounds as well as differences. In this respect the past year and a half have shown certain useful developments. There has been a great development in the exchange of individual visits of our citizens, and this constitutes a breakthrough. Both the Chinese and the American peoples want to be friendly....
>
> And President Nixon, at Kansas City on July 6, 1971, when he spoke to journalists, said that at the end of World War II the United States never dreamed that its prestige would sink so far [because of Vietnam] during a quarter of a century. I think it was honest of him to say this....
>
> Moreover, even if the Democrats elect the next president, they won't be isolationist either. President Nixon put it frankly when he openly expressed his opposition to isolationism. It is odd that in the past it was the Republicans who favored isolationism and now it seems to be the Democrats. But neither will achieve it.

Australia's Liberal prime minister, Gough Whitlam, voiced similar views that year (1973). He told me (Sydney, March 1973) that he was "encouraged" by U.S. policy. "What President Nixon has done to achieve entente with China and Russia is salutary. These are very great milestones." (This represented a big shift from Whitlam's earlier anger at Nixon for ordering heavy air raids on North Vietnam.)

It is interesting to include in this assessment by foreigners of an American chief of state the views of Kurt Waldheim, the Austrian president who in December 1985 had just completed his term as secretary-general of the United Nations.

> Nixon had little regard for the United Nations. However, I am obliged to say that in the field of foreign policy, one could not but appreciate his knowledge, vision, and skill. Of the four presidents with whom I have dealt, he was the best prepared for his diplomatic responsibilities.
>
> I particularly admired the way in which he managed the opening up of American attitudes toward the People's

Republic of China. I doubt that any American president who did not have strong backing from American conservatives could have run such a high political risk. I also appreciated his management of the détente policy toward the Soviet Union. Both these initiatives contributed materially to an improvement in international relations at the time, and their effect was quickly and beneficially evident at the UN.

The most complete analysis of Nixon as a statesman was given to me (January 22, 1986) by Maurice Couve de Murville, a former prime minister of France and probably the finest French foreign minister since Talleyrand. Couve told me:

> It's not easy to give a judgment, but it seems to me that Nixon was a very good president for the United States. I mean in terms of foreign policy, because I can't judge otherwise. The question, of course, is what was the respective merit of Nixon and of Kissinger, because Kissinger played an immense role in foreign policy and gave the impression he could decide and do everything on his own. Which is probably not so true as it seems....
>
> A good example is the Vietnamese affair and the respective roles of Nixon and Kissinger in leading the United States to peace. I suppose that the decision in principle and all the big decisions afterward were taken by Nixon. And that Kissinger was more of an instrument than a decision maker, it seems to me, but I don't know. You see, what gave us at the starting point a good impression of Nixon was his journey in Europe, beginning with France. I think it was in the year 1969, when he took office. It was immediately after taking office. When he came he stayed two days, and we had discussions with him, and it was entirely on his initiative, and it was he who spoke all the time and who took a position on most of the big problems....
>
> He gave us his opinion on the most important points of French foreign policy from NATO to nuclear weapons. So of course that made a good impression, and when he was gone we had the idea that he was taking things personally in hand in order to have a policy that would be much more satisfactory to us than the policy of his predecessors. After that, of course, a few weeks, some time, I don't know who was secretary of state, he is forgotten now; yes,

that was Rogers then. He was forgotten even when he was in office....

When Kissinger took the job, of course, everything concentrated around him. And he gave the impression that he was deciding everything, which I think is not true as we said, for instance, on Vietnam. Nixon had made the decision a long time ago. I would say from the beginning. And Nixon was, I think, of the opinion that we had been avoiding establishing official relations with China. I mean he was very free in his judgments. And especially, that point is even more astonishing because before he was elected as president he had never done anything special. He wanted to finish with the Vietnam affair. He knew he couldn't win; therefore he wanted to get out....

And then Nixon played rather cleverly, using his Chinese policy to affect his Soviet policy. First China itself. He felt it was silly to continue the policy that had been followed since the war, that meant not having anything to do with Mao. It was normal, sheer common sense to establish relations with Mao. That was one part. The other part was linked to relations with the Soviet Union and the fact that it was the time things were beginning to change between East and West. In fact, the starting point, the point at which things began to change, was with the Berlin Wall, which was an evident demonstration that neither the Soviet Union, who announced their intentions and decided to be defensive, nor the West, who did not interfere whatsoever, wanted war. I mean it began to change at that time....

Things began to change before Nixon came in, but he saw China was a way to strengthen his position vis-à-vis the Soviet Union, and in fact it's exactly what happened....

I have a feeling that Nixon really started the U.S.A. on a policy of détente and people forget it.

Couve spoke willingly and well. He had known Truman, Eisenhower, Kennedy, Johnson, and briefly Carter; he never met Ford. But Nixon he had seen several times, and he thought Nixon was the best U.S. president this century on foreign policy.

Couve thought Nixon had been a true "statesman" in foreign policy, although it was never easy to distinguish in American foreign policy of the time what was Nixon's. Kissinger played a well-publicized role. This was especially true on Vietnam. Nixon and Kissinger worked together toward peace and extricating the

United States from the war, but the big decision, as all major decisions then, had been taken by Nixon.

France had much praise for Nixon's policy because, like France's own, it was based on facts, on realities, not on prejudices or presumptions. Nixon made the basic decision to make a peace and get out of Vietnam. Nixon did the decision making and Kissinger did the negotiating.

Helmut Schmidt, the brilliant former Social Democratic chancellor of the German Federal Republic, wrote to me (March 7, 1986):

> In my opinion Richard Nixon was, indeed, quite a successful international leader whose reputation still is much higher abroad than in his own country. Undoubtedly, Americans lowered their esteem for him considerably after Watergate had happened.
>
> The size of the United States, its vitality and dynamic energy, the fact that it has a genuine common market consisting of 235 million people, with a single currency and a single legal and tax system and, finally, its superior military strength, mean that the leadership role of the Western world can be assumed only by the United States.
>
> American leadership emanated from Harry Truman, George Marshall, and Dean Acheson. it was refined in Dwight Eisenhower's pragmatism, John Kennedy's vision, and Richard Nixon's outstanding ability to assess strategic situations and make the corresponding decisions.
>
> In free countries with democratic constitutions, leadership must reflect both strength of conception and the will and ability to engage in compromise and arrive at a consensus. As regards foreign politics, Richard Nixon showed this kind of leadership during his presidential years.

Considering Nixon's widespread unpopularity among so-called liberal and leftish forces both at home and abroad, these observations show the accuracy, intellectual honesty, and generosity of vision that always marked Schmidt as a singular personality, unaffected by emotional prejudices.

There is an impressive universality in these statements on the subject of Richard Nixon by his political peers abroad. As recently as March 27, 1986, Lord Home of the Hirsel, who had served his country both as foreign minister and prime minister (as

Sir Alec Douglas-Home, in order to take a seat in the House of Commons), wrote me admiringly of Nixon: "President Nixon was always extremely well-informed on international affairs. He traveled the world extensively and listened to people who told him of the problems facing their countries. He had a very retentive mind. He understood above all that a balance of power must be real, and he was therefore a consistent advocate of a strong NATO alliance. He also initiated fresh relations with China."

To summarize my impressions of what so many of the world's leaders felt was the solid success of Nixon's foreign policy, I was struck by two facts. Although Nixon came to the top in American politics as a rather right-wing conservative, foreign statesmen were not blinded by labels. He seemed to be at least as admired by left-wing and Marxist leaders as by so-called conservatives. All had compliments for this man of the right who had used his reputation as a conservative to accomplish more successful diplomacy with the left than any other U.S. president. Even Emperor Hirohito of Japan, who had met Nixon briefly as the former passed through Alaska en route to Europe, speculated with an admiring chuckle (Tokyo, March 2, 1972) on the link between Nixon's Peking visit and his trip to Moscow, admitting with evident appreciation that he saw the obvious "connection."

A second factor struck me on assessing Nixon's record as a statesman. This was the limited criticism of Nixon by foreigners with respect to the Vietnam War. Could this be because of acceptance of Nixon's formula for ending it or because of an inclination to view that conflict as one initiated by Kennedy and vastly enlarged by Johnson (both Democrats)? In other words, it wasn't "Nixon's war" —even though he was in the difficult position of trying to extricate the United States from the morass into which it had so foolishly strayed. And, despite everything, Nixon was the man who disengaged and struggled out of that swamp at immense ultimate cost.

Nixon was being a shrewd American politician as well as a wise statesman when he traveled around the world acquainting himself with foreign leaders and foreign problems. On June 23, 1967, I had a good talk in Washington with Vice-President Hubert Humphrey, who already hoped that he might be Nixon's Democratic opponent in the 1968 presidential election.

I told Humphrey it was my belief that Nixon, an expert national politician, was being very clever by traveling all around and making himself genuinely familiar with foreign policy issues as an international statesman, because he recognized that this would be issue number one in the next election. Humphrey agreed emphatically. He said:

> Nixon is pushing this. You are quite right. Don't underestimate him—even as a candidate. I wouldn't have a chance to get identified with foreign policy as vice-president because all vice-presidents are overwhelmed by their president. Don't forget that Jack Kennedy had the solid Catholic vote, the solid Jewish vote, and a lot of other solid strength, and yet Nixon ran so close behind him that a shift of only a county or two would have changed the outcome [in 1960]. He is still very much there. And he has been very responsible in his foreign policy statements.
>
> As a Republican candidate—and I think he will probably be nominated—he will run against an incumbent of his own age and not against a young nonincumbent as he did in 1960. He will run against an incumbent with scars, just the way he himself has scars, and not against an unscarred young nonincumbent. Nixon will be a very strong contender. He is no fool. And he knows that foreign policy is the issue of our day—more than ever.

Humphrey opposed Nixon in the 1968 presidential election. Nixon won.

And, not surprisingly, Nixon's successor, Gerald Ford, chosen by him as his vice-president after the disgrace and resignation of Spiro Agnew, sent me an assurance once both he and Nixon had retired from public life (February 7, 1986) that while Watergate had "initially" weakened the president's position as director of U.S. foreign policy, this was not true "in the long run." It was "essentially" true that the strength of American democracy was sufficiently vibrant to restore the nation's international position amid the detritus of Watergate. Nixon's policy had been confirmed by Ford's own retention of Kissinger as secretary of state when he became president. "Most assuredly," American foreign policy had remained steady despite the crisis.

II

Learning as an Exile

In 1746, as a septuagenarian, François de Callières, the great diplomat and statesman, published his classic book on statecraft, *De la manière de négocier avec les souverains (On the Manner of Negotiating with Princes).* It is still regarded as a primer in many foreign ministries.

In this elegant work Callières argues that "the occupation of the lawyer, which is to split hairs about nothing, is not a good preparation for the treatment of grave public affairs in the region of diplomacy."

Richard Nixon was by profession a lawyer. Nevertheless, while in the role of chief of state, he proved to be a skillful negotiator with his opposite numbers from other countries. He had prepared himself well by global travels and diplomatic interviews. And, as president, he was well served by several exceptionally able career envoys including Ambassador Charles E. Bohlen and those polished and experienced nonprofessionals he selected, like David K. E. Bruce and Ellsworth Bunker. As president, Nixon was also wise enough to name a brilliant historian, Henry Kissinger, as his right-hand man for external affairs. He heeded both him and his chosen diplomatic envoys in formulating his own policy views, both strategic and tactical.

Nixon flawed his unusually successful record of analysis and action overseas by permitting the Watergate affair to develop into a cancerous, malignant growth. This smudged his record as a president and certainly allowed some foreign policy aims to become blurred.

Only one other American chief executive suffered from a somewhat comparable fate, although it stemmed from wholly different circumstances. This was the egocentric, thoughtful, idealistic, and scholarly Democrat, Woodrow Wilson, who underestimated the opposition in Congress that could and did block his dream of a peace treaty skein, including U.S. membership in a League of Nations that would remake the world after World War I. Then, after suffering a stroke while hustling about the country in a vain fight to achieve his goals, Wilson was bedridden for the rest of his life. Although patently unfit to continue in office, he refused to hand it over to his vice-president. This was not a moral lapse, as was Nixon's, but one of political wisdom if not ethics. Yet its ultimate consequences for the United States perhaps strengthened the isolationist tide with far greater global consequences than did Watergate, half a century later.

Wilson lacked no moral core; quite the contrary. But, encouraged by his ambitious wife, he was consumed by the presumption that his noble political ideals required his own presence as a guiding factor—a vanity that tortured his sickbed and discombobulated the world.

Wilson's career and splendid place in history were seriously scarred by this accident of fate and his refusal to recognize that he was unable to fulfill his role as president, which in effect he left to his wife to carry out in secret for him. Nixon's career was immediately spattered with the disgraceful mud of Watergate and the cover-up, but the long-term effects of this scandal were perhaps less harmful to the nation and the world than those of Wilson's tragic thrombosis. I do not compare the innocence of Wilson's egocentric error in judgment with the evident guilt of Nixon's; yet the latter was less consequential to the course of history.

The first discussion on foreign policy I ever had with Nixon was in Washington on July 25, 1958, while he was vice-president. I noted that what he said was sensible and well phrased. When I asked what he considered should be the basic aims of U.S. foreign policy, he answered readily:

I would say that our foreign policy begins with the major consideration of protecting the independence of the U.S. We recognize that the independence of our nation and the freedom of our people cannot be considered as separate from the independence and freedom of other nations.

Therefore, especially since World War I, we recognize that when the independence of our allies is threatened, we have a stake in helping them to defend it. This was a primary consideration in both world wars and in the Korean War.

Up to this point, you will find general agreement among most American people: that the U.S. must help other threatened countries when the threat is of a military character.

Until the time when the imperialist Communist movement began to be effective—since the latter part of World War II—I think this kind of policy was relatively adequate to protect our security. But now we find that the Communists have developed, to a degree never before reached, the tactics of indirect aggression. Therefore, we must expand our concepts.

This is why we have interest in mutual defense pacts in Europe and Asia and why we have supplemented the military aspects of these pacts with arrangements for foreign aid on a massive scale.

This foreign economic aid is often misunderstood and misrepresented. Its fundamental purpose is to enable countries abroad to become economically strong enough to maintain political stability and to resist...political and economic infiltration [by] nations whose ultimate purpose is to dominate them. This is the greatest danger faced by the U.S. and the free world, and in this particular area our policies are most inadequate. The leaders of our government have been unable to develop enough support to enable Congress to vote sufficient funds for these purposes.

Let me summarize my ideas of policy. First of all, we should protect the independence and security of the U.S. Secondly, we should give military support to those nations who will stand beside us. Thirdly, our economic program should shore up the independence of other countries. Fourthly, we must recognize that any world war would destroy or warp our freedom, and, consequently, we have the obvious objective of finding useful solutions to international problems; that is why we support the United Nations.

The people of this country and perhaps its policymakers cannot stress too much that we are devoted to peace at almost any price. And there is an important ingredient of our foreign policy which we have not adequately conveyed abroad: We are not wedded to the status quo. We recognize that the world, above all the world outside the West, is in a process of change and that the popular masses want a better way of life. Unfortunately, the image we present to many people abroad is precisely the opposite of this desire on our part. We are not for change merely for the sake of change as Russia is, but we do not oppose change.

In the Middle East, we are presented as taking a position of opposing change in the status quo and opposing Arab independence and economic improvement. This is not true. Regardless of ideology, I think we should aid any independent nation. The security interests of the U.S. require this. Therefore, for example, I am for helping Spain and Yugoslavia. My own view is that we should take chances like granting economic aid to Poland to encourage the independent forces in nations that are not really independent.

I asked Nixon what he thought was the proper role of an opposition party in our nation's foreign policy decisions.

An opposition can bring about changes in two ways. First of all, it can have an influence on public opinion. Key senators can speak out and influence public opinion, and in its turn, public opinion will influence the administration.

Secondly, the opposition can exert influence through direct consultation. In this way, we have seen Senator Humphrey discussing the Middle East with Secretary of State Dulles. The administration hopes to gain bipartisan support on these matters. Thirdly, the opposition can exert an influence through legislative control of the purse strings. For example, one can see this in terms of foreign aid. The tools with which an administration implements its foreign policy can be denied by Congress.

I asked if Nixon would give me the names of three men he would consider eligible for the position of secretary of state if he should be elected president in 1960. He looked a bit coy.

It would be presumptuous of me to comment on anything I might do if I were elected president. I don't even mention such things to my wife. In those terms, I can't answer your question. I don't like to speak of names.

But then, somewhat to my surprise:

As a secretary of state I think that first of all, a man should be able to talk to various people and get their various views on foreign policy, even though the secretary of state should have the final word.

Since the president, constitutionally, has the final word, I took this as a gibe at Dulles, whom Nixon disliked.

A president should have several broad-gauge men sophisticated in international affairs in his cabinet. There is a continual and extensive political campaign in the world. The propaganda and political struggle is constant. Therefore, just as in wartime, when several members of the war cabinet participate in making decisions, a president nowadays needs to call on the best men in his administration to help guide his decisions on foreign policy. For example, such ministers as the attorney general, the secretaries of commerce, treasury, and defense, should join with the secretary of state, the head of the Atomic Energy Commission, the head of the CIA, and others in making decisions. All of them can contribute something to the thinking of the chief executive.

I was very interested to see Nixon put the attorney general at the head of the list. His own closest personal friend in the cabinet was Bill Rogers, the attorney general, whom he subsequently chose as the first head of his State Department but never empowered to surpass Kissinger, national security adviser.

It is dangerous for an administration to confine itself to too narrow consultations in the field of foreign policy [another dig at Dulles]. I would not venture to suggest who would be a good man to follow Dulles, but he would have to have a basic understanding of the world struggle and how the international Communist movement operates. He would have to be able to work with the people in the foreign service and inside the State Department.

As much as anything else, we need a man with initiative, creativeness, and a recognition of the necessity to break out of old patterns of thought. It is easy to say that we need a bold new program in foreign policy today. But Dulles is extremely able.

Nevertheless, as we move into the period ahead, I do not think that the struggle will be determined by the military strength of the U.S. and Russia. It will be decided by things like the Middle East today and what I saw in Latin America on my recent trip. Therefore, we must have people who understand the political and economic aspects of this struggle. I must emphasize foreign economic aid.

He said he thought there was a definite need for a longer-range system of budgeting instead of the present year-to-year basis and that Congress must recognize this. He also said it was very difficult for us in analyzing foreign movements to distinguish "the voice of the mob from the voice of the majority."

He thought our propaganda was inadequate. The crux of the problem was in the very name of our government radio, the Voice of America.

This voice tells people abroad how we live, and so forth. But instead of trying to be the voice of America, we should seek more to be the voice of other peoples. The Communists have done this. They have identified themselves with the aspirations of other peoples, but we only speak for the Americans. Our propaganda should associate itself with the voice and aspirations of peoples like the Tunisians.

We are inept in presenting a true picture, even of ourselves. We do not adequately let other peoples know that we do not want to dominate them and that we believe in their economic progress for their *own sake as well as for the simple reason that it is in our own best interest. We should be the voice of others, them, not of Americans. We must get across to other nations that ours is the true revo-*

lution. We should talk more of the promise of the American revolution and less of the menace of the Communist revolution. But we must make it plain that we do not expect other peoples to share all our views and to imitate us in all their actions.

As so many of my friends in Washington and in the Democratic party were savage in their mocking criticisms of the man, I was impressed by Nixon far more than I had expected. Although he was only vice-president and had no direct foreign policy responsibilities, he had already traveled considerably on missions for Eisenhower and he spoke readily and fluently with good sense and a knowledgeable manner.

While he was still in his first federal office I saw him again a few times, but the next occasion I had a chance for good talks was in July 1963 in Paris, where we lunched at Ambassador Bohlen's and also played golf. John F. Kennedy was president. Nixon had been traveling abroad as part of his deliberate effort to educate himself on world affairs in preparation for another try for the White House. I noted in my diary immediately after our conversations:

> Nixon told me he had taken with him on his trip a column I wrote saying one result of the Sino-Soviet fight was to make communism look more respectable and to heighten the danger of popular-front movements in Europe. He had successively tried this idea out on the leaders of Morocco, Egypt, Greece, Italy, and Germany and found they all agreed.
>
> Nixon agreed with Adenauer that it would be a mistake for the West to get too mixed up in the Sino-Soviet row; we should be in a position to play both sides rather subtly and to see if we could not develop some kind of indirect contacts with the Chinese—not recognition but at least a means of "keeping in touch." They were both against us and we should not put all our eggs in Khrushchev's Soviet basket.
>
> Essentially there were really no major differences between [the] foreign policy attitudes of the Democrats and of the Republicans, and it wasn't any use talking about Cuba (meaning the Bay of Pigs), because that was an affair of the past. The main issue in the 1964 elections would be foreign policy and not race. The race issue was simply too big. Both parties were devoured by it. It would be impossible for the

Republicans either to run on a platform such as that Senator Javits (a GOP liberal) wanted—of promising even more than Kennedy—or on a kind of lily-white, retrograde, and outright racist platform.

Nixon said he was (in 1963), technically speaking, titular head of the Republican party...as the last defeated candidate, and he proposed to use his influence when he got home to achieve three things: (1) to ensure that there will be an internationalist and nonisolationist foreign policy plank; (2) to ensure that there is no retrograde racist plank; and (3) to ensure that there is a sound economic plank, "because after all I am a free enterpriser myself."

From his conversation it seemed he was definitely anti-Goldwater, the Republican aspirant:

> *A time comes when any politician has to cut the umbilical cord that ties him to a party group and [Barry] Goldwater, as Republican candidate, will face that problem—probably between now and January, but certainly before the New Hampshire primaries—vis-à-vis the John Birchers and the right-wing lunatic fringe. They have a lot of money. I know that because they used it against me. But he is going to have to make a choice.*

In September, 1964 I had another interesting conversation with Nixon in New York and found myself increasingly impressed by his potential as a guide and executor of American foreign policy. I observed in my diary:

> He was very sensible, presenting his position with calm and logic. If he were the Republican candidate this year I might very well be inclined to support him. He has grown a great deal in modesty, humanity, wisdom, and stature in the four years since he was defeated.
>
> Nixon regrets that foreign policy has not been properly discussed in the campaign and thinks the only issue that has been brought up has been the nuclear one—and that in a confused and unsatisfactory way. The real question is not how nuclear weapons should be used but how to apply policy in such a way that they will never be used.
>
> He considers President Johnson, the Democrat, dangerously egocentric and power-hungry and that it is imperative

> to have enough Republicans in Congress to keep the president from being corrupted by his own power. Nixon has no illusions about the outcome of the election.
>
> He expresses admiration for Johnson's political techniques but doesn't like the moral tenor of his administration. He thinks Johnson is wise not to engage in debates with Goldwater, and that he has been mistaken both in mentioning Goldwater too much and in using members of his cabinet in the political campaign. Johnson has a bad television personality, and it would help Goldwater a great deal if he put his own attractive personality on television more.
>
> Nixon thinks the situation in Vietnam is drifting more and more and that if we don't come out with some kind of a policy we are going to lose it within a year or two or have no chance to influence the outcome. Then, through Indonesia, Communism would threaten the frontiers of the Philippines and Australia.
>
> He says Goldwater never asked him before announcing that he would name Nixon his secretary of state and that he [Nixon] had learned himself four years ago that it is "counter-productive" to talk to cabinet appointments before election.

As the above indicates, Nixon was always thinking back to his defeated ambition to be elected president and working throughout the years of his political exile to learn lessons from past mistakes, also studying the problems and methods of international leaders, whom he visited whenever possible. I believe it was probably a useful development in his career that forced him, through the 1960 electoral loss, to travel, read, and study not only how to reach the presidency but how best to accomplish his policy desires when he got there. In this respect he acquired considerable understanding and sympathy from General de Gaulle, who had also passed years in a wilderness of powerless contemplation between two periods at the helm of France. For both leaders the period of undesired reflection helped them to mature their consideration of world political issues and to devise new formulas to solve the problems they would eventually have to face.

III

Becoming a Statesman

Nixon captured the White House in 1968 perhaps for the reason that he was regarded as *the* foreign policy expert—as Humphrey had discerned. And he embellished this ability by proceeding to become the most traveled president in American history, the leader who met most of his foreign peers.

Following his election he set about activating many ideas he had developed while he was removed from political power. Vietnam, however, he soon discovered was virtually insoluble. He floundered manfully about that morass, seeking to subdue the Communist north by heavy bombardments of key points and supply lines, by trying to cut off Vietcong bases in Cambodia, by shifting U.S. commanders, and by trying to prop up and clean up the corrupt Saigon government as his predecessors had done before him. But he failed, and his weakened position at home didn't help when he wished to protect U.S. troop withdrawals.

The Southeast Asian mess was too far gone. It proved incapable of being tidied or swept away. Its denouement was seemingly inevitable by the time Nixon entered the White House. American weakness, constantly growing since Kennedy had sent the first troops to intervene, became a horrible cancer under

Johnson. Nothing Nixon attempted in playing against each other the two powerful supporters (Soviet Russia and Communist China) of Ho Chi Minh's North Vietnamese government worked.

By the time he reached the White House, Nixon had had considerable experience of foreign affairs, having made a point of doing much overseas traveling and meeting as many world leaders as he could.

I first went abroad on our honeymoon. To Mexico in 1940. Then in 1941 just before we were in the war. Mrs. Nixon and I saved our money. She was teaching and I was making very little as a lawyer but we saved and took a cruise. It was the last banana boat cruise leaving from New Orleans and we went to Panama and to Havana and another place in Central America. So that was the second trip. I became very interested in Central America at that time. I went back in 1955 as vice-president and visited the same places.

Then there was my war experience as a lieutenant in the navy But the war experience was limited to the South Pacific. That's Noumea and New Caledonia. I became well acquainted with that.

In 1947, as a member of the important Herter Committee of Congress, he toured Europe and helped prepare the way for the Marshall Plan. After that, his travels burgeoned, both during his exile from public office (1960–68) and his time as a public servant (congressman, senator, and vice-president), when he became the most extensively traveled American official ever to reach the White House. He sums up his experience in learning the diplomatic game:

My major interest in foreign affairs [began] even before I came to Congress. I grew up, of course as you know, in Whittier and went to a Friends school. The whole background was in terms of trying to build a more peaceful world and so forth. We had that drilled into us in the family and in the church and the college and so forth. So I had an interest in it early. But the Herter Committee was the first practical opportunity that I had to see the world and to have contact with world leaders. On that trip we had some very good teachers. Chip Bohlen was one of those that briefed us on the Queen Mary *going over. Chris Herter was a first-class man. Then we visited En-*

gland, France, Germany, Italy, and Greece and saw firsthand how the world worked.

In his preparation for a political career and for his ultimate role as a statesman, Nixon sees three principal fields to which essential attention must be paid: travel, reading, and personalities. (He once listed for me the eighty-one countries he visited during his career, in which he conversed with political leaders.) He is now (July 2, 1986) appreciative of the fact that, thanks to his 1960 electoral defeat by John F. Kennedy, he had eight years in which to indulge the first two of these studies.

That was a very useful period, and I would recommend such to anyone who is defeated for office or retires from office but who is still able to run or plans to run again. The best thing he can do is take a holiday from politics to travel and to study and to think and sometimes to write. I found that it was the best period in my life. I was able to spend more time reading, more time traveling. When you are in office you are so busy doing things, talking to people, entertaining people, making decisions, and so forth that you have very little time to think about things. I think that de Gaulle found, Adenauer found, Churchill found that being in the wilderness, as it has been described, was a very important part of their development as strategic thinkers. Traveling abroad and meeting people: That is important because you need to get the feel of a place. You've got to smell it—to sense differences as well as similarities—among people and leaders.

But it's also coming back and reflecting on it. In fact, having to write about it, having to make a speech. I once talked to Foster Dulles about it after he was returning from one of his trips and I said, "Boy, speech writing is tough," 'cause he came back from his trip and had to make a speech and report on it. He said, "I know it's tough, but it's very important. I find that having to write a speech forced me to think through the problem and ideas came as a result." I agree with that. Writing a speech, writing a book, forces one to think through the problem, very important for the education.

Finally, wide and intense reading is a useful prerequisite for the would-be statesman:

I think somebody has written that history is the great mistress of wisdom, and I would agree with that. You read biographies, Talleyrand, Bismarck, Metternich, for instance, and it doesn't mean that you try to become like them, but by reading about them and how they handled great affairs it forces you to engage your mind and to break out of the rather parochial tunnel vision that most of us have.

You come out of college or a university and you tend to have a very narrow parochial view. It's hard for me to pick one of these great figures out and say he would be my idol. You must not become focused on one individual and one approach and so forth. You must read very broadly and then develop your own concepts.

Among American statesmen he admires, Nixon enumerates:

Considering the very small and weak country that he represented, John Quincy Adams, by an objective evaluation, has got to be put very high on the list. But I would have to put T.R. [Theodore Roosevelt] pretty high too. I know that he was bombastic and all the rest, but he was important. And, curiously enough, I have always had a very high regard for Woodrow Wilson. In retrospect, however, as I look at the world today from a different vantage point, I think that Wilson's policy doesn't work in the real world.

Nixon readily acknowledges that the importance of a negotiator's political position and personal prestige is a key factor in a negotiation, and that was true for both himself and Kissinger during his presidency.

As people got to know him, got to know me, in the conduct of policy, that greatly increased our bargaining leverage and our credibility with our opposite numbers. Success builds on success.

I first saw Nixon, as chief executive, at the White House on May 19, 1969. I wrote in my diary:

Good talk with President Nixon and then lunch with Henry Kissinger, Nixon's special assistant for national security and foreign policy matters. Nixon was sitting at his massive desk. Behind was a table stacked with folders of classified documents.

The president expressed himself well, never fumbling for a word. Kissinger told me later that he writes far more of his own speeches than any other political figure Kissinger has known.

He recalled his visit to Paris in February and his talks with de Gaulle. De Gaulle had told him it would be easier for the United States to leave Vietnam than it had been for France to leave Algeria. Had Nixon been in his place, "I would probably have done the same thing. He saw the way history was going and knew withdrawal was inevitable. He carried it out with vision and courage."

Nixon said de Gaulle had known all along he couldn't achieve certain things, such as the unification of Europe. There wasn't any chance of unifying Europe today, "and we all know that. Of course, I'll go on making the proper noises—but it isn't going to happen. Things are moving in another direction. Just as with NATO. It isn't possible anymore to return to the military emphasis on NATO. The Left would simply object too much."

The present trend was one of disintegration rather than unity, and this was true all over the world, in Europe, in Asia, in the free world, and in the Communist world. The stress was now on national states and national policies working for national interests. We had to look at reality and base our policy on it, not on inherited dreams. France was more nationalistic, and so was West Germany. But inside each country there was less unity, more fragmentation.

This, he said, was the particular problem of the United States. There was a need for unity at home if we are to persist in Vietnam. And he meant everything he had said about our determination "not to fold" and to adhere resolutely to "our very modest objectives."

The U.S. can't fold. A great nation sometimes has to act in a great way. Otherwise it destroys its own moral fiber. The British knew that. There is more to this war than just prestige, and I am not speaking only of the thousands of people who would be slaughtered if we just pulled out. I don't know what you think of the domino theory, but it is obvious that if we pulled out other countries would crumble.

And think of Europe. No matter what some of the politicians say about hoping the "dirty war" will end and that then America can pay more attention to Europe, they really know this wouldn't happen. They fear this would be the start of isolationism and a weakening, not a strengthening, of the American position there. We would be forced by isolationism to go home from there too.

A great power like ours sometimes has to meet challenges elsewhere in the world. The British knew that and there was something valid in the pax Britannica. *It worked. Well, some people talk of a* pax Americana. *But we have to stay with it.*

And we would destroy ourselves if we pulled out in a way that really wasn't honorable. It might take our people a year or two to realize what had happened, but they would know in the end. And the reaction would be terrible. I hate to think of it. It would be destructive to our own morale.

You know our objectives in this war are very limited. We only want to establish a real peace. The true objective of this war is peace. It is a war for peace.

He said the true moral crisis in the country was a "leadership crisis."

The trouble is that the leaders, not [the] country as a whole, are weak and divided. By the leaders I mean the leaders of industry, the bankers, the newspapers. They are irresolute and lack understanding. The people can be led back to some kind of consensus if only the leaders can take hold of themselves.

Briefly, he touched on China and Russia. He said China clearly had no intention of leaving Russia alone. At this point Kissinger looked at me, and I realized from the clock on the wall that it was almost twenty minutes of two and well past presidential lunch hours. I went with Henry to lunch in his office.

I said I thought the most disturbing thing that had struck me on returning from abroad was the moral decline of the United States; even distinguished Americans were declining official jobs offered to them by the president; the old

> idea of serving the nation was dead. Kissinger said: "This is our biggest challenge, the loss of moral fiber. This is why Nixon worries so much about what he calls the leadership problem. There is a real crisis of authority. The leadership class has lost its will. To restore it we need some sort of success—preferably on something they disagree with. I don't mean that we should look for an artificial field in which to achieve this."

As a political exile the president had learned a great deal about the world. If one adds to this newly acquired knowledge what he had already absorbed as vice-president when Eisenhower sent him abroad on representational chores, he was probably better qualified in terms of foreign policy than any other U.S. president at the time he entered the White House.

One trip he took as chief of state in 1970 was a visit to Marshal Tito in Belgrade. Nixon had come to realize the value of having a personal contact with someone close to another leader of importance to the United States. The president had no intention of requesting any assistance from Tito in extricating the United States from Southeast Asia. He and Kissinger had built up a small network of useful contacts with North Vietnam, largely through experienced Frenchmen. But Nixon recognized that Tito had "very useful credentials" with Nasser, the Egyptian president guiding the new wave of revolutionary Arab nationalism.

The Tito-Nasser link didn't pay off. Nixon's persistent efforts to bring about a Palestine settlement and Middle Eastern peace never produced definitive results. Yet he kept on trying, as he continued also to cultivate good French relationships in the hopes these would help end the Vietnam stalemate. In February 1970 he invited President Pompidou on an official visit to America, but this backfired when hostile Jewish crowds, angry at France's arms sales to Arab states fighting Israel, demonstrated against him.

Nixon used Kissinger discreetly and effectively in his search for a solution to the Vietnam crisis. Kissinger told me (Paris, January 9, 1973):

> Nixon doesn't give me instructions. We simply meet at great length and work over what he likes to call "the game plan." We discuss what provision we must get for a settlement, and then he leaves me on my own to do it. The presi-

> dent took the decision that we must end the type of conversation that was going on when the previous negotiations broke off [December 13, 1972]. He based his decision on three reasons:
>
> 1. The trickery of the North Vietnamese. There was a basic difference between the English text and the Vietnamese text concerning the phrase that would have established an "administrative structure" in South Vietnam. Hanoi tried to pull a fast one and gain more sovereignty for the opponents of Thieu than we were prepared to concede, and they did this by deliberate mistranslation of the Vietnamese text.
>
> 2. They were going to start another offensive which was timed to coincide with the application of the agreement that had tentatively been reached. For this reason we wanted adequately large international machinery on the scene to supervise the agreement, but they wanted to keep this at a ridiculously small level so it would be impossible to check what was going on.
>
> 3. The president was worried about a showdown with Thieu at that time (late October) and he wanted to postpone any such showdown until after the presidential elections on November 7, 1972. The record of the negotiations will show all of this.

Kissinger also said Washington had now achieved what it wanted in Saigon and that it was clear Thieu was prepared to accept whatever deal we found acceptable here.

Henry insisted that despite widespread international criticism of the United States touched off by the Hanoi-Haiphong bombings, Moscow and Peking had been surprisingly soft in their reaction. They were "even softer" in their private reactions to Washington than in their public statements.

Kissinger said: "The North has lost the war. But this hasn't helped us. The trouble is that if we could continue to hit them for two months more as we hit them in December, we could end the whole thing. But as things are—in the condition they are in today, even if they have been badly hit—they can endure."

We munched, he talked, I scribbled notes. He said: "This president always promises a little less than he can actually deliver. He wants to know what all the possibilities are before he moves. I can't tell you what we might feel necessary to do if Hanoi pushes its offensive."

At this point I observed that in Vietnam I felt the basic problem was to relate internal and external U.S. capabilities and policies more tidily. "Precisely," said Kissinger. "We've run out of the policy concepts of the thirties, the liberal theories that we had no inherent conflict with any people, that economic action can solve political problems. In this respect Kennedy wasn't the great innovator; he was the sunset on an era."

On March 8, 1974, I had an interview in the White House with Nixon of about an hour and twenty minutes. To my surprise, he summoned a photographer who took several pictures. "You might want one of these," said Nixon with a friendly grin. "Just in case you are planning to write another book."

He looked relaxed, sunburned. When I remarked on this he said: "If I didn't know how to stand up under the heat I'd have no business being here." He gave the impression of being self-confident, contained. He was wearing gray-blue slacks and a darker-blue jacket. He ordered a cup of tea for himself and coffee for me.

To start his summation, the president said:

I would strongly commend to you my second foreign policy report. It sets forth new policy directions and outlines the goals we hope to achieve—the goals not only for this administration but for subsequent administrations. A long-range effort.

The irony today, for those who look at the Washington scene, is that the great internationalists of the post–World War II period have become the neoisolationists of the Vietnam War period and especially of the period accompanying the ending of that war. And it is ending. This is also true of the attitude of those former internationalists with respect to our defense posture and defense spending. And, for some, it is even true of our foreign trade policy.

The point is, why has this happened? Why have many former internationalists developed neoisolationist tendencies, at least in some degree? Part of the answer is simply that Americans, like all idealists, are very impatient people. They feel that if a good thing is going to happen it should happen immediately.

And a great many of these people are very disillusioned with the

United Nations. I am not, personally, because I never expected it could settle all problems involving major powers but could nevertheless play a useful role in development and in peacekeeping in areas where the superpowers were not directly involved.

The older a nation and a people become, the more they become conscious of history and also of what is possible. Now I will explain to you what I mean. I rate myself as a deeply committed pacifist, perhaps because of my Quaker heritage from my mother. But I must deal with how peace can be achieved and how it must be preserved.

With this in mind, I am deeply devoted to a desire that the United States should make the greatest possible contribution it can make to developing such a peaceful world. It is not enough just to be for peace. The point is, what can we do about it?

Through an accident of history, we find ourselves today in a situation where no one who is really for peace in this country can reject an American role in the rest of the world. Of course, we had our own period of colonial expansion, as typified by Theodore Roosevelt and the idea of manifest destiny. But that period is fortunately gone.

Since then this country has fought in four wars which we didn't start, and really what they have in common is the effort to bring about a better chance for a peaceful world. And this applies for the Vietnam War as well as the two world wars and Korea. Obviously it was a political temptation when I started office to state simply that we would get out right away without any responsibility for what came next.

But I knew too much about history, about Asia, about the basic feeling in the United States. If we failed to achieve our limited goal —to let a small country exercise the right to choose its own way of life, without having a Communist government imposed upon it by force—if we failed to achieve this, we would not help the cause of peace.

For a time, perhaps, we would be seen as a kind of hero. But soon it would be seen that we had left behind a legacy of even greater dangers for Southeast Asia and for the Pacific region. And, after all, we are a Pacific power.

In 1966 and 1967—culminating in 1968—the American people began to tire of playing a role in the world. We had fought four wars, selflessly and for no gain. We had provided some $100 billion in foreign aid, much of it to former enemies who are now our competitors, like Japan. And we found ourselves committed in Vietnam, in a *war where there are no heroes, only goats. Our people became sick of Vietnam and supported our men there in order to get them out—after this period of change in mood. Somewhere a great change had taken place.*

We had used our power for peace in four wars, but this new attitude gained force: "If we can't handle this one, to hell with it."

We got caught up in a vicious crossfire, and it became increasingly difficult to make people understand. I must say that without television it might have been difficult for me to get people to understand a thing.

The crossfire I referred to was this. The superdoves opposed our commitment in Vietnam and all world responsibilities—Korea, the Philippines, the Middle East, Europe. This was the kind of isolationism of those who felt the United States shouldn't have played any role at all in Southeast Asia from the very start. For these people, Vietnam was a distant, small foreign country in just the terms Chamberlain mentioned concerning Czechoslovakia at the time of Munich [1938]. These were the superdoves.

But on the other side, the opposite crossfire came from the superhawks. This group stood by their commander in chief, the president, but became fed up with war for their own reasons. They felt that if the United States can't handle a stinking little war, why then let's just pull out and build up our strength at home. And they want to develop a fortress America at home and cram it full of missiles, while the superdoves want us to pull out of the world also, but reducing our strength at home.

In between there are those of us who stand in the middle of the crossfire. The superhawk feels it is his duty to support the president even if that same superhawk isn't sure he wants to see us do what we are doing. The superdove has a different attitude. He is a goodhearted fellow, but, when he looks around and sees the problems of the poor, the blacks, the Indians, the poor whites, the pot-smoking kids, crime in the cities, urban slums, the environment, he says: "We must get out of the war right away and concern ourselves only with problems at home."

The fact is, however, that there has never been so great a challenge to U.S. leadership. This war is ending. In fact, I seriously doubt we will ever have another war. This is probably the very last one. In any theoretical question of a war on the basis of "either them or us," I am sure everyone in the country would join in behind, but this is not the case in a small country so far away involved in a situation so difficult to explain.

I am certain a Gallup poll would show that the great majority of the people would want to pull out of Vietnam. But a Gallup poll would also show that a great majority of the people would want to pull three or more divisions out of Europe. And it would also show that a great majority of the people would cut our defense budget.

Polls are not the answer. You must look at the facts. The Soviets now have three times the missile strength [ICBM] of ourselves. By 1974 they will pass us in submarines carrying nuclear missiles.

All of these things are very directly related. For example, when Mrs. Meir, the Israeli prime minister, visited me, she understood me right away when I said that if America winds up the war in Vietnam in failure and an image is developed that the war was fought only by stupid scoundrels, there would be a wave of isolationism. This would embrace the U.S. role everywhere—including the Middle East. Mrs. Meir saw the point immediately.

As I see it, we have to take certain specific steps. First of all, what we now have to do is end the war—as we are now doing—in a way that gives South Vietnam a reasonable chance to survive without our help. But this doesn't mean we would withdraw all our responsibilities everywhere.

As I stated in first explaining the Nixon doctrine, our idea is to create a situation in which those lands to which we have obligations or in which we have interests, if they are ready to fight a fire, should be able to count on us to furnish the hose and water.

Meanwhile, in Europe, we can't cut down our forces until there is a mutual agreement with the other side. We must stand with our European friends if they will only do a bit more themselves in NATO—as they have indicated they will do.

And we cannot foolishly fall behind in the arms competition. In the United States we remain ahead in the navy and in the air, but the Soviets are ahead in ICBMs and soon will pass us in modern submarine strength.

But each has a kind of sufficiency. The Soviets are a great land power opposite China as well as having far-reaching interests elsewhere. We are a great sea power, and we must keep our strength. I am a strong navy man myself. I believe in a strong conventional navy, which helps us to play a peacekeeping role in such areas, for example, as Latin America.

These are all elements that must be considered with respect to each other. The main thing is that I'd like to see us not end the Vietnamese War foolishly and find ourselves all alone in the world. I could have chosen that course my very first day in office. But I want the American people to be able to be led by me, or by my successor, along a course that allows us to do what is needed to help keep the peace in this world.

We used to look to other nations to do this job, once upon a time. But now only the United States plays a major role of this sort in the world. Our responsibilities are not limited to this great continent but include Europe, the Middle East, Southeast Asia, East Asia, many areas whose fate affects the peace of the world.

We must above all tend to our national obligations. We must not forget our alliances or our interests. Other nations must know that the United States has both the capability and the will to defend these allies and protect these interests.

Unless people understand this and understand it well, the United States will simply retreat into isolationism, both politically and diplomatically. We would, of course, continue to be an economic giant, but that is not enough.

Only the United States has sufficient strength to be able to help maintain a balance in Europe and other areas that might otherwise be affected.

What I am saying is not a cold war philosophy. I hope that we can further develop our negotiations with the Soviet Union. For, although we recognize that their ideology is expansionist, they know what it means if the genie comes out of the bottle and that their interest in survival requires that they avoid a conflict with the United States. This means that we must find a way of cooperating.

For obviously pragmatic reasons, therefore, we can see peace slowly shaping up. First, as we are doing, we must end the war in Vietnam. We must continue our Soviet negotiations and open the door of cooperation to China. And in this way there will be a chance of building a world that is relatively peaceful.

I deliberately say relatively peaceful. That doesn't mean everyone will be disarmed, safe, and loving everyone else. The kind of relative peace I envision is not the dream of my Quaker youth. But it is realistic, and I am convinced we can bring it about.

The day the United States quits playing a responsible role in the world—in Europe or Asia or the Middle East—or gives up or recedes from its efforts to maintain an adequate defense force—on that day this will become a very unsafe world to live in.

I can assure you that my words are those of a devoted pacifist. My very hardest job is to give out posthumous medals of honor. I don't question the motives of those who oppose me. But I know this world. I have traveled about and talked to many leaders, and I know we have a chance to play a role in this world.

What is going to happen if we ignore such basic facts? The United States, as I said earlier, is a Pacific power. And the SST will be built—if not by us, by someone else. And then we will be only three hours' flight from Japan.

There will be 400 million people in non-Communist Asia relying ever more upon us. Why, Prime Minister Sato said not so long ago that Japan depends on U.S. nuclear strength.

In past times, the Number One nation was always in that position because of military conquests. But the mantle of leadership fell on American shoulders not by our desire and not for the purposes of conquest. But we have that position today, and how we handle ourselves will determine the chances of world peace.

Do you know, in all my travels, not one leader I have talked to ever said to me in private that he feared the United States as a nation bent on conquest. And I have met many Communist leaders, as you know. Whatever some of them may pretend in public, they understand our true troubles and they are also thankful that the United States wants nothing—nothing but the right for everyone to live and let live.

But the real problem that worries me most is: Will our Establishment see it that way? I am not talking about my critics but about a basic, strange sickness that appears to have spread among those who usually, in this country, can be expected to see clearly ahead into the future.

These are the people who, after World War II, supported the Greek-Turkish aid program, the Marshall Plan, NATO. But today they are in disarray because of two things. They are terribly disillusioned about Vietnam, which is so hard a problem to understand. And they have an enormous concern with home problems of a sort and a degree that did not face us a generation earlier.

I understand these factors. There is a vast need for reforms, for improvements in health, education, and environment. But we have to assume our resposibilities both abroad and at home. We have to do both. After all, if we manage to improve the environment and living conditions in this country we must also assure that we will be around to enjoy those improvements.

China was the keystone in the arch, Nixon's policy there was preceded by the effort to show, via India (China's opponent) that the United States was tough. If Washington implied it would react violently over India, Peking could assume we would react even more violently over China, should the USSR strike at its former ally. And the United States knew Japan would remain its permanent ally in the Pacific despite our improved relations with China. This was a subtle and complex game, and it was played by Nixon as a grand master at a chessboard, with Kissinger at his right hand.

The final piece in the China game was played at Moscow, where Nixon first saw Brezhnev (May 1972) and agreed on the SALT I arms control treaty. It was a classical and complex diplomatic maneuver whose results were a revolution in Chinese-American relations, with ultimately profound changes in the Chinese internal and economic system; a significant improvement in Soviet-American relations, which was to falter after Nixon was weakened and then ousted by Watergate; an angry India that could do little more than grumble at the United States; and a contented Japan.

Senator Mike Mansfield, then Democratic majority leader of the Senate (later Ambassador to Japan), summed up for me Nixon's achievements (Washington, March 29, 1972):

> I think what has been happening is a decline in the influence of the State Department and an increase in the influence of the foreign affairs adviser of the president [still Kissinger]. The person closest to the president's elbow will always have great influence. The base of operations has shifted from the State Department to the White House. The result has been an increased concentration of power for foreign policy in the White House and a decrease in the usage of the State Department....A metamorphosis has taken place....
>
> Nixon's trip to Peking was a great success. The important thing is that he took the first step in what will be a long

journey. I'm delighted that he's going to Moscow. He has been the first president in office to travel to the two most important Big Power areas, and I have nothing but words of praise for this, for the Chinese and Soviet visits, and for getting the SALT talks going. They have all been necessary, worthwhile, and indicative of the shift of foreign policy in a changing world.

IV

Techniques of Diplomacy

During his lengthy period of preparation to be a statesman, followed by a briefer but momentous period of practicing the art of statesmanship, Nixon learned a good deal about the techniques of his chosen profession. The first requirement, he discovered, was also a necessity in internal politics—the art of measuring individual human beings or analyzing their personalities and their motives and of getting along with them after a mutual search for satisfactory resolution of differences and attainment of mutually beneficial goals.

Nixon warms up when he talks about specific people rather than abstract theories. On July 2, 1986, I remarked to him that I had often wondered which of the many statesmen he had met he liked most, not admired most, and—after carefully reading his memoirs—I had come to the surprising conclusion that the answer was Leonid Brezhnev. What about it? I inquired. He spoke freely and somewhat surprisingly on this theme.

Well, let me respond to that by first saying the obvious—that if you read my book Leaders, *you see a description of great men and people that I've met. I've been a very lucky person to have known such pople and just to sit and talk to them. Because when I talk to people I listen and I learn a lot. Many times when you talk to somebody you talk, and when you're talking you're not learning anything. And so I have had one-on-one conversations with some very, very able people. The second thing is, I've always had good personal relations with them, not the get-drunk-together sort, and we share intimate stories and that sort of thing.*

I've never been very familiar with people, and I'm somewhat like de Gaulle in that respect. Most of the leaders that I have met have a deep sense of personal privacy. They keep a little distance. But consequently, because I approach it that way, I must say it is hard for me to think of any one leader that I didn't like.

I mean like you meet somebody like a Churchill, an Adenauer, a Yoshida, or a Lleras-Camargo of Colombia, Syngman Rhee, de Gaulle—they are people I respect and people that I like.

I find that world leaders have their idiosyncrasies. Some are vain, some are not as smart as others, and so forth. I liked Khrushchev. We had some pretty fair goes, but I greatly respected him. He had a fast-acting mind. And he could be at times very Russian and very warm, just as Brezhnev could be. But of all foreign leaders I met, I think I liked best Sir Robert Menzies, [the] former Australian prime minister. A fine man, good talker, intelligent, forceful, [an] excellent sense of humor.

As for your idea, I liked Brezhnev as a person and we hit it off extremely well. But this will probably surprise you. The one I think if I were to select, if I had a choice to bring him back and spend an evening with, . . . would be Menzies the Australian. It's a shame that he was in such a small country (small in terms of population). He would have been a great Churchillian prime minister, in my estimation. But to sit and talk to Menzies was really an education. He was a strategic thinker of the first rank, and he was a good storyteller, but he always came back to the point. He liked the good life, he liked a good drink, liked to smoke a good cigar, and that sort of thing. In terms of his personal life, I would say that he would have to come very high on the list. I must say he did come from a small and less important country, but in England he had an enormous reputation. The English respected him exactly the same way as I did. He was a big man, and for his full appreciation I can see the time is coming.

Reflecting on the actual working of statesmanship, as he learned as president, Nixon told me (July 2, 1986):

Too often negotiators seek an agreement for the sake of getting an agreement. Diplomacy is an end in itself rather than a means to an end. Now, they would not agree that that is a fair criticism, but often it is. What they believe, therefore, is that you can take any subject and if you can reach an agreement on it, that is a plus. That is a "victory" insofar as diplomacy is concerned: Untrue.

Trade, for example, should not be sought as an end in itself. The Commerce Department disagrees with that; the State Department usually disagrees; and the reason that I say that is that trade (for example, with the Soviet Union) is one of the major tools we have to affect their foreign policy. They want it, they need it. We should provide it. I'm not among those who think we should squeeze them economically and they'll collapse. But we should provide it only so long as they conduct themselves in a way that is not injurious to our interests.

And here's where a great mistake is made by those who believe in linkage. When we negotiated the most-favored-nation agreement with Brezhnev in 1972, Scoop Jackson came forward with the Jackson-Vannik amendment. The Jackson-Vannik amendment conditioned the most-favored-nation privilege on the basis of Jewish emigration.

What happened then was that the Russians cut the number of visas they gave the next year in half. When I came into office only six hundred visas were issued for emigration by those who wanted to leave, primarily Jews. In 1972, as a result of confidential diplomacy, thirty-four thousand went out; the next year, seventeen thousand. One Soviet leader expressed it to me and to mutual friends by saying, "We are not going to trade goods for bodies."

Now, what they mean in effect by that is you can't put a nation into the position where in order to get what they want economically they're going to change their internal decisions or their foreign policy decisions. In fact, however, it must operate that way. In other words, what you do is simply say, "Fine, we'll go forward." Then you drag your feet—you drag your own feet. But you do not put them in the public position of having to make it appear that they are giving in. You must always give a government a chance to back down gracefully and don't make it appear that it's been a trade-off.

Now, you must recognize that linkage is all-important in diplomatic negotiating. Think of this as a basic technique both sides can use. With regard to linkage, arms control has to be linked to political conduct. Now, I don't mean by that you do not make an arms control agreement unless the Russians get out of Afghanistan. But you have got to make it clear to them that what torpedoed SALT II was the Russian invasion of Afghanistan. And we cannot have a situation where they engage in adventurist activities which are adversarial to our interests and then expect the Senate to approve any kind of an agreement. So linkage is a concept that must be practiced.

But it is not a concept that you put in communiqués. It is not a concept that you put in legislation. The point on linkage is that it is the offensive-defensive linkage that applies to the present as it did in 1972. In 1972 they wanted to limit our ABM defensive systems because they knew our technology was better. We wanted to limit their offensive arms because they were moving faster than we were. Finally we got a deal. It wasn't the best deal, but it was better certainly than nothing.

We agreed to an arms agreement limiting offense weapons and at the same time the ABM treaty limiting defensive weapons. You see, it makes no sense to have to build defense unless you can limit offense. Otherwise you have a spiral in which your offense outruns the defense. So if you want real arms control the two must be linked, and that gives the basis for whatever trade-off is arranged. SDI [Strategic Defense Initiative], the whole concept, should be used as a bargaining chip. Research has to go forward because they have a program, we have one. Second, it is not verifiable; third, if it is possible to develop a defense of populations we should proceed.

But insofar as deployment is concerned, I'm referring particularly to those aspects of strategic defense that have to do with missile defense: [where] our deployment is concerned. You only deploy your system of defending populations if you eventually develop it to the extent that you have an offensive threat. If they reduce the offensive threat, the amount of deployment is thereby reduced. That is linkage in practice.

Without any remote connection with linkage, the concept comes into our relations with China and with Russia. Nixon admits:

There is no question but that the Russians were concerned about any move we would make in China. And there is no question to that as far as the Chinese are concerned. Their interest in us in the first instance, back in 1972, was not as some rather naive observers believed. They said the first question Mao is going to ask you is, "What is the richest country in the world going to do for the poorest and most populous country in the world?" That never came up.

Economic matters were never discussed in the first Peking meeting in '72. They were all geopolitical matters, the relations between the United States and China, Japan, the Soviet Union, etcetera. So we were brought together because of the fact that the Soviet Union was a potential threat to them at that time and the United States was not. Now, looking to the future, we have to bear in mind that you cannot assume that relationship will continue. I believe that, as long as the Chinese have an economic stake in good relations with not only the United States but the West generally, we can offer far more to them for what they most desperately need—the instruments of progress for a country that is very primitive. And they are the first to tell you that. We can offer more than the Russians can, but on the other hand we have got to remember that if you look far into the future, into the next century, China is a country of a billion people. They are potentially among the ablest people in the world; they have enormous resources.

They are not going to be subversive. They are not going to be subordinate to any other people. They are simply going to play a bigger and bigger role. I've always felt that it's very important to have a dual policy. We seek good relations with the Chinese, but we do not do it at the expense of Russia. We seek good relations with the Russians but not at the expense of the Chinese. It must be parallel. We must say that, we must believe it, we must do it. And it always disturbs me when people say, Well, we're going to play the Chinese against the Russians, the Russians against the Chinese. That's short-term politics, but it's not long-term strategy.

President Roosevelt probably without knowing it did a very brilliant thing when he insisted on Chiang Kai-shek and his China being permanent members of the Security Council, because it didn't mean Chiang Kai-shek was going to be able to sit there—it meant China. It just so happens that the symbol of China was Chiang.

I then asked if Nixon didn't think President Johnson should formally have declared war on Vietnam and put it through the normal machinery, in order to make the institution of military censorship legal. I had covered a war with United States forces, and there was military censorship, and nobody had a legitimate beef. It worked. And I had a feeling that the lack of military censorship in Vietnam enormously complicated the position of the government back home. I didn't mean political censorship at all.

In retrospect I would say yes. Let me give you a little background. First insofar as the war that you covered, you have to remember the country was united because it was a popular war, if any war can be popular, because there was a very unpopular enemy—the Germans in the one case, the Japanese in the other. In this case it should have been the same, because when we see what has happened now that the Communists have prevailed in Vietnam and in Cambodia, the genocide that has occurred, we realize that we were certainly on the right side, however ineptly we may have carried it out.

Eisenhower felt very strongly that Johnson should declare war. He told me that when I saw him in 1967 and 1968. His arguments were in relation to a suggestion I'd made at that time about the possibility... of a naval blockade. He said, "I don't see how you can do that without declaring war," and then he went on to make exactly the same point as you did. He said we really should declare war because you could have censorship; his point was, too, that's a way to unite the country. You aren't going to have so much draft dodging, draft evading, and all that sort of thing if the Congress makes the declaration decision.

That was Eisenhower's point. Now, the argument against it is one that prevailed in my own mind, because I had that option when I came in, of course. I think Johnson did not want to do it because of what later proved to be in my view too much concern about how the Chinese would react. I had the same concern early on; and [about] what the Russians would do.

Later on I realized that should not have been the prevailing factor. What is involved, I'm sure, in Johnson's case is that he was concerned that if we declared war that... would activate the mutual defense treaty that the North Vietnamese had with the Chinese. And I also understand they had some sort of agreement with the Russians. In other words, if you declare war you are throwing the gauntlet down, and it forces them to react, and it expands into a bigger war.

I had the same concern. A second concern I had, however, went beyond that. A magazine [Foreign Affairs] *article of mine pointed out that Vietnam, our obsession with Vietnam, had blinded Americans to the opportunities and challenges we had in other areas of the world. Our relationship with the Chinese, with the Russians, with the Third World, and so forth. We were spending so much, not just of our men and our money and our resources, but also of our creative thinking and leadership in this one small area. That's why I wanted to talk about Asia after Vietnam, which was, incidentally, the title of that piece.*

I believed we had to go forward at the time we were winding down the war in Vietnam with both the Chinese and the Russian initiatives. These began after I became president. We called Dobrynin in and set up the meetings in 1969 with Henry on the Russian diplomatic front. We also started dancing with the Chinese. Step by step we went along.

What I was concerned about [was] that if we declared war in Vietnam... it would possibly have had the effect of destroying both those initiatives. That was my concern. But in retrospect I believe such would probably not have been the case. I do not believe the Chinese and the Russians would have reacted if I had declared war. I believe they would have objected, but that under the circumstances they would have understood. Later on both understood when in May 1972 we bombed Hanoi and Haiphong just before the Russians met us in Moscow. The Chinese objected; the Russians objected; but we went forward with it.

I believe also that in peacetime a military draft would be in the interest of this country. I think it would have a very positive influence on the Europeans and a very positive effect on the Russians. It would be a diplomatic asset, I think, in terms of men and so forth.

I remember talking to Eisenhower and he said, "I think it would be good for the hippie generation." He was talking about universal military service; he told me that in 1967. My feeling is that we must get away from this concept which grew up in Vietnam, that only... (to put it in the vernacular) the "dummies" go out to fight wars and the brightest and the best go to the universities, and if they can't do that they fly off to Canada. That is simply unacceptable. I hope we will never have another war. We all hope that. But I believe that from the standpoint of the country at this time, clearly apart from what the economics would be, it would be better to have the draft than the volunteer army. The volunteer army is an idea that I supported. It was developed by Martin Anderson, one of the bright young men I had with me. The Young Conservatives and others all supported this.

But as time passed I could see that a military peacetime draft was the best solution for U.S. defense. And it improved our posture for diplomatic negotiations; it gave us permanent strength without stretching our resources. At first, like others, I was inclined to support the argument that conscription was involuntary servitude. I backed the concept that military service should be voluntary. And I remember the day after we finished the Paris peace agreements on Vietnam, we got rid of the draft. But in retrospect I would say that today I believe that a draft across the board with no exceptions, except of course for health, would be good for the country, and I think it would be a very positive foreign policy move as well.

Economically or financially it would cost less, of course. And it should, because you know one of the problems we have at the present time when we compare Russian military expenditures with ours is like comparing elephants with pygmies. Because basically, with our military expenditures, I think over 50 percent of our budget goes for personnel (don't hold me to the numbers) and about 20 percent of theirs goes for personnel.

Let me just address one other thing that is current. You take the drug problem. You know it's mythology that the people who served in Vietnam are greater drug users than those who stayed home. Not true. Studies have since been made that with those who are [in] the same age bracket, who are in the best schools, and so forth, the incidence of drug use is about the same as those [who were] in Vietnam. What I am suggesting here is that with this drug thing, which really concerns me, I am inclined to think that military service curiously enough rather than making it worse could make it better.

Nixon believes Congress can intervene too much in foreign policy.

Let me quote de Gaulle on that. The last interview I had, he made a very perceptive statement: "Parliaments can paralyze policy, they cannot initiate it." Now, he took a dim view of parliaments, as we know. In this country, the president can take a dim view of Congress because we are coequal branches of the government. But what we have to bear in mind is that five hundred senators and members of Congress can't develop a foreign policy. They will develop a number of foreign policies. The Congress cannot take the leadership, because the Congress itself speaks with many voices. In the field of foreign policy it is necessary to speak with one voice. The second point you have to bear in mind is this: Whenever the Congress preempts the president in the field of foreign policy, the Congress then takes responsibility for what happens.

If it is bad, they take responsibility for that. If it is good, then of course they get credit. It is far better for them not simply to rubber-stamp but to argue, to debate, to be consulted, and to amend it. But in the final analysis the president must make the decisions. Congress must not inhibit him, particularly in superpower relations where he has access to secret information and where he has the power to do something about it. They must not inhibit him in the conduct of foreign policy.

That is one of the reasons I vetoed the War Powers Act, and I think that I would hope that the Supreme Court in the future might reverse its position on the War Powers Act. In today's world it simply provides too many inhibitions, too many restrictions, when you may have to make the decision with regard to war or peace in thirty minutes. It isn't like the old days where you could take several weeks.

Another aspect of our foreign policy which I find is unique in the world and very inconvenient, and I'm not sure that the inconvenience does not outweigh the convenience, is the fact that we have so many rather well-organized special blocs—Jews, Catholics, Italians, Irish, blacks, Hispanics, Asians, Poles, etcetera—and their emotions can be appealed to easily in the cheesiest way. They'll swim along and vote for the man who backs their view.

There is no question about their lobbies. The IRA is an organization that is denounced by many good supporters of Ireland, yet it is backed here. What is called the lobby for Israel has an enormous effect on members of Congress whenever subjects like arms for Jordan or Saudi Arabia come up. It is true that those who oppose it in this country in the American Jewish community in many cases are far more opposed than the Israeli government is. And then you have got other ethnic groups, [like] the Poles who are concerned about what the policy should be toward Solidarity.

And then, of course, you have the various religious blocs, but that is just a fact that we have to deal with. On the other hand, I think it is very important for whoever is the president to make the decisions. He must take into account views of different groups. He has to take into account these views, because no senator or congressman wants to be "Percyized." You remember Senator Percy, who in my view was never anti-Israel? To the contrary, he was the reverse. But because he had not taken as hard a line against the Palestinians as some people thought he should, many believe that was the cause of his failure to be reelected. You take the average senator who is up for election; he is not going to put his head in a buzz saw.

It is very important to have in mind that we live in a world of power politics. On the other hand, Americans do not like power politics. We never have. We are dragged into it against our will. For Americans to support any foreign policy initiative, it must be cast in idealistic terms. Wilson, for example, talked about making the world safe for democracy. That was in his mind. And a lot of Americans believe that was also the case when they walked in and supported World War II.

Look at Franklin Roosevelt. He practiced power politics. But, on the other hand, he cast it in terms of the Four Freedoms, not just against the Nazis and the Japanese, who were very convenient enemies, but in terms of what we would gain positively from it.

I think at the present time it is very important for the United States in its position of leadership to cast its role not just in terms of balance of power, arms control, etcetera, but in idealistic terms. That is why I think it is very important that despite the traditional unpopularity of foreign involvement, Americans respond to a positive initiative. They should see that we're not just spending all this money to defend outselves and all the rest, but that we want peace for ourselves and everybody else too.

We want progress for ourselves but for others too. And the way, for example, that Americans respond to humanitarian pleas, like the way we contribute to hunger programs for Ethiopia and others, indi-

cates that's an untapped reservoir of support out there. Of course, a good dose of idealism exists in American foreign policy. We should practice power politics because that's the way the world is. But it must be cast in idealistic terms in order to get people to support it.

By 1986, Nixon had another precise idea on policy he would have wished to formulate, to reduce the tide of terrorism that has been felt increasingly by the U.S. government and by its citizens.

I take a much broader view of terrorism than many do. I think first you have to define it. What is terrorism? Terrorism is the attack on innocent civilians to accomplish political ends. That's the way I see it. Now, there are other kinds of activities that are classified as terrorism, crazy people, people who kill just for the sake of killing, but generally speaking in the world today you have real terrorism. The most commonly known is the Palestinian terrorism. Its purpose is for political ends. There is the IRA; the purpose is for Northern Ireland. Also Italy's Red Brigades—what they're after I don't know—the German gangs, and so forth and so on.

However, when we look at terrorism I think we have to go back a way and see how war changed between World War I and World War II. I always thought of World War I as being the most horrible war in history because of the trench warfare and number of famous offensives, the German offensive of March 21, 1918—sixty thousand dead.

But only fifteen million people were killed in World War I, fifty-five million in World War II. What is the difference? The difference was not simply the atomic bomb; that's only two hundred and fifty thousand. The difference was—and the Germans did it first, perhaps, some say the British did—but the difference was that the deliberate killing of civilians became an accepted military tactic to assure victory. Break the will of the people to resist. Once you have crossed that line morally, then what are you going to do about the others?

I mean you have the example the Palestinians point to: [Menachem] Begin and the bombing of the King David Hotel. In Algeria terrorists didn't kill the French, they killed the moderate Algerians. In South Africa the radicals are killing not so much whites but blacks they think may be cooperating with the whites.

Now, taking that as an example, someone would say that is okay because the end is good. And my view is very hard line: One cannot justify terror and still have a civilized society. You cannot justify the killing of innocent civilians to achieve political purposes. Once you start with that proposition then that means all civilized nations have got to recognize that terrorism is not an attack on one but an attack on all. And it has to have a response by all. The response is not only in terms of gathering the intelligence, of sharing the operational capabilities and developing them together, acting together economically.

Sanctions don't work. They don't work if you have leaks, but you have got to remember that sanctions have been practiced by the British against Napoleon in the Napoleonic War[s], the British against the Germans in World War I and World War II. Sanctions will work provided there are not any leaks. I often think, for example, in terms of Libya. Had the Europeans acceded to the Reagan administration's request that we all join together in economic quarantine against Qaddafi, that would have been far more effective than bombing a few places. But nevertheless, looking to the future, I think we have to recognize that there is a very different attitude in Europe among Europeans than there is in the United States about terrorism. You have to realize too that out of 950 people last year that were killed by terrorists, only 23 were Americans. But when Americans are killed and shown on the TV screens, Americans are going to do something about it. What I am coming back to here, getting away from the philosophical point, what I come back to is that I look at terrorism as being an attack on international order. And it needs an international response. That's why it is important to bring the Russians into the game.

Now, the Russians are making the right noises, but let's face it, the Russians gain from a destruction and a weakening of the status quo, a weakening of established government. So consequently they support terrorism, because they believe that any means should be used to accomplish the end of "liberating" a country from a so-called capitalist government. And we cannot accept that on their part, and on the other side we cannot indulge in it on our part. Here you see the double standard for a lot of Vietnam. Mylai, that was terrorism. Yet the media gave hardly a stitch of coverage to the terrorism of the North Vietnamese, because for them it was policy; for us it was a violation of policy.

Put yourself in President Reagan's position. In 1986 he had warned that in the event there was another incident involving Libya, and we were able to identify the individual and the target, we would respond. He had to respond. A great country cannot warn and then back down; you lose all credibility. And it has had some deterring effect. But we must recognize that Qaddafi is only a pimple as far as the problem is concerned. The boils, the carbuncles, are other countries, other states, who deliberately sponsor terrorism and justify it as a legitimate means to accomplish political ends. I think we in the West and the Russians should go along with this: We must reject the proposition at the outset, and incidentally this means in war or peace. Destroying civilians, killing civilians to accomplish political ends is not justified. Now, when you talk about war, that gets you down to the difference between counterforce strategy and mutual assured destruction. You get my point?

A president should warn only once. If, after a warning, a terrorist again attacks and the president does not retaliate, he would lose all credibility for the balance of his term [when] there were attacks on America's interests. The president used military force as a last resort only after he was unable to get cooperation from our allies for diplomatic and economic sanctions. It is particularly distressing that hostages held by terrorists may lose their lives because of reprisals for the United States action against Libya. If we allowed that to be the case, it would only encourage the taking of more hostages.

Drawing together the divers threads of Nixon's ideas on foreign policy techniques, he would recommend: (1) learn to know the individual leaders with whom you deal; (2) don't negotiate as an end in itself; (3) employ linkage subtly but pragmatically; (4) improve the negotiating position of the United States by restoring the peacetime military draft and wartime military censorship; (5) limit congressional power to intervene in foreign policy matters; (6) stress the idealistic motives of practical power policy approaches; and (7) work internationally to curb terrorism but never allow U.S. policy to become hostage to the fate of American hostages held abroad.

V

Chile—Waiting for Jefferson

Many major Nixon accomplishments in foreign policy occurred for the most part (if not entirely) during his second term in office under the cruelly extending shadow of Watergate. However, Chile and its international role were almost wholly exempt. The White House began to worry seriously about Chile and the U.S. position in Latin America in 1970 after Salvador Allende Gossens, a left-wing pro-Marxist liberal socialist, had won the presidential election by a plurality, but it was only tempted to meddle in Chilean affairs by a constitutional quirk there. This provided that a leader in the race for president could be confirmed as representing the majority only after being endorsed by a parliamentary vote. The first important American intervention was produced by an attraction to meddle in this last constitutional provision by blocking the constitutional majority Allende required in order to take power.

When King Henry II of England became fed up with Thomas à Becket, his archbishop of Canterbury, who claimed more rights for the clergy than the sovereign was prepared to concede, Henry exclaimed petulantly in front of some of his courtiers: "Who'll rid me of that meddlesome priest!" Four of Henry's liege knights interpreted their lord's words literally. They set off on their horses for Canterbury, where they murdered the prelate in his cathedral. It is generally assumed that the king was merely expressing irritation rather than uttering a command or pronouncing sentence.

Could the death of Salvador Allende, president-elect of Chile, be considered a vaguely comparable case? President Richard Nixon and his right-hand executive, Henry Kissinger, had both made no secret of their irritation with and diplomatic fear of Salvador Allende, who had narrowly won Chile's 1970 presidental election and was awaiting parliamentary confirmation in accordance with Chilean law. Nixon and his national security adviser had made it clear to high U.S. officials that they considered Allende a menace to our interests whose removal would be welcome.

I do not think there is any convincing evidence that Nixon's intention was as murderous as Henry's turned out to be; he was indeed irked, to say the least. Yet it is highly improbable that he ever gave an instruction to the CIA to liquidate the Chilean Socialist. Moreover, it is known that Richard Helms (CIA head in 1970) had stated to certain of his fellow officials that he would have nothing to do with assassination plots.

This bears pointing out to those who like to imagine the worst about the coup d'état that took place on September 11, 1973. It was staged by a right-wing army general who claims he acted entirely on his own, with no CIA or other U.S. advice or assistance. Furthermore, Allende was not murdered, like Thomas à Becket, but blew his own brains out when he saw the uprising was going against him. I have no doubt that Nixon was just as pleased by this result as King Henry was when, to his possible embarrassment, he learned of his archbishop's demise. Nevertheless, satisfaction is not the same thing as guilt.

On September 4, 1970, Allende gained a plurality of little more than 1 percent of the votes in Chile's election, thus, in the absence of a majority, throwing the decision to the nation's parliament in accordance with the constitution. This event precipitated an effort by the Nixon administration to block Allende's confirmation—an instruction given to CIA director Richard Helms, who was told to use up to ten million dollars and not to be concerned at the risks involved in order to "save Chile." By presidential command the American ambassador in Santiago, then Edward Korry, was kept ignorant of this order and the consequent activities of American agents and undercover policymakers. At the president's command, moreover, neither his secretary of defense nor his secretary of state were advised; only his national security adviser, Kissinger, was involved in the Chile problem from its very inception.

Kissinger, who from the start was executive officer of Nixon's Chilean policy, concluded of Allende's portent to the United States:

> It was the first, and so far the only, time in modern history that a democratic process has come so close to producing a Communist takeover. For Allende was not the classic Chilean President who would serve his six-year term and then be replaced through another democratic election. Once he was in office, his proclaimed intention was to revise the Chilean Constitution, to neutralize and suppress all opposition parties and media, and thereby to make his own rule—or at least that of his party—irreversible.
>
> Allende's later martyrdom has obscured his politics. Socialist though he may have proclaimed himself, his goals and his philosophy bore no resemblance to European social democracy. Allende had founded the Socialist Party of Chile, which set itself apart from the Communist Party by being more radical in its program and no more democratic in its philosophy. . . . He had been a founder of the Organization of Latin American Solidarity, a Havana-based coalition of leftist groups dedicated to armed struggle against the United States and to violent revolution throughout the hemisphere.[1]

I cannot refute these assertions by the stalwart Dr. Kissinger, but I cannot forget either that he had made similar assertions about the Portuguese socialist Mario Soares, when he took the lead in post–Salazar Portugal and was saved from American-stimulated ouster only by Western European Socialist leaders. Soares became the detested enemy of the Communists when he consolidated the Democratic Socialist regime.

Two clandestine U.S. operations were aimed at destabilizing Allende's control through economic pressures. The first also toyed with a brace of Chilean brigadier generals who had been involved in previous political coups and were known to oppose Allende. The clandestine schemes were code-named Track I and Track II. They involved sponsorship of a former president, Eduardo Frei Montalva, and the man edged out by Allende in the 1970 balloting, Jorge Alessandri Rodriguez. Frei and Alessandri were not conspirators.

The rationale for such scheming was fear that Allende, a well known left-wing Socialist, might easily pave the way for an outright Soviet-backed regime in Chile, comparable to that of Fidel Castro in Cuba. Presidential adviser Henry Kissinger told American newspaper editors on September 16: "I have yet to meet somebody who firmly believes that if Allende wins, there is likely to be another free election in Chile." These opinions, while not shared with Nixon's cabinet or with his envoy to Chile, were discussed in an interagency group chaired by Kissinger, the "Forty Committee."

What was accomplished by the conspirators in Washington is not wholly traceable, but the Chilean army commander, General René Schneider Chereau, an opponent of military coups, was accidentally killed on October 16 in an unplanned shoot-out. Six days later the Chilean Congress voted in secret ballot to confirm Salvador Allende Gossens as chief of state.

Korry was to cable Washington right after the Chilean election that gave Allende his initial edge:

> Chile voted calmly to have a Marxist-Leninist state, the first nation in the world to make this choice freely and knowingly.... *His margin is only about one percent but it is large enough in the Chilean constitutional framework to nail down his triumph as final.* There is no reason to believe that the Chilean armed forces will unleash a civil war or that any other intervening miracle will undo his victory. It is a sad fact that Chile has taken the path to communism with only a little more than a third (36 percent) of the nation approving this choice, but it is an immutable fact. *It will have the most profound effect on Latin America and beyond; we have suffered a grievous defeat; the consequences will be domestic and international;* the repercussions will have immediate impact in some lands and delayed effect in others.[2]

The italicized sentences were underlined by Nixon when Kissinger sent him Korry's report.

Régis Debray, a left-wing French intellectual, visited Chile shortly after the election to write a book about Allende. Debray is not formally a Communist, but, as is not uncommon in France, has at times been even to the left of the French Communist party. He is an admirer of Fidel Castro and was in Bolivia with Che Guevara, where he was captured but eventually freed by the Bolivian authorities after French diplomatic intercession. I know and rather like Debray but do not trust him entirely either in judgment or accurate recounting of facts. Kissinger was impressed by his assertion that Allende had told Debray he was seeking to "overthrow" the "bourgeois" state in Chile. Thus, with Kissinger convinced of Allende's pro-Communist intentions as Debray reported them, Korry was preaching to a converted national security adviser (although it is worth noting that Nixon first ordered Korry to be omitted from his short list of key officials dealing with Chilean affairs and then replaced him as ambassador, with no new assignment).

Kissinger concluded: "The myth that Allende was a democrat has been as assiduously fostered as it is untrue. The fact is that various measures taken by Allende's government were declared to be unconstitutional and outside the law by the Chilean Supreme Court on May 26, 1973, by the Comptroller General on July 2, 1973, and by the Chamber of Deputies on August 22, 1973. It is the opposition he aroused *within* Chile that triggered the military coup of 1973, in the conception, planning, and execution of which we played no role whatever."[3]

On March 8, 1971, I had a long talk with President Nixon in the White House, the first I had had since he became president. At the end, after well over an hour of conversation, he asked where I was bound and I told him Chile. "You lucky fellow," he commented. "I wish I could go there." I told him Kissinger had asked me to write him a letter after my trip—to show to Nixon—expressing my opinions. He said: "Yes, I wish you would help me by doing that. Tell me straight what you think." The next day I saw Secretary of State Rogers (who had been dealt out of consultation on Chile, by no less a person than the president). Rogers told me that the United States was not pursuing a policy of hostility (toward Chile) "of the sort we developed against Castro in

Cuba.... We are trying to maintain proper and friendly relations and to take no action detrimental to the Chilean government. We will frame our future policies in accord with Chile's policy toward us. Obviously we don't want to look as if we are rewarding anti–U.S. policies in other countries. We do not wish to appear hostile simply because Chile has a different form of government from ours—like Yugoslavia, for example, a country with which we have good relationships. But if the Chileans develop an anti–U.S. policy we will adjust our own policy in reply."

Rogers said Chile was still run by a minority government, stressing that Allende and his coalition were in the legislative minority. He claimed that the Chilean leftist tide did not seem to be spreading among its neighbors and that our relations with Peru had improved as a result of the new regime in Chile. Other South American countries were worried about a Communist takeover. Chile was so far from Russia that it was less likely to become a superpower battleground like Cuba; and we shouldn't forget that troublemaking in Cuba was costing the Russians a lot.

While I was in Chile shortly afterward, I had a two and a half hour visit one evening (March 23, 1971) with President Allende in his office. I found him a likable, garrulous man of sixty-two, small, stocky, quick moving, with a gray mustache, a ruddy face (he liked sailing), and wavy brown hair untouched by white. He wore thick, heavily rimmed spectacles and had a determined, obstinate face with small cleft chin. He preferred to walk up and down, gesticulating as we talked, referring all the time to our discussion as "a dialogue," not an interview. I observed in my notes: "He resembles a slightly overweight, agitated fox." Allende said:

> Today, in our popular unity government, the Socialists, Communists, and other left-wing groups hold equal roles. The Chilean Communists are a very serious party, known for its political honesty, which has taken an engagement to fulfill our announced governmental program. And the Chilean Communist party is sufficiently realistic to know any policy that might subject Chilean interests to those of another country would have disastrous effects here.
>
> Furthermore, even if they have very skillful people in the Chilean Communist Party, I assure you they don't have any monopoly of intelligence. Don't forget, I am the presi-

dent, and I run things, a Socialist. I have no need to import strength from outside.

In thirty years' political life, I never failed to do what I said I would do. It could be possible that the dynamic of events might eventually create a revolutionary party, one party of the revolution. The dynamic I refer to—which certainly does not exist now—would be a profound harmony of thinking in Chile and a homogeneity of views on the best tactical approach to our problems.

But this is not possible for the imminent future. After all, the Socialists don't want to be changed and the Radicals, who in Chile have had a party for 110 years, surely won't commit suicide. Don't forget that Karl Marx foresaw a time when there would be no governments at all. But when? It hasn't come yet.

The strategy of socialism must depend on the realities of any country where it is attempted. To be a Socialist is obviously not the same thing as being a Communist.

There are different roads to socialism. Yugoslavia is a socialist country. So is Rumania. So are China, Cuba, the Soviet Union, and many others. But all of them have followed different paths. I think capital must be placed at the service of man. I think that man must come before everything and anything else. Our existing constitution was drafted in such a way that we had to reform it even in order to pass the necessary legislation to nationalize our mines. I hope, for the time being, to utilize the existing constitution and our present laws in order to achieve the reforms we urgently need. But as a second step—some time later on—I envisage proposing an entirely new constitution.

If I were to die tomorrow, no one in Chile would ever dare to abolish the system I instituted of giving every child free milk. No one would ever dream of taking away from illiterate citizens the right to vote which they have been legally granted. Nevertheless, if we are defeated, another party would certainly take over. I can assure you, however, that we don't think we will be defeated.

My word is formally engaged to respect all the fundamental rights of man. No matter how extensive our economic and social reform[s] will be, we will not only respect human rights but actually increase them. So far they exist only for a minority. Human rights are not merely political;

> they are also social and economic. Freedom alone is just a fiction for the poor.
>
> Not the slightest violation of freedom of the press exists. Such allegations are unfounded. How can we be accused of an unfree press when only two days ago the most reactionary party in Chile started its own new paper called *La Tribuna*?

I asked: "Do you foresee the possibility of any violent confrontation in Chile as a consequence of opposition to your program?" Allende replied:

> Sadly, very sadly, I admit this possibility exists. That is the lesson of history. There is no doubt at all on this point. It would come from the Right. I know it would come from the Right because it has already done something that never before occurred in Chilean history—namely assassinated the army commander, General Schneider. What they really wanted to do was kill me. There have already been two attempts on my life.
>
> Certain groups in the United States, groups including the copper mine owners, who have always been influential in your policy, are trying to upset my government, to interfere with our program. What I mean is that there are local plots, inside Chile, supported or encouraged by certain interests in the United States. Obviously I do not think that the United States government would lend itself to such efforts, to a policy that would clearly violate the principle of self-determination.

He promised to give financial compensation to foreign companies with interests in Chile that are being nationalized, adding: "This is not a process of confiscation. We fully accept the principle of compensation."

He said Chile intended to stand by its existing international commitments.

> We will honor every single commitment Chile has undertaken. We are, indeed, very active in the Organization of American States. And we have not changed any of our

relationships with the United States. We want respect for our policy and understanding of our insistence that a Chilean citizen has the right to work, the right to improve and educate himself, the right to rest and recreation....

The United States should recognize that our democracy here is authentic democracy and that we will never do anything against the United States or contribute to injuring its sovereignty. For example, we will never provide a military base that might be used against the United States. Chile will never permit its territory to be used for a military base by any foreign power, by anybody.

What we are doing in terms of our internal reform is simply to improve our own country and our own society and standard of living. The United States should understand that if we nationalize copper installations in which there have been U.S. interests and U.S. investment, it is because we need to do so, because it is vital in the interests of the Chilean nation and the Chilean people. I simply cannot imagine that the United States government would make common cause with private enterprise on an issue like this and frame its policy accordingly. Unfortunately, history does teach that on occasion in the past this has been the case.

On March 30 I sent Nixon the letter he and Kissinger had requested. I sent it by embassy pouch from Buenos Aires, Argentina, to avoid even the slightest chance of any kind of leak. After reflecting on my talk with Allende and the rather limited past background I had in Chile plus more recent reading, conversations with Ambassador Korry and other foreigners, as well as ex-President Frei and other Chileans, I dispatched my own suggestions as Nixon had proposed. I indicated in a covering note that I had personally liked Allende and felt he was probably more sincere in his statements than many people in Washington admitted. My letter said:

Every country has the right to reform or revolutionize its social system if this is the desire of its citizens. There can be no valid U.S. objection if the Chilean people wish to revise their economy and society without bloodshed and by electoral means.

But the United States has a legitimate right to see that such changes are not produced at our expense. We have a fair claim to compensation for property sufficient to cover insurance commitments otherwise chargeable to the U.S. taxpayer. And we must try and safeguard against the spread across South America of an obviously anti–U.S. movement deliberately encroaching on our legitimate interests—especially if (as in Cuba) hostile military installations are permitted. We cannot tolerate a Monroe Doctrine in reverse....

My impression of Allende is that of a clever but not profound man, energetic but undisciplined, intuitive but not intellectual; a man being rendered giddy with success. He is bound to face serious economic and political problems.

There will be inflation, declining production in key sectors, sizable unemployment. Although the anti-Allende parties have displayed timidity and an inability to unite, those leaders who don't flee the country are destined to coalesce in an opposition to the right of the President....I would recommend:

1. That Washington should never allow any development to precipitate a break in relations with Santiago, thus sacrificing the ultimate potential of being able, someday, to influence developments from within. The error of Cuba should not be repeated in Chile, even if humble pie sometimes features on the menu.

2. That a single individual, directly responsible to the president's staff, be assigned to coordinate all Chilean affairs (diplomatic, economic, propagandistic, military, financial, commercial, and intelligence—including the private sector). Thereby, policy can be directed effectively from the top on both a long-range basis and, should such be needed, an immediate ad hoc basis.

3. That the U.S. ambassador and his entire staff be rigidly enjoined to assume an unruffled, infallibly courteous, low-profile posture, regardless of what develops. They should never lose their cool when attempts are made to affront the United States, damage its property, or even menace its representatives.

4. That this attitude should be coordinated with a deliberate, subtle policy of isolating Chile—at this moment—from its normal commercial and financial contacts with our allies in Western Europe and Japan....

5. Ultimately it will be in our interest to see our friends expand their contacts and influence in Chile. The long-range political effect would be benign as today the flag follows

> trade. But during the immediate future our friends must be dissuaded from rash moves and postpone efforts to move in before Santiago negotiates satisfactory accords with us to move out....
>
> 6. Until such accords, U.S. diplomacy must persuade our friends to freeze the ball; not to rush into a Chilean vacuum and ease Allende's problem with us....
>
> 7. In the long run we should seek to take advantage of Chile's isolated geographic position (the Pacific, the desert, the Andes) and deter other South American nations from trying to follow Allende's example—at our expense....

I received no acknowledgment from Nixon until my return to Paris after a long trip around Africa, Madagascar, Mauritius, the Comoro Islands, and the Middle East. The president thanked me and said the approach on Chile being followed by our government conformed with my recommendations. This pleased me, not out of vanity but because I felt my proposals were sensible and might avoid the disastrous results that could be expected from rather more dramatic ideas I had heard discussed in Washington.

Unfortunately, I have since realized that a more dramatic course was in the process of being elaborated, one that ultimately, if not directly, produced death for Allende and a cast-iron regime for the Chilean people. I don't mean to imply that Allende was murdered as a consequence of American plots. I have no reason to believe this was the case, despite the fact that at least some CIA agents had dickered with Chilean opponents of Allende, including members of the military up to the rank of brigadier general. When the plot exploded, Allende shot himself to avoid capture by the insurgents. But the regime installed to succeed him was and is an old-fashioned military dictatorship that justifies all its harshness in the name of "anti-Communism."

In much the same fashion that President Nixon was to use so deftly and wisely in his China policy, largely confining it to himself and Kissinger (who became the point 2 man I had suggested), Nixon limited access to the scope of his Chile policy to Kissinger and, to a lesser degree, CIA Director Helms. Helms was a known opponent of violence in Chile and refused to countenance assassination as a method the agency might employ under his supervision.

Thus I am personally convinced, on the basis of available evidence, that the CIA was not involved in the assassination of Allende, first of all because I don't believe he was assassinated but that he killed himself, and that there was no such conspiracy under way in the United States government and its agents despite an attempt to kidnap General Schneider, during which he was killed by adherents of one of the CIA's "tame" operations. The evidence is befogged. But I have been convinced that there is no conclusive evidence that the CIA was involved in Schneider's murder, despite Nixon's direction to Helms that Chile should be "saved." On October 15, 1971, Kissinger, on the president's behalf, ordered the CIA to call a halt to any Track II operations. Thenceforward U.S. policy sought a covert economic squeeze with an unruffled embassy under Ambassador Nathaniel Davis, who replaced the energetic Korry. Kissinger's role in Chile was similar to that recommended in my point 2 but preceded it.

It appears to me that there was no diminishment of pressure against Allende. However, to those involved at the heart of American policy in 1970 it became plain that there was to be no fatal violence. Instead, Ambassador Korry was authorized by Washington to advise his contacts in the Chilean armed forces (which included earlier known coup-makers) that they could expect no further U.S. military aid if Allende were seated as president.

This warning was underscored by the closing of U.S. military facilities, two in mainland Chile and one on Easter Island in the Pacific, which monitored Soviet missile testing in the Pacific as well as French nuclear experiments near Tahiti. However, Admiral Elmo Zumwalt, U.S. Navy chief of staff, had urged that Washington approve a visit to Valparaiso by the nuclear aircraft carrier *Enterprise*, and Allende made an official invitation public—only to be openly rebuffed by Washington on orders from Nixon.

In November 1971, Fidel Castro paid an official visit to Chile, heating up the alarm felt in the U.S. government concerning Allende's intentions. The trip came only a month after Allende, despite his promises, had announced that the three great U.S. copper mines of the Kennecott and Anaconda companies would receive no compensation for their seizure by Santiago. But Castro proved unable to convert Allende to his own wholly pro-Soviet views, thus leaving the Chilean president stranded between Chilean moderate left-wingers and outright extremists. One result of this predicament was a rash of unsuccessful coup attempts in 1972 and early 1973.

At the start of 1972, General Augusto Pinochet Ugarte was inducted into the important Chilean office of army chief of staff. One of his early moves was to instruct his Directorate of Intelligence to produce a study of the internal security position. This produced a paper stressing the dangers to the regime of the extreme-left activists of MIR, the Movement of the Revolutionary Left, and also analyzed the possibility of a left-wing extremist coup against Allende. It was already becoming apparent that the Chilean president faced his most difficult political hurdle on the far left, an analysis borne out by future events. I am firmly convinced that Allende was brought down in the end by the MIRistas of his far left and its enthusiastic supporters rather than by pressures from the right or by the United States.

The tensions between right and left and between extreme left and moderate left rendered the situation inside Chile uneasy. Pinochet said subsequently that a "conflict between the executive and legislative branches did not allow for a constitutional solution" of the problem and that, together with some colleagues, he had started to analyze "the possibilities of carrying out a coup." More than a year later he acknowledged that his ideas then started to "coincide" with those of his more restive officers.

On November 16, 1975, I had a two-hour talk with General Pinochet, the sixty-year-old officer whose coup displaced Allende and who became chief of state. It is widely assumed that the United States encouraged, supported, and collaborated in the Pinochet coup that ended in Allende's death. When I observed to Pinochet that it was believed in the United States that he had collaborated with Washington in preparing and staging his operation, he said:

> I can swear to you as a Christian that I never had any kind of contact with any ambassador, with anyone from the CIA or with any ambassador, U.S. or otherwise. I wanted to be free of any obligation to anyone, to any other force or faction. And, of course, I wished to protect my plans by total discretion. Why, afterward, even my family asked me what kind of help I received from the United States. I told them:

"Not even good will. And in that I am very much disappointed."

In the absence of any convincing evidence to the contrary—that Pinochet was aided to the seat of power and (even worse) that the coup's supporters murdered Allende—I tend to believe Pinochet, a man who is not blessed with a winning personality but whose unvarnished arguments have a telling ring. He says of his role:

> The Chilean army was the only organized force in a position to take over. It was the least Communist-infiltrated institution in the country. Even the navy and the air force had been infiltrated. Even the police. But the army managed to escape because the then-commander, General Prats, was believed to be a friend of Allende, and the Communists left it alone.

Pinochet told me that he began to plan his action as soon as Allende became president in 1970. He had become convinced Allende favored the Communists, who were not just a left-wing party but "a perverse doctrine" seeking to install a "materialistic system." He feared Allende's election "was the end for Chile" and that Allende would fire him as soon as he was in power, but another General Pinochet was dismissed in error. Allende named Augusto Pinochet army commander instead, and in August 1973 the general ordered the Army War College to prepare a game plan on national security—"on a defensive basis, against riots, strikes, etcetera. Later I had this modified on an active and offensive basis."

"When this had been done," Pinochet continued, "I had to decide on D day, the date to take action. I thought that the most appropriate date would be September 14—four days before our Independence Day parade on September 18, when all the units that would take part in the parade would be in the Santiago area. Thus I could organize the required units without provoking any alarm. . . . But the situation changed on September 9."

He explained that the air force commanders, an admiral, and a general visited him and said they were worried about the situation, but "I didn't confide my plans to them, for reasons of discretion. I only said I would take some kind of action and agreed on the date they wished. I moved up my projected D day to September 11 because of a very excitable speech made in Valparaiso by Carlos Altomirano [an extreme left-wing Socialist, more extreme than the Communists]. He threatened to produce chaos throughout Chile if he was removed from his position as senator, which some people were demanding. And he was trying to work up the youth, the students, by inflaming them."

Pinochet claimed that he acted to forestall efforts by Russia and Cuba to assume paramount control. "Russia and Cuba are trying to recuperate their position, to make Chile the Latin American base for their activities that it was under Allende. This was then the center for weapons and for their money throughout Latin America. But China has not participated in this. China has behaved well." (Later the general told me Chile had arranged a large Chinese loan, offering access to Chilean copper in exchange.)

It is obvious that Pinochet could make such statements even without factual basis, but I have a feeling that he staged his coup as he described it and didn't take fellow officers from the navy and air force into his complete confidence until the end. The coup was probably stimulated by the revolutionary ardor of the MIRistas—the left-wing extremists from the Movement of the Revolutionary Left—who were violent activists and had adherents placed in key positions including Allende's personal bodyguard. The excessive actions of the MIRistas in seizing land and property, especially in the south, did a great deal to promote counterrevolutionary sentiment and plotting, turning against the regime even a considerable body of liberals who might otherwise have been prepared to tolerate Allende.

By March of 1973 it was common knowledge that a group of colonels and brigadier generals was inviting fellow officers to join them in a conspiracy, but Pinochet's activities were far more discreet. An unsuccessful plot against Allende in June of that year showed that the president was prepared to fight off illegal action with paramilitary forces. It is interesting to note, incidentally, that Pinochet's senior, General Carlos Prats Gonzalez, when asked by Allende whether he felt Pinochet should be named commander in chief, replied: "I am confident that he will know how to support you with the same loyalty I have shown." Prats later said: "It is my conviction that he [Pinochet] only climbed aboard the chariot of the coup-makers at the last minute."

There is no doubt that the United States worked under cover to support the liberal and conservative opposition to Allende. During Allende's first year at the helm, covert expenditures approved by the "Forty Committee" of American officials and their advisers amounted to more than $2,500,000. The conservative Santiago newspaper, *El Mercurio*, was given almost $2,000,000 in U.S. financial support, which must have seemed satisfactory to its owner, Agustin Edwards Eastman, an émigré from Allende's Chile living in the United States. Edwards was also owner of a Coca-Cola bottling plant and through this a friend of that company's chairman, Donald Kendall, a personal friend and occasional adviser of President Nixon.

William E. Colby, who directed the CIA from 1972 to 1976, said he had "no problem in testifying and answering questions before a congressional investigating committee on all of the CIA's covert political action operations" (in Chile) up to Allende's election and after his installation in office—our so-called Track I activities. But there was Track II, although it lasted only six weeks and was cut off after Allende was inaugurated. In Track II, Washington had indeed looked for a coup. But President Nixon had ordered Helms (Colby's predecessor) and the CIA to keep that activity in the strictest confidence, reporting it to absolutely no one. (In fact, however, Colby did confide information on Track II to one congressional committee member.)

Nathaniel Davis, American envoy to Santiago at the time of Pinochet's coup and Allende's death, writes in his excellent memoir of his mission: "Both Richard Nixon and Henry Kissinger had deeply held emotions and convictions about Chile."[4] But whether these "deeply held emotions" were more tangible than those Henry II confided to his knights on Becket is impossible to say. The Church Committee of Congress, which examined most secret CIA, Pentagon, State Department, and White House documents, concluded: "Was the United States *directly* involved, covertly, in the 1973 coup in Chile? The Committee has found no evidence that it was." Now, of course, not having found any evidence (which could have been destroyed) is not a wholly conclusive statement. Nevertheless, the exceedingly reputable Ambassador

Davis, who made many private inquiries on the Chilean affair after his retirement from the foreign service, believes: "According to everyone I asked, the U.S. military was conducting only normal intelligence activity in Chile during the 1971–1973 period. Clandestine military action programs would have been contrary to operating instructions and interagency ground rules, and the Church Committee staff report gives no indication of such programs."[5] (This was a proposal of a rumored secret Track III task force 157, which apparently never existed.)

And Colby, another honorable civil servant, said in his memoirs: "CIA sent clear instruction[s] to its station in Santiago in May and June 1973 to separate itself from any contact with the Chilean military so that it could not be misunderstood to have been involved in any coup action the military might undertake."[6] Of course, the CIA supported opposition publications and labor unions, using "third-country intermediaries." This is normal in today's world.

I have a suspicion that in 1971 Kissinger was still spending too much time looking for camouflaged Communists. Even in 1974 he was labeling as a "Portuguese Kerensky" the socialist Soares, first foreign minister and then president after the Salazar dictatorship ended. Soares, a staunch democrat, was perhaps the last man in Portugal ready to permit a Communist takeover as Kerensky unwittingly did with Lenin. My own surmise—although these things never can be proved—is that an Allende government would gradually have mellowed into a liberal democratic regime, driven in that direction by its own fanatical MIRista wing.

Willy Brandt, the former German chancellor, wrote me on this subject (April 10, 1986), discussing Kissinger and the post-Salazar Portuguese regime, with particular reference to Mario Soares, today's president of NATO Portugal. It is well known that Brandt was never one of Kissinger's favorite statesmen, and vice versa. Nevertheless he comments:

> It is well known that Henry Kissinger at the time had been in a rather pessimistic mood with regard to the prospects in Southern Europe. He feared that the region might have been lost to "Marxism."
>
> In 1975, I urgently talked the point into Brezhnev that

he should not draw any false conclusions and that he should not make any miscalculations about Portugal. At about the same time I urged upon President Ford—in Kissinger's presence—that he should take Mario Soares seriously and that he should not assume that Soares and his democratic socialist partners would by necessity be overrun by the Communists.

Questions like this can never be answered. What the Pinochet regime did was to establish a tough dictatorship, outlaw leftist parties, "recess" center and rightist parties, and dissolve Congress. Castro, who had visited Chile in 1971 as Allende's guest, was already dubious about the latter's "pluralistic" approach to socialism. Moscow, which envisioned as a dream what Kissinger fancied as a nightmare, obviously hoped that Allende would indeed prove to be another weak Kerensky. And David Phillips, the CIA's Western Hemisphere section head, said that the famous and short-lived Track II operation "just faded into oblivion." The attitude of the State Department toward the Pinochet regime has been coolly standoffish but correct, avoiding the abrasive incidents that have marked U.S. relations with Castro's Cuba. Nixon was no latter-day Henry II, nor was Allende.

Undoubtedly the United States was pleased to see Allende overthrown, although I cannot imagine it was delighted by Allende's death. Personally, I suspect that Allende was by no means the horned devil he seemed to be in the White House, either in the Oval Office or the cellar suite at that time inhabited by Kissinger as security adviser. Although the disappointment of both Moscow and Castro at seeing a more sympathetic regime established on the continent of South America was clearly regarded as a plus in Nixon's own foreign policy book of records (the fact that the people of Chile are consequently having a pretty thin time is an unfortunate spin-off), neither Allende nor Pinochet nor what either of them represented was "made in" Russia or America.

A great deal of emotional outpouring among ill-informed U.S. liberals followed the disappearance of Allende and his regime. On the whole, stripped of verbiage, Nixon and Kissinger pursued a shrewd policy in defending U.S. interests and are certainly not responsible for the Chilean president's death and almost certainly not responsible for the installation of General Pinochet and his brutal regime.

The most knowledgeable, objective, and well-informed observer I know who lives in Chile (but is not a native) has a wise analysis of Allende with which I thoroughly agree. He writes:

> In my judgment, Allende was a Third World socialist whose ideological roots derived their sustenance from the Chilean political soil. By social origin, he was from the "national bourgeoisie." His grandfather had been surgeon general of the Chilean army during the war of the Pacific and he himself, a physician. He entered national politics as minister of health in the Popular Front government of 1938, representing the Socialist party, to which he belonged all his political life.
>
> Although the Chilean Communist party (very Moscow line) wound up supporting his presidential candidacies in 1964 and 1970, it was with little enthusiasm since Allende was never Marxist-Leninist and nurtured the dream of "another road to socialism."
>
> He thought he saw elements of this approach in Cuba. The problem in making a judgment on whether Allende was pro-Communist or pro-Soviet is that he thought he was using them, and it turned out to be the other way around. And this was not for lack of opportunities to have worked out a modus vivendi with the United States.
>
> But this would have meant breaking with the radical left in his party and the Havana-run Revolutionary Left Movement (MIR). Instead, he waffled and maneuvered to gain time when what was needed was consolidation of the center. In effect, he opened the door to the radical right and the praetorian government of Pinochet.

In terms of Nixon's policy prejudice he could be considered lucky to have seen himself rid of the specter of a hammer and sickle waving above La Moneda, seat of the president of Chile. Nor was he put to the test of having to attempt new means of confronting a threat to the spirit of the Monroe Doctrine. That doctrine had been partially directed against Russian advances by its author, John Quincy Adams. But those were direct advances and in Alaska, not South America. Nixon felt his presidency was being threatened by a new kind of doctrinal aggression—by indirect and third-party interference of a sort that neither Adams nor his president, James Monroe, could even have imagined.

Nixon's basic aim (as later in Nicaragua), to keep from the mainland of the American continents ideological or political bases for movements considered hostile by Washington, was accomplished by what the White House could cynically see as good fortune, no matter how the Chilean people felt. They weren't asked.

My own hunch is that the proposals I sent Nixon that tended to spell out careful diplomacy might gradually have toned down the impact of Allende's policy and avoided a bloody coup. History is not written by untested hunches.

Nixon himself takes wry comfort that in Pinochet's Chile:

> *Critics focus exclusively on political repression in Chile, while ignoring the freedoms that are a product of a free economy.... Rather than insisting on instant perfection from Chile, we should encourage the progress it is making!*

He wrote unabashedly in *The Real War*:

> *In Chile the ruling junta has embarked on what has been labeled "a daring gamble... to turn the country into a laboratory for free-market economics."*[7]

Bill Colby who headed the CIA at the time of the Pinochet coup and Allende's suicide, says in his memoirs: "I am not trying to whitewash CIA's activities in Chile, but only to put in true perspective what the Agency did there. Certainly Track II [the six weeks' abortion it fostered] in 1970 sought a military coup at the direct order of President Nixon."[8]

But Nixon can claim honestly that neither he nor any branch of his government played a role in the successful 1973 coup of General Pinochet. He had given CIA chief Helms a clear order to block any chance that Allende would win a 1970 parliamentary majority confirming Allende as Chile's legal president. But this plot, which never came off, vanished in failure together with Track II. Because Nixon was clearly ready to sanction Allende's end, if need be, in 1970 does not legally convict him of Allende's end by suicide in the face of a coup in 1973.

However, to say the least, there was no innocence of intent. As Colby writes in his memoirs, "In Track II we had indeed looked for a coup."[9] The moral blemish is obvious; but there was no involvement by the United States in a Chilean crime in 1973. And, as Kissinger writes in *Years of Upheaval*: "Over time, Chile gradually faded as a major issue both in American public opinion and for American policymakers."[10]

Not for Chileans, alas, but it was their coup, happily not ours. Nixon's foreign policy toward Chile was not criminal (except in its early stages, and then it was only criminal by intent). Nor was it very high-minded, to say the least. Yet Nixon argues:

> *In Cuba there are neither political nor economic rights. In Chile, the latter may well be the precursor of the former. Rather than insisting on instant perfection from Chile, we should encourage the progress it is making.*[11]

VI

Chinese Checkers

It is extraordinary to recall that the greatest diplomatic coup achieved by Nixon was the recognition of China and consequent exchanges. Yet the entire secret and brilliantly successful negotiation that brought this about occurred within the time span of the dirty Watergate affair. This was not permitted by the Chinese to interfere with their objective of a friendly America; if anything, that goal was achieved more easily by the personal intervention of Mao Tse-tung and Chou En-lai. They were fully briefed on the whole Watergate business that had infected not only U.S. internal political health but also, when statesmen abroad sought to play on American weakness, its position in many aspects of foreign policy. And Mao subsequently showed his alarm unabashedly.

Kissinger admired Chou immensely, but it was clear that he had been even more enormously impressed by Mao, whose personality seemed to fill a room. Kissinger told me: "He was grossly overweight but he had a remarkable capacity to dominate things around him. Physically he exuded will power. He dominated by this feeling of will."

Kissinger observed some time later: "Very recently I reviewed the transcript of our conversation [with Mao] and I found it like the overture of a Wagnerian opera. Every single thing we [Nixon and Kissinger] discussed in the subsequent conversations with Chou En-lai was previously mentioned in that single talk with Mao."

It was perfectly plain that, although the People's Republic of China did not yet have a liaison office, much less an embassy, in Washington, it was completely informed on Watergate's potential significance to the Nixon presidency; yet the worried Chinese leadership resolved to stick by its planned new friendship with Washington. This was obviously a fundamental step that did not depend on the personal links of the two chiefs of state as individuals but on government-to-government relationships and sometimes dubious calculations of strength.

Possibly, one might conjecture, the Chinese speculated that they might obtain a better deal in their bilateral negotiations with the Americans if the latter were maneuvering from weakness. I personally do not believe this for a minute. Much as they clearly admired Nixon, who took the initiative in recognizing Peking, and liked Kissinger, who handled Washington's negotiating with superb skill, I am persuaded that they had taken a basic decision and apparently resolved to stick by it, come what may.

On October 26, 1973, when I was in Peking on an extended tour, I asked Chou whether the Watergate scandal had had any effect on Sino-American relations. He said it had had no effect. He added; "We think it perhaps reflects your political life and you have had such things occur in your society and undoubtedly will again. There are many social aspects interwoven into it, and it is better not to discuss this issue. I hope your president will be able to overcome these difficulties. Do you think he will?"

One of the many remarkable aspects of the Nixon-Kissinger negotiations with Mao-Chou is that it was wholly contained within the Watergate time span. This began June 18, 1972, when a group of men was arrested in the Watergate complex in Washington; one was an ex-CIA man, another had been a minor White House consultant. These connections caught the eye of editors, and the wolves were soon baying. Finally on August 9, 1974, President Nixon resigned under fire.

Bracketed between these dates was a foreign policy achievement such as few American presidents could boast of and a striking change in the existing world power alignment. Fortunately, President Nixon was able to hang on to the reins of government long enough to ensure that this historic step became a fact in international life. Its effects on all the world's major nations and power blocs persist.

Nixon's greatest foreign policy coup even produced an easing of tensions with a Soviet Union that was clearly worried by his success in arranging a friendly accommodation between Washington and Peking. The operation was carried out by Nixon and Kissinger, at that time national security adviser to the president, with great vision and discretion, style, and dignity. Befitting his constitutional role as chief executive, Nixon laid out the goals and sketched out the basic strategy to be followed while Kissinger—with finesse, subtlety, and impenetrable secrecy—made the initial arrangements, primarily through Pakistan, an ally common to both China and the United States.

Even during his political exile after his defeat by Kennedy in the 1960 presidential race, Nixon had quietly discussed China with foreign statesmen he visited, including the Indonesian chief, Sukarno; the Rumanian, Ceauşescu; and General de Gaulle as well as some of his top French aides. In 1967, the year before his successful candidacy against Hubert Humphrey, he wrote an article in *Foreign Affairs*, in which he said:

Taking the long view, we simply cannot afford to leave China forever outside the family of nations, there to nurture its fantasies, cherish its hates and threaten its neighbors.

Subsequently he wrote:

One of my first acts as President was to derect that we explore privately the possibilities of a rapproachment with china. This proceeded at first as a sort of slow ritual dance, but the steps rapidly gained momentum in 1971 until, on July 15, I made the surprise announcement that I would visit china early in 1972.[1]

Nixon proudly commented on his rapprochement with Peking that the 1972 accord

may have been the most dramatic geopolitical event since World War II, but the most significant geopolitical event was the Sino-Soviet split that preceded it. This split made the later rapprochement with the United States possible. Together with continuing Soviet belligerence, it also made the rapprochement indispensable from both the Chinese and American viewpoints.[2]

Nixon (as well as Kissinger) had taken pains to study long-term and contemporary Chinese developments, and when he first arrived in the White House, he recalled:

There were... a few things in our favor. The most important and interesting was the Soviet split with China.[3]

From his studious preparation for his voyage of political exploration he learned that Sun Yat-sen, father of modern China, had estimated that the Russian sphere of influence in his country included some 42 percent of its territory. The Chinese hope that the new communist leadership that took over in Russia in 1917 would repudiate the expansion into China of past czarist regimes was grievously disappointed. Indeed, the fifty Soviet divisions maintained on China's border after World War II were regarded with deep suspicion despite the initial years of Sino-Soviet amity following the defeat of Germany and Japan.

Neither Nixon nor Kissinger had ever been infected by the insidious racial prejudice that referred to both Japanese and Chinese as the "yellow peril," a phrase of sinister implications that was often used by Kaiser Wilhelm II of Germany earlier in the twentieth century and later even by Brezhnev. Moreover, although the Taiwan question with its overtones of a "two Chinas" policy had to remain formally unresolved as the new relationship developed between Peking and Washington, Nixon banked on the obvious fact that the United States (unlike Russia) coveted no Chinese territory, and that China realized America was the only nation strong enough to be capable of checking Moscow's possible designs. Thus there were certain underlying political bonds that could overbalance any vestigial ideological ties between the two giants of communism. And both Nixon and Mao favored the priority of national interest over national ideology.

In October 1969, almost two years before Nixon's Chinese journey was publicized, Nixon had called in Anatoly Dobrynin, the experienced Soviet envoy in Washington, and cautioned him:

Anything we have done or are doing with respect to China is in no sense designed to embarrass the Soviet Union.

It was a wise precaution to take Moscow at least that much into our confidence, because sufficient preliminary contacts with the Chinese had by then occurred to stir Soviet suspicions when their intelligence sources made their reports. The American ambassadors in Warsaw, Islamabad, and Bucharest had all met with their Chinese colleagues—a set of facts that could not have escaped the Soviets indefinitely. Through Pakistan also, Kissinger had made arrangements for his first most secret journey to Peking to prepare for a Nixon visit. In reporting to the president on that clandestine mission, Kissinger said: "If we can master this process we will have made a revolution."

On July 15, 1971, the White House announced: "Premier Cou En-lai on behalf of the government of the People's Republic of China has extended an invitation to President Nixon to visit China at an appropriate time before May 1972. President Nixon has accepted the invitation with pleasure." The announcement declared that the purpose of the journey was "to seek normalization of relations." Before leaving for Peking the following year, at Kissinger's suggestion, Nixon invited André Malraux to the White House. The famous French author, who was the member of de Gaulle's cabinet closest to the General, cautioned Nixon: "China's foreign policy is a brilliant lie! The Chinese themselves do not believe it. They believe only in China. Only China." The Frenchman had spent a part of his life in French Indochina and in China itself and had acquired a reputation—perhaps transcending the facts—for expertise on Chinese aims and methods.

The historical background favored a U.S. rapprochement with China. Although Americans had fought Chinese on occasion between the Boxer Rebellion and the Korean War, I never encountered even a hint of anti-Americanism while traveling around China for more than a month in 1973. I visited the 196th Infantry

Division outside Tientsin and was shown with great pride a display of weapons captured from U.S. forces in Korea. There was no hint of lingering animosity for the United States, whose troops the 196th had defeated on several occasions. That friendly attitude was in sharp contrast with the attitude of anti-Russian chauvinism that was deliberately fostered by the division's propaganda apparatus. This benevolent legacy undoubtedly helped the Chinese regime to accelerate its sudden swing to an openly pro-American line.

It was obvious that Nixon's flight to Peking might never have occurred had not the Russians started a private Marxist cold war against the Chinese, a development that appreciably narrowed the gulf between Washington and Peking. Both capitals had strong suspicions of Moscow. Nixon himself recalled later with undisguised realism:

> *When I traveled to China in 1972 to meet Mao and Chou, it was in the interests of both nations that we forge a new link based not on common ideals, which bind us to our Western allies, but on common interests.*[4]

And in the single long conversation between the two heads of state (and interpreters) Mao observed: "In America at least at this time those on the right can do what those on the left can only talk about."

Understandably Nixon has cherished a particular affection for China ever since his first trip there succeeded so well. Even at the height of the Watergate crisis, he was welcomed as an honored guest and treated with just as much affectionate dignity as in 1972.

Still today, more than a vestige of personal sympathy for China remains in Nixon's heart. He has always appreciated the fact that China in no sense "demoted" his reputation as did many other nations on the heels of Watergate.

It was and is obvious to any observer of the latter-day Sino-American friendship that the door to China was opened to Nixon as soon as it became crystal clear that the split between Moscow and Peking was not only genuine but very deeply sited and clothed in undisguised hostility that reached into all forms of the immense society comprising today's China. Yet neither Nixon nor Kissinger was tactless enough at any time to suggest that the United States was using China as a tool or that it sought to prise Peking loose from its Moscow ties or in any way to influence its choice of ideology. Nixon wrote:

China may now be at an important turning point. The People's Republic is in desperate shape economically and its leaders are finally acknowledging that they could use help from the West. The internal convulsions of the period when Mao and the extreme leftists tried to run the world's largest country on revolutionary rhetoric have now ended, at least temporarily. The present Chinese leaders are trying to tackle China's greatest task—modernization—in a more sensible way.

They openly acknowledge that they can learn from the West. The success or failure of their effort over the next few years to bring some measure of modernization to the Chinese people may determine whether China continues in its more moderate stance or reverts to revolutionary chaos, isolation, and belligerence. It is obviously in our interest that the Chinese remain open to Western ways. The boost that trading with the West, especially with Japan, gives to their modernization plans will be crucial to the decisions they make about their future path. That is why we are justified in giving MFN [Most Favored Nation] status to China and denying it to the Soviet Union. The Soviet Union threatens us; China, as of now, does not.

Whether dealing with China, the Soviet Union, or Eastern Europe, we should ensure that the bottom line in our trade policy is its impact on our geopolitical objectives. We should make a deal with the Soviets only when it involves a significant diplomatic or political payoff for us. As much as possible, we should seek arrangements that allow us to withdraw advantages if the Soviets do not keep their end of the bargain. We should not put our faith in their future goodwill. We should use our economic power to give the Eastern Europeans an option and to encourage them to pursue independent and nonadventurist foreign policies. We should use our economic power to help build a less vulnerable China and—by making it in their own interest to do so—to encourage the Chinese to follow the path of moderation.[5]

He added:

The Chinese formerly referred to the Soviets as their "Elder Brother"; now China has become the Soviet Union's bitterest enemy, a giant that shares 4,000 miles of border with the USSR and claims parts of its territory.

There has been a great deal of talk about "playing the Chinese card." This talk is insulting to the Chinese, who do not like to be considered a "card" to be "played." Some say we sought closer relations with Peking during my administration so we could use the Chinese against Moscow, and that Moscow was then forced to seek better relations with us. This is a valid assessment, but it is only a half-truth. Even if there had been no differences between Russia and China, it would still have been in our interest to improve relations with China. Further, as Henry Kissinger has pointed out, the notion "that we use China to annoy the Soviets as a penalty for Soviet conduct" is dangerous for two reasons: because "China is an extremely neuralgic point for the Soviet Union and they may not react rationally," and also because "it may even have a bad effect in Peking. If we improve our ties with Peking in order to punish the Soviet Union, this may leave the implication that if we want to improve our relations with the Soviet Union or if the Soviet Union makes some concessions to us, we may lower the level of our activities with Peking. So we ought to have a settled, long-range policy."

It is in our interest to have a strong China, because a weak China invites aggression and increases the danger of war. We and our European allies should do what is necessary to see that China acquires the military strength necessary to provide for its defense. For their part, the Chinese want to see a strong and resolute United States. If they see us backing down before the Soviets, they may decide that their interests lie in a rapprochement with the Soviet Union—not because they will suddenly agree with the Soviets or stop hating and fearing them, but because the combination of Soviet strength and U.S. weakness will cause them to reassess where their interests lie.

Promoting Sino-Soviet rivalry cannot, in and of itself, be a U.S. policy. But the rivalry is there, and it provides an opportunity, an environment, in which to design a policy. Triangular diplomacy can work to our advantage or our disadvantage. As long as that rivalry persists, however, it not only ties down a large portion of the Soviet forces militarily and affects the overall balance of power; it also seri-

ously undermines the Soviet position in the Third World. In speaking to many Third World leaders China has credentials the United States cannot match. They will listen to Chinese warnings when they might discount our own.[6]

This last point was always regarded as one of paramount importance by David Bruce, the brilliant first ambassador accredited to Peking by Washington. A shrewd observer and tactfully adroit envoy, from the start he saw the special value of the People's Republic as a friend and companion of the United States in relationships with the underdeveloped nations who, despite their miseries and troubles, comprised the great majority of the United Nations.

Nixon had the confidence of more experience in foreign affairs than any American president since Buchanan, who had been secretary of state before he became president. (The others were John Quincy Adams and James K. Polk.) Because of his familiarity with the main global problems and because of his recognition of the need to have a particularly brilliant right-hand man, he designated Kissinger as his first national security adviser and then confided in him far more than in Secretary of State Rogers, whom he had chosen for that post because he trusted him and knew he could rely on him.

Kissinger, from the start and until 1973 when he was moved into Rogers' position as the Watergate scandal unfolded, used to advantage the propinquity of his White House office to the president's. And the indefatigable "Henry" from the very start dominated the president's attention on foreign policy matters, playing the key role on problems as important but far removed from each other as Chile and China. Rogers had had slight experience in diplomatic affairs and was treated in cavalier fashion by Nixon, who didn't take him into his presidential confidence on either Chile or the unraveling of the Chinese problem. Kissinger was placed in a position of total authority (subject to presidential approval) on all matters dealing with Chile, and he personally handled the China affair for Nixon, even arranging the Pakistan connection and subsequently flying on a secret mission to Peking. Kissinger likewise helped arrange the Nixon trip to Rumania in 1969, where China figured in the conversations, and the entire series of clandestine negotiations with North Vietnam that took place in Paris. Rogers was told nothing in advance about the Rumanian journey (which irked the Russians, who saw it as an intrusion into Moscow's sphere of influence), and although he accompanied Nixon to his talk with Mao Tse-tung, the secretary of state, keeper of the Great Seal of the United States, was excluded from the meeting of the two leaders, attended by Kissinger.

The State Department suffered from this unusual presidential behavior, and it was occasionally responsible for ignorance among senior U.S. diplomats on matters with which they should have been acquainted. But the country benefited from this procedural method, which saw Kissinger wholly charged with secret negotiations on Vietnam and a variety of contacts in the Middle East, including a direct link from the security adviser to President Assad of Syria. The planning of foreign policy, its execution, and attendant publicity were all held closely in the White House until Kissinger was finally moved to the State Department to replace Rogers when he resigned.

The results of Nixon's opening to China are still developing. There is a natural economic relationship in the availability of American industrial products and know-how to a huge nation still in a stage of underdevelopment and commensurate economic progress. And it is striking that from a tiny trickle, Sino-American trade has already expanded to the degree that it is now more than twice that between the United States and the USSR. And the Chinese have always taken pains to be especially polite and hospitable to Nixon, even after his demise as president.

The artistry of Nixon's remarkable China policy was not only to gain a vitally important friend where once a bitter enemy had existed but also to earn a new respect in Moscow, which was leery of the new ties between its most powerful antagonists. But Russia, despite several attempts, was unable to drive a wedge between America and China.

It has been interesting to see how little the new Peking-Washington amity has in fact rebounded to our discredit in the Kremlin. Neither the opening of the China door not the bloody battleground of Vietnam, which was being overrun by a dauntless communist tide openly backed by both Russia and China, was allowed to unbalance the new triangular relationship or to poison Moscow's attitude toward either member of the Sino-American partnership. Indeed, the Soviets have attempted to explore new and friendlier avenues with China and, although the course of the Reagan-Gorbachev relationship has yet to develop, the fact that the United States has a friend on Russia's eastern border with a huge army and a growing capability in the realm of nuclear weapons plays a significant role in the world power balance. I think it fair to say that indications show a heightened respect in the Kremlin for both the White House and the Forbidden City.

Nixon never made a secret of his maneuverings either to Moscow or to Peking. He accepted as a basic definition of his foreign policy efforts that there was, this century, only one door opening a road to real peace and that two keys are required to open it, keys held by the United States and the Soviet Union respectively. Thus, it becomes ultimately clear that he regarded China's role not as itself a player in the "finals" of this diplomatic game but as a potential partner to one or the other of the tourney's finalists. He saw China as a decisive factor in this quintessential challenge, saying:

Unless the [two] superpowers adopt a new live-and-let-live relationship, the world will not see real peace in this century. If we fail to work toward that end suicidal war is inevitable.

It is axiomatic to Nixon's thinking that both war and peace are evidently not absolute but relative terms. "War" includes the obvious all-out cataclysm but also local wars with conventional weapons, terrorist and guerrilla campaigns and also the more esoteric competition limiting actual bloodshed but playing for the highest kind of stakes with threats, diplomacy, and the kind of game designed (as with China) to transform the world's power balance. In the last of these categories, Nixon feels that the Soviet leaders understand that one of the greatest dangers to the Soviet system is contact between their ideas and ours, their people and ours, their society and ours. These separate but connected contests fall within the realm that has come to be called "cold war" in this century.

With regard to the increasingly complex cold war competition, Nixon placed much stock in the nonbelligerent aspect of global cold war and professed great faith that the more the United States and its allies maintain contact with the Soviet Union and its allies, "the more we open it to the force of Western example. This will inevitably add to those internal forces that are generating change" (as, it has been convincingly demonstrated, is the case with China, whose economic system is increasingly based on a non-Marxist and competitive market system, no matter how it is labeled). Nixon believes that the more contact we have with the East, the more we open it to the force of Western example.

His administration certainly introduced a refreshing and sensible element into American policy formulation as regards our adversaries. Unlike Truman, Eisenhower, Kennedy, and Johnson, he took pains not to treat the countries of Eastern Europe as if they were part of a monolithic bloc. Those who insist that we do so make the same argument as some did when we opened the door to China in 1972. They say that all these nations are Communist, that communism is evil, and that they are therefore all potential enemies and should be treated as such. They fail to recognize that it is the essence of geopolitics to be able to distinguish between different degrees of evil.

However, a narrowing of political differences between America and nations with Marxist ideologies can have significant and rapid effects. Nixon said in 1982:

> *Less than a decade has passed since the opening to China in 1972 and already our relations have been transformed—and so has China's approach to the world. Mao had the authority to make the turn toward the United States; his successors have had the wisdom to make use of it, and to change Mao's policies so that the opportunities it created can be used.*

U.S. policy has taken a gradually more visible line of differentiation in this respect, and in graduating from an awkward devil-or-angel view of foreign countries whose political ideas are at variance with ours. By the time Nixon had left the White House, and thanks in considerable degree to his own efforts, Washington had come to view through differing prisms the professed Marxist socialism of Yugoslavia, Hungary, Rumania, China, Poland, North Korea, North Vietnam, and Albania—some for the better, some for the worse.

Because the Soviet Union is the lodestone of all but three of these differing systems (China, Albania, and Yugoslavia), because it is the original birthplace of Marxism-in-power, and because it is the only superpower of the various specimens of that ideology, U.S. policy as directed toward Moscow is more important than any other facet. Even the highly successful China policy inaugurated by Nixon may be seen largely in this light.

Nixon is still persuaded that the Soviet challenge is total and therefore the U.S. response must be total. When nations are menaced by Moscow it is in our interest to help them defend themselves. This concept was first formulated by Truman through his Truman Doctrine and pointedly elaborated by Kennedy in his promise to help nations threatened by Russia. Nixon says:

We must provide military and political support to governments threatened by Soviet-supported revolutionary forces. While this sometimes poses a difficult choice, it is rarely between a bad regime and a potentially good one. Rather it is usually a choice between an imperfect regime and a post-revolutionary regime that would be far worse.

In no sense does this aspect of Nixon's policy break with preceding tradition. It is simply more refined in a more complex world. And it is a direction on the diplomatic map that is dictated by new world concepts. The United States was in no organized position to help Hungary against a Soviet invasion in 1956. But it did help Yugoslavia to stand up against threats from Moscow and its Cominform allies in the 1940s and 1950s. It was unable to halt flows of Soviet and Chinese matériel into Vietnam. But it has learned through more skillful and larger CIA operations how to help Russia's enemies in Afghanistan in ways somewhat more sophisticated than the dispatch of supplies to Vietnam. This American policy has been favorably received by China, which has a common frontier with Afghanistan and which fears being encircled by a Soviet East-bloc in Afghanistan, North Korea, North Vietnam, and, perhaps someday, India.

This new and subtler turn of U.S. diplomacy now plays a perceptible role in Sino-Soviet estimates of each other. When Brezhnev met Nixon at Camp David in June 1973 he expressed a fear that China would soon become a great nuclear power. When that moment came, he intimated, Russia feared Chinese aggression, and he quoted to the American president the well-known words (although it is difficult to confirm that they were actually uttered) of Mao: "Even if China loses four hundred million men in a conflict, that would leave more than half a billion still alive." This old story has been bruited about for years with various ramifications and twists; it may even be true.

Nixon's great diplomatic achievement, which is so especially admired in France where diplomacy is seen—if not always practiced—as an art form, bore fruit in 1972 after three years of careful preparation. He recalls:

When I went to Moscow in 1972 I had no illusion whatever about the aggressive nature of Soviet intentions. During my first three years in office the Soviets had tested us in Cuba, in the Mideast, and in South Asia; they tested us again in Vietnam just two weeks before the summit. The fact that we had stood firm in each case, and had even met with the Soviets' deadly enemies in Peking before going to Moscow, did not "torpedo" the summit, as some had predicted it would. On the contrary, I am certain that our firmness helped to convince the Soviets that they had no choice but to negotiate with us.

I did not expect that personal meetings with the Soviet leaders would change their views. I knew that Brezhnev and his colleagues were all dedicated communists. However, I believed then, and I believe now, that while such meetings will not erase major differences in basic philosophy, they can be useful for narrowing the areas of potential conflict and exploring the possibilities of cooperation for mutual benefit. In a broader sense, the Soviet Union and the United States are the only two world nuclear superpowers; we therefore have an obligation to ourselves, to each other, and to the rest of the world to explore every possible avenue to see that our awesome power is not used in a way that could bring massive devastation to ourselves and to civilization as we know it.

It is essential to keep in mind the limits of what détente can achieve. It is equally important to know our adversaries and how to deal with them if we are to achieve even these limited goals. The Soviet leaders I have met, going back to 1959 when I first visited Moscow as vice-president, are very different from the old stereotypes of the bomb-throwing Bolsheviks.[7]

He liked to point out to visitors that an apparently firm line of policy could produce soft results; that the first Soviet-American Moscow summit came only after the Soviets had first agreed on the terms of a Berlin settlement in 1971 (a great compromise on what the United States wanted but nevertheless a hard position compared with those previously elaborated by Washington). And it was in 1972 that he set forth his attitude—later reiterated by Reagan and Gorbachev—that "We must develop a process of annual summits between the leaders of the United States and the Soviet Union; these meetings can both reduce the chances of war and help restrain Soviet behavior."

In all these subtle maneuvers between the United States and its ideological opponents, Nixon never forgot the necessity of keeping U.S. allies well briefed and adequately informed, a position received with gratitude by our partners in Europe, Japan, the Americas, and throughout the world—an appreciated position. Referring to these friends, he warned of NATO members:

They are going to look closely at the United States to see whether we have the power and leadership with the will to use it, not just in our own defense, but also in defense of our friends and allies in the event that they become targets of Soviet aggression.... If our conduct in Asia or in any other part of the world leads them to conclude that we are not a credible friend or ally, they will, in the interest of their own survival, seek an accommodation with the Soviet Union despite their territorial, ideological, and personal quarrels with the Russian leaders. The role the Chinese play in the future is as much in our hands as theirs.

Prior to the fruition of Nixon's blazingly successful China policy, when the Soviet Union considered its strategic position, it essentially looked westward toward NATO and America's European allies and eastward toward Japan, which—although demilitarized—was such a dynamo of economic power and potential armed strength that Moscow maintained military and naval forces between Khabarovsk and Vladivostok with an eye toward Japan, which had so strikingly crushed Russian forces in 1905. China was not the potential target of Soviet Far East planners. Now all that has changed. Japan has not vanished from the list of Soviet concerns. But enormous China, armed and financed by the

United States and industrialized by Japanese enterprise, moves steadily forward on the list of Soviet defense priorities and as a subject of concern in Moscow's major diplomatic negotiations. From Finland to Pakistan and on eastward to Tokyo there was admiring applause as Nixon's China game progressed, and even Emperor Hirohito did not fail to see and appreciate the ultimate goal of Nixon's China game.

By November 1973, when he had a second Peking meeting with Mao, Kissinger had begun to worry about whether the Sino-American friendship structure might not also be corroded by the insidious Watergate rust. The new secretary of state wrote:

> I was the foreign minister of a country that had the physical means and shared the geopolitical analysis but in post-Vietnam, Watergate conditions lacked the domestic consensus to execute its conceptions....
>
> It turned out that Mao's principal concern was not our Soviet policy but our domestic situation, specifically Watergate. What good was a strategy of containment if at that time we sapped our capacity to implement it by our domestic divisions? He simply could not understand the uproar over Watergate. He contemptuously dismissed the whole affair as a form of "breaking wind." The incident itself was "very meager, yet now such chaos is being kicked up because of it. Anyway we are not happy about it." He saw no objective reasons for an assault on a President who had done a good job.[8]

Mao then discussed U.S. attitudes between the Eastern Mediterranean and India and wondered how much American domestic upheaval would vitiate its position in that vast area. Kissinger saw that "a Washington riven by strife was a less interesting partner for China. Our credibility was bound to decline with the evaporation of Presidential authority, whatever my brave words to the contrary."[9]

Mao urged Kissinger that the United States should increase its naval strength in the Indian Ocean, and Kissinger commented in his notes: "He was the quintessential Cold Warrior; our conservatives would have been proud of him," adding, in a slightly mischievous tone: "The last thing Mao wanted at that point was the very domestic upheaval in America that his political theory foresaw and advocated."

Although Watergate matured as a sad counterpoint to the fruition of Nixon's dramatic China policy, it had no lasting negative effect on that policy. It is strange that the two extraordinary events should have occurred conjointly.

One is forced to deduce that Mao Tse-tung, as a matter of deliberate and conscious decision, resolved to play down the implications of the swelling Watergate scandal. There isn't any doubt that the Chinese leadership was fully informed about the Watergate affair and its possible consequences to the United States. But the Chinese ladership was nevertheless inclined to push forward with the policy of friendship between the world's largest industrial power and the world's largest population center.

Nixon himself played out the part of innovator with good courage and style. He was brilliantly assisted by Kissinger, who obeyed his strategic orders from Nixon with shrewd discretion and with wisdom. The policy has proven durable.

VII

Third World Problems

The trouble for U.S. foreign policy, both in the Third World of former colonial possessions and in Europe, stemmed partly from the fact that all of our European allies except for Greece, Luxembourg, Iceland, and Norway had been imperial powers as recently as the twentieth century. Even Denmark—with the huge land mass of Greenland, the largest colonial agglomeration at a time when all other empires were shedding their last freeholds overseas—could understand aspects of the colonial nostalgia that dogged so many European countries. Forced to look inward rather than support distant commitments, the shift from imperial to national state could have been a unifying impulse that brought the Europeans closer together in a dynamic, relatively small community. They had all experienced the shock of collapsed imperial enterprises: Germany, Italy, Turkey, Portugal, Belgium, Holland, France, and Britain.

Yet the economic and psychological strains were difficult to accept. A compact European dynamism made up of separate nationalities could not wholly and easily replace the colonial system. This, for example, had seen Belgium and Holland, respectively, investing huge sums in profitable enterprises in the Congo and Indonesia or given rise to the vast and intimate social and administrative fabrics of Britain and India or France and Indochina and North Africa, which provided psychological and traditional heritages militating against integration into a tight European community.

Moreover, not only did the United States find it virtually impossible to develop a system of European unity with which it could deal as a massive ally in what used to be called the Twin Pillar system, an American (United States–Canada) pillar on the western shore of the Atlantic and a European pillar on the eastern shore; it even made for economic and commercial difficulties in former colonies that were in the habit of depending on their erstwhile protective administrative and financial centers in Europe. One result was that previous colonial capitals resented the fact they could no longer receive adequate sustenance or shelter from former nursemaids, and the latter often resented it when the United States seemed ready to move at least partially into the geopolitical vacuum. France particularly disliked the idea of "Cocacolonization" of its once-enormous, wealthy imperial domain.

This understandable but fruitless resentment of the friendly United States as heir to past history could not help but infect European attitudes with a certain jealousy of the insouciant legatee. One can speculate that this influenced the indifferent allies who largely ignored the Nixon message, voiced by Kissinger, of a "Year of Europe." Likewise, lingering ties to their former imperial wetnurses undoubtedly influenced some of the Third World attitudes to America on the part of newly independent states as far apart as India and Senegal.

For natural psychological and socioeconomic reasons of adjustment, it proved more difficult than one imagined possible for the United States to elaborate either a tidy Third World foreign policy or one for a cohesive Europe. And many accumulated tensions, both among our European partners and our Third World friends, erupted amid the flare-ups in the Middle East, especially the 1973 war between Israel and Egypt and Syria.

U.S. broad policy toward the Third World had never been very coherent. It seemed to be an injudicious mixture of charity and sometimes the imposition of obligations like support in UN votes. Fortunately for Washington, the Soviet Union had not been especially successful in its own policy among former colonial states, with the possible exception of its most costly investment, in Cuba. China was the only large power with a logical Third World policy, and it was compounded more of hospitality and prestigious satisfaction of injured feelings of pride than of more serious tangible aid.

The Third World can make the unhappy boast that it has provided virtually all the wars that have festered around the earth since the last global conflict. A large number of these were at least tacitly encouraged by great powers. The list includes the Korean War, when the North was prompted by China and Russia to invade the South; Vietnam, when first the French and then the Americans sponsored resistance to a Communist-led independence movement; and the Cuban Bay of Pigs invasion, fostered by the United States.

However, the great majority of the ruckuses were part of the growing pains of newly free states beset by tribal and regional problems as well as by violent factionalism. The most peculiar of these was the on-and-off Somalia-Ethiopia war, in which both were sponsored by superpowers. (When the Russians, originally backing the Somalis, gave up and switched sides, sending their number one agent in Somalia to Addis Ababa, the Americans shifted likewise and stopped helping Ethiopia by switching to Somalia.)

Other neocolonial or postliberation conflicts in the Third World have been between Libya and Chad (helped by France), India and Pakistan (helped by China), Iran and Iraq (helped by Russia), and North Yemen and South Yemen and civil wars in the Philippines, Malaysia, Burma, Nicaragua, Indonesia, and Nigeria. Of course, there has been the continuing regional war in the Middle East, with Israel backed by the United States. And there has been Afghanistan.

The Third World had been largely pro-American when the United Nations first started up, but Soviet propaganda and clever assistance programs won over many such states despite more generous, less effective U.S. aid payments. There is no doubt, looking backward, that Moscow has gained support in the Third World sweepstakes since 1945, as compared with the United States. The Nixon administration tried, with unremarkable success, to reverse this situation, but it was an effort more marked by failure than by positive results, the most blazing failure being, of course, Vietnam.

Nixon demonstrated much interest in the Third World, starting with Latin America. The first foreign country he ever visited was Mexico, on his honeymoon. As Eisenhower's vice president, he took a much-publicized tour of South America, giving a good account of himself for courage and self-control during vicious hostile riots against him as his country's symbol, staged in Peru and Venezuela by communist-organized mobs. Later, his personality and straightforward simplicity were to be particularly well received by distant leaders as far apart as Indonesia's Sukarno, Egypt's Sadat, and Saudi Arabia's King Faisal. There is a good deal of valid evidence confirming that these and numerous other Third World dignitaries genuinely liked Nixon personally and found him sympathetic and understanding.

General Charles de Gaulle, despite his understanding of Nixon's policy and sympathy for his personality, took an early lead in stressing the dichotomy between European conceptions of the national interests of former imperial powers and those of the immensely powerful and occasionally brusque new giant from North America. De Gaulle insisted that Europe must remain free to pursue its own interests even when they differed from those of the United States. The General had even blocked Britain's initial application to join the Common Market on the grounds that it would serve as a "Trojan horse" for American policy.

Nevertheless, it soon became evident that Nixon was not embarrassed by the concept that a more united Europe should be able to conduct its own policy. Indeed, in many respects Washington encouraged this approach, hoping to build a coordinated Europe that could serve as a valid, organized partner of America and recognizing that the interests of the two on fundamental matters would almost certainly be parallel.

This assumption ran into serious trouble during Nixon's administration when Israel was attacked by Egypt and Syria in October 1973. From Britain and France to Greece and Turkey, our allies showed a surprising independence from Washington's policy of preventing at all costs the defeat of Israel, and they even balked at the use of their conveniently located airfields by U.S. transport planes reinforcing Israel's battered weapons systems.

Washington managed first to bolster Israeli logistics sufficiently to turn the tide of battle in its favor. Then, after the war was brought to a halt with battlefield deadlocks unfavorable to the Arabs, Nixon and Kissinger were successful in arranging a valid cease-fire, the last signal foreign policy success of the Nixon administration before it was trapped in the Watergate morass.

Kissinger pays tribute to Nixon on this achievement. He wrote in his memoirs: "The disintegration of the Presidency was painful to observe. Nixon's self-discipline was extraordinary, but it only masked his vulnerability."[1] His account also said: "As always in crisis, Nixon was clear-headed and crisp.... He had taken the responsibility and faced its implications with panache and determination."[2] When a tough Soviet line was followed by Brezhnev's backdown after Nixon ordered an alert of his airborne troops, he recalled that the United States had bombed North Vietnam prior to a summit meeting that was nevertheless not called off, and "that is what made Mr. Brezhnev act as he did."[3] Referring to the October Middle East War of 1973, Nixon called it "the most difficult crisis we have had since the Cuban confrontation of 1962."[4]

The armistice that put a stop to the October fighting provided no clear-cut victory for either side. Israel had saved itself by a heroic effort and massive American aid, but it had lost the renown that had in the past made its troops appear ever victorious. The victory was limited, reestablishing prewar frontiers, but this proved to be a tactical gain; strategically, Sadat recovered Egypt's former territory in the Sinai peninsula although it took time and negotiation to achieve this.

On November 6 the Egyptian-Israeli armistice line was stabilized in a six-point plan between the two combatants, an accord shepherded by U.S. diplomacy. Nixon was elated and hoped that this token of his foreign policy achievements would buttress his insistent claim to remaining in the White House, but it was patently clear even then that no overseas success could expunge the insidious stains at home.

It was noteworthy, however, that Sadat, Faisal, and Assad in Damascus all expressed their respect and admiration for Nixon, as did the Israeli leadership, which knew it owed him an immense debt. And at a Geneva conference that December, the door to a true peace between Israel and Egypt was opened and Nixon, who had understandably been privately jealous of Kissinger's diplomatic triumph, generously said: "The American people are proud that it was their secretary of state who brought it about." Kissinger said of the president that Nixon was "extraordinarily proud that even in the midst of domestic crisis his Administration had managed to play the decisive role in turning the Middle East toward peace."[5]

Nixon's confidence in Kissinger became excessive when he wrote Brezhnev that Kissinger, who was en route to Moscow to arrange the superpower frame that would encompass a Middle East cease-fire, had full authority to make commitments that would have the president's complete support. This actually weakened the secretary of state's hand by depriving him of the tactical privilege of delaying proposed accords on the pretense of having to consult his chief of state when in reality he was seeking better terms and opportunities to consult Israel through diplomatic channels. Brezhnev saw precisely what he had gained. He immediately sent a letter to Nixon saying he noted that Kissinger could speak and make commitments with the President's wholehearted advance support.

Although Vietnam and the Middle East absorbed so much of Nixon's attention, to the virtual exclusion of other sectors of the Third World, there were obvious ancillary if unrelated problems. Thus, for example, after Britain recognized it could no longer afford any military presence in the area east of Suez, it had withdrawn its small remaining forces from such regions at the end of 1971. Within six months Moscow had moved in, and the Soviet Union had signed a friendship treaty with Iraq.

In a similar way, as the western empires terminated and withdrew to their original matrixes, the superpowers—sometimes only in economic terms, sometimes with more political and military emphasis—often moved in. It is significant that the last important foreign tour made by Nixon was to the most prominent Third World region of them all—the Middle East. In June 1974 the president flew to Cairo, to Jidda, to Damascus, and to Jerusalem, in all of which he was received with friendship and respect.

There had been deeply divisive issues between the United States and many of its allies at various points during the Vietnam

War and also during the permanent Middle East crisis and the battles it produced. Nixon saw this and worried about the consequences. He said in his 1973 foreign policy report: "The United States will never compromise the security of Europe or the interests of our allies," and he asked that "we . . . close ranks and chart our course together for the decade ahead."

Unfortunately, for a considerable period, Nixon felt that good relationships were being hampered by the private biases or machinations of Prime Minister Heath in Britain, Chancellor Brandt (and his adviser, Egon Bahr) in Germany, and Foreign Minister Jobert in France. But by spring 1974, these men had disappeared from the active international scene, and a period of amiable and quiescent relaxation suddenly replaced a hitherto strained relationship with Washington, mostly dealing with U.S. and European views of the two principal Third World arenas. Unfortunately for him, this era came too late to affect Nixon's problems, but it eased the transfer of power to Gerald Ford in August, always with the faithful Kissinger in attendance. Alas, the "Year of Europe" launched by Kissinger's speech on the subject in April 1973 had been virtually forgotten in between.

From the start of his presidency, Nixon realized that the greatest threat to peace today is in the Third World. The most unhappy page of that book was turned on April 30, 1975, when North Vietnamese tanks rolled into conquered Saigon. In an effort to avoid this dismal conclusion, Nixon had been trying since 1969 to follow de Gaulle's formula of withdrawing American troops—but not too precipitously—and arranging a peace settlement thereafter. De Gaulle had urged evacuation but not with undue haste. This precaution proved impossible to fulfill, largely because of internal American politics. De Gaulle had also suggested contacts with Hanoi, which Nixon attempted by clandestine links to Ho Chi Minh via the French Indochina expert, Jean Sainteny; through subsequent direct secret conversations with North Vietnamese leaders; a Kissinger visit to Hanoi; and the persuasive efforts of Nixon's willing Communist contact, President Ceauşescu of Rumania.

These attempts died aborning, not because there were inadequate tries in the Third World itself (Hanoi and Saigon) but because of Watergate, which had become synonymous with

"Vietnam" as a code word for anti-Nixonism in the United States and which ultimately came to signify all that opponents of the president considered wrong. Nixon himself concluded:

> *Watergate had become the successor to the Vietnam War as the rallying cry for anti-administration critics. [It had become] an obsession in Washington.*[6]

This vindictive political mood came at a particularly unfortunate time for Nixon, who had already established an effective and amiable working relationship with Peking. China was just as eager as the United States to prevent a Soviet hegemony in Indochina and Soviet humiliation of the United States, the only possible force that could block such an event. And although on January 27, 1973, Secretary of State William Rogers had signed the Paris peace agreements for Vietnam, the war had been deliberately restarted by Soviet-backed Hanoi, and with disastrous effect.

Despite its conscious realization that the Third World was the danger spot, the United States has not shown much ability in producing effective military operations there. The Bay of Pigs was one example; Nicaragua was to become another. But the most disastrous by far proved to be Vietnam. Ever since President Eisenhower allowed a military mission to observe French efforts to win the first phase of an ongoing war, the United States had been sucked more deeply into a vortex: sixteen thousand troops under Kennedy and about thirty times as many under Johnson—a figure to be reduced, but unsuccessfully, by Nixon.

In 1963 the Kennedy administration applied pressure on Prime Minister Diem with instructions to U.S. ambassador Henry Cabot Lodge that "If he remains obdurate, then we are prepared to accept the obvious implication that we can no longer support Diem" and that plans should be made to "bring about Diem's replacement if this should become necessary." Diem was murdered by a hostile military faction—Vietnamese, not American, although the same cannot so surely be said of the instructional button that was pushed.

It is impossible to measure the effects of Watergate on world power balances. When the tragedy reached its zenith Nixon's reputation in Europe and, indeed, around the world was still high. Foreigners regarded the scandal as the result of a political coup by Nixon's adversaries. They saw it as the unbelievable result of a petty, trivial offense—a clumsy attempt at an office break-in by incompetent hired burglars. But statesmen as far removed from each other as Saudi Arabia's King Faisal, Soviet Foreign Minister Gromyko, and his boss, Leonid Brezhnev all took pains to send personal messages of encouragement to Nixon.

The United States invented the word "Vietnamization" to cover its troop withdrawals behind a larger South Vietnamese army screen. Kissinger met one North Vietnamese negotiator secretly in Paris and another in February 1970. On April 30, 1970, American troops hit Communist sanctuaries in Cambodia. In 1971 the *New York Times* published damaging classified "Pentagon papers" on the war, and Nixon sent Kissinger on secret negotiating tours to both China and North Vietnam. On May 20, 1972, Nixon held his first summit with Brezhnev in Moscow. On June 17, 1972, the five "plumbers" broke into Democratic National Committee offices in Washington's Watergate complex. On January 8, 1973, an agreement with North Vietnam was reached by Kissinger and signed four days later by Secretary of State Rogers, to be undercut and wrecked by both Saigon and Hanoi. On August 22, Kissinger replaced Rogers as secretary of state. In January 1974, Hanoi resumed war against the south and the United States. On May 9, the House Judiciary Committee opened hearings on Nixon's impeachment. On July 30 it recommended impeachment on three counts. On August 9, 1974, Nixon resigned, to be replaced by Ford, who pardoned him September 8. On April 30, 1975, Saigon fell and the south surrendered.

After Hanoi's victory its field commander for the final offensive said: "The reduction of U.S. aid made it impossible for the puppet troops to carry out their combat plans and build up their forces."[7] Nixon added:

In April, May and June of 1973, with my authority weakened by the Watergate crisis, retaliatory action was threatened but not taken. Then Congress passed a bill setting August 15 as the date for termination of U.S. bombing in Cambodia and requiring Congressional approval for the funding of U.S. military action in any part of Indochina. The effect of this bill was to deny the President the means to enforce the Vietnam peace agreement by retaliating against Hanoi for violations."[8]

As Nixon wrote following his retirement:

Congress proceeded to snatch defeat from the jaws of victory. Once our troops were out of Vietnam, Congress initiated a total retreat from our commitments to the South Vietnamese people. First, it destroyed our ability to enforce the peace agreement, through legislation prohibiting the use of American military power in Indochina. Then it undercut South Vietnam's ability to defend itself, by drastically reducing our military aid.[9]

Nixon wrote in his diary in 1972:

I have no illusions whatever. . . . The U.S. will not have a credible foreign policy if we fail [in Vietnam]. And I will have to assume the responsibility for that development.

He returned to this thought by saying the U.S. defeat in Indochina

paralyzed America's will to act in other Third World trouble spots and therefore encouraged aggression on the part of those who had made them trouble spots to begin with.[10]

In the same book he said:

Increasingly the world balance of power will be determined by who wins these key conflicts in the Third World. To play an effective role, the U.S. must at times side with authoritarian governments that do not come up to our standards in protecting human rights in order to keep from power totalitarian regimes that would deny all human rights.[11]

On November 28, 1983, I had an interesting talk with Nixon in New York. He said:

The United States should direct its long-term objectives not toward a Marshall Plan type of economic recovery program but to a general "starting up plan" for tackling Third World problems. And I believe all the developed countries of Europe as well as Japan should join us in such an endeavor.

It is an odd thing now that the Communists talk mainly of critical problems in the Third World while we talk mainly of the Communists. We must think of the whole Third World. It is there that the greatest danger of war lies. I don't foresee a war arising from a Soviet attack on the United States or Europe. But a rubbing together of conflicting interests and policies among Third World nations, in the Middle East or the Persian Gulf or Africa could ignite such a conflict.

We need to talk of the need to reduce Soviet and Western armaments to create stability. But the next great war is more likely to come not through any direct confrontations between the superpowers but through conflicts in the Third World area.

Citing the economic and financial problems of Latin American countries like Mexico and Brazil, he said:

We must get our friends in Europe and Japan to show an interest in helping solve these problems in the Western Hemisphere.

It was not the tawdry Watergate break-in that brought down the Nixon administration but the furtive and irrational cover-up attempt, and it was the dubious efforts of some of the more meager figures of the governmental groups involved that ignited the glowing embers already fanned by the Vietnam misadventure. All this combined to collapse what proved to be a house of cards built from a badly shuffled deck. But, with the exception of Indochina, the strong framework of a successful foreign policy remained substantially intact. For this President Nixon deserves ample credit.

Nixon and Kissinger distinguished three Third World diplomatic crises as starting in September 1970, all unrelated except in timing. As defined by Kissinger, these were the civil war in Jordan, which saw King Hussein beat off an effort by Palestinian guerrillas to assume control of his state; the Soviet attempt to create a nuclear submarine base at Cienfuegos, Cuba, in violation of the Russo-American understanding that ended Kennedy's showdown with Khrushchev on missiles by a Moscow pledge to refrain from establishing military installations on the island while America promised not to invade it again; and the establishment of the Allende regime in Chile, which Nixon and Kissinger saw as the first stage of a communist takeover.

As things turned out, these three events proved to be just a warm-up for a dramatic series of tensions that were to mark the end of Nixon's first term and the beginning of his second. In late 1970, when Moscow was confronted with the evidence of its new Cuban mischief at Cienfuegos, it backed down, although its intention to establish some kind of installation didn't vanish. The Chilean problem, already discussed, was to my mind exaggerated; but Washington was in no sense responsible for the eventual overthrow and death of Salvador Allende.

Two major events with which the United States was only indirectly connected, if much concerned, were the civil conflict in Jordan and the 1971 war between India and Pakistan, both of which were to have enduring importance. Ever since the creation of Jordan after World War II, comprising the former emirate of Transjordan and a large portion of Arab Palestine (primarily what is now commonly called the West Bank), there had been a growing power struggle between the king—supported by desert Bedouins and the British-created, highly professional Arab Legion, which was fiercely loyal to Hussein—and the newly created Palestine Liberation Organization (PLO), then headed by Yasser Arafat and determined to seize control of Hussein's kingdom before destroying Israel.

I had a long talk with Arafat in his command post at Amman after his Al Fatah guerrillas had been defeated by Hussein's well-drilled loyalists. The PLO leader, a short, plump man with sensual features, glittering eyes, and in dire need of a shave, was carrying a Kalashnikov (Soviet tommy gun) by the barrel and fiddled with it throughout our conversation. He said:

> We are Palestinians; we are not concerned with Transjordan although we believe in the unity of our people on both sides of the Jordan.... We are only seekers of national libera-

> tion. We consider ourselves a progressive revolution.... Our staff studies the experience of revolutionary warfare. We have sent our men to be trained in Algeria, Cuba, Vietnam, and China.
>
> We suffered a ferocious attack by the imperialist Zionist forces. This attack was carried out by the Jordanian army and King Hussein.

He said with wild exaggeration that the royal army had fired 120,000 tons of explosives at the Fedayeen guerrillas he commanded, adding, "six times the amount of Hiroshima" (the first nuclear bomb exploded in war).

I asked the calmly courageous little king, Hussein, whom I saw in his modest palace, whether the accord that had just ended the civil war was operative, and he said somewhat wearily and with the lack of genuine conviction born of experience dealing with the wily Arafat: "The pact, as far as it goes, appears to be working. I have every confidence that the end result will be the establishment of law and order in Jordan."

With the staunch support of the desert Arabs, he had put down Arafat and his Fedayeen guerrillas, helped by the discreet backing of the United States, which wanted the trustworthy, firm ruler on his throne as a stable element in the treacherous Middle East. Washington worked deftly to attain this goal, which has not substantially changed since, despite frequent, and often violent ups and downs. By helping to keep Arafat's Palestinian Arab rebels from grabbing all of Jordan and then attacking Israel, Washington attained a measure of stability in an inherently unstable situation.

The other Third World war of that period that caused great strain amid American policymakers was the 1971 civil conflict between India and Pakistan, in fact a civil conflict between Moslems and Hindus quarreling over the independent states that were formed when imperial Britain withdrew its control and handed over divided self-government to the quarreling sects on the Indian subcontinent. From the first, the United States helped Pakistan, the smaller, poorer heritage, largely Punjab, Baluchistan, and Sind in the west and East Bengal in the east. Burt Marshall, a CIA veteran, helped draft a Pakistan constitution that tried to knit a skein containing these vastly different and geographically distantly separated sectors, bound only by religion and hatred for India in between.

Encouraged by Moscow, which had its eyes on Afghanistan and a piece of West Pakistan if and when it should disintegrate, India finally launched an attack on East Pakistan, to force its excision from the west and Islamabad, the national capital. The war was short and sharp. The Nixon administration was openly critical of the Indian cause, irritating the sturdy body of pro-Indian sentiment among American liberals who had always been strongly sympathetic to India. They tended to mistake for the teachings of Gandhi the practice of some of those political leaders who assumed power in New Delhi and who never made any bones about their contempt for the United States.

Washington made no effort to disguise its preference for the Pakistani cause during the 1971 war, which ultimately ended by smashing East Pakistan and replacing it with the new republic of Bangladesh. When the conflict began, Washington was powerfully influenced by the fact that Pakistan was its only contact and communication with the Chinese People's Republic during the intensive secret negotiations culminating in Nixon's visit to Mao Tse-tung. This ultimately brought about an exchange of ambassadors with Peking and a brand-new friendly relationship between those former enemies, the most populous and the most industrially advanced powers of the world.

Determined to prevent India from smashing West Pakistan, regardless of the atomization of the Bengali East, Washington ordered a naval demonstration in the Indian Ocean as a gesture of caution to New Delhi and gave Pakistan material to help its defense should that prove necessary.

The superpowers have always eyed the Indian subcontinent with avid solicitude and eagerness to gain favor. Nixon's famous "tilt toward Pakistan" during the India-Pakistan war of 1971 is but one example; the Soviet Union had already, if more discreetly, indicated its own preference for India and encouraged a truculent attitude in new Delhi.

Shortly after he first took power, Pandit Nehru acknowledged to me that, while he looked with sympathy on Russian socialism, in the event of a world war India would be forced to favor the Western powers because it depended so much on maritime shipments for food, fuel, and vital industrial supplies; and Britain and the United States had overwhelming naval superiority. Yet he gradually modified this view as the Soviets built an enormous fleet in postwar years. Finally, the Soviet presence in a huge base at Vietnam's Camranh Bay on the South China Sea, twinned with its known aspirations toward Baluchistan on the Indian Ocean and the Arab world to the West, has served to balance this concept of dependence on foreign naval superiority.

Nehru's daughter, Mrs. Gandhi, also Indian prime minister, told me some years later (March 10, 1969): "Some people in the United States say that we are too close to Russia and that we vote too often on the Soviet side in UN. But this really isn't so; it is only true on such issues as those involving colonialism and racism, and here it is not a question of us following the Russians but a question of the Russians taking the stand that happens to agree with ours."

The contemporary fact is that Soviet attitudes have gained ever-greater currency in India; and Pakistan, as India's opponent and China's ally, is currently Washington's Number One friend in Southern Asia.

Both directly and indirectly, the Nixon administration was faced with Third World problems from its very start, and on the whole it survived them with commendable skill. But the biggest and the longest-enduring Third World problem was the war in Vietnam. This was inherited originally from the shattered French empire and subsequently from three American presidents whose administrations had failed to stabilize Indochina against mounting pressures. In Hanoi a powerful Communist regime was determined to seize every inch of the former French empire in Southeast Asia, and did. And in pursuing this goal it contributed to the fall of Richard Nixon, whose desperate efforts to frustrate Hanoi's drive fostered an atmosphere of poisonous bitterness among the American people.

VIII

The Watergate War

In terms of what transpired afterward, the unluckiest day in Richard Nixon's life might well have been November 5, 1968, when he defeated Hubert Humphrey for the presidency of the United States. Humphrey, although he was personally a far more popular type of man than the brooding, competitive Nixon, could perhaps have been an easier symbol for his country in the Vietnam War. Yet—and I discussed this on several occasions with Humphrey—he in fact loyally shared the Vietnam policy of his boss, Lyndon Johnson, who had become almost as unpopular over Vietnam as Nixon was soon to be. It was said by Humphrey's admirers that his attitude on Vietnam was much more dovish than Johnson's. Yet Humphrey in effect denied this. And Johnson was as much a hawk as Nixon.

On May 11, 1965, Humphrey told me: "Above all I try to keep myself informed. I am the first vice-president to be totally incorporated into the information system of the president. He made it that way. I have become a member of the innermost team of the president on foreign affairs."

On June 4, 1966, he said his own position on Vietnam was "not just a Lyndon Johnson position." He had drawn up a paper in August 1964, before he was elected vice president, in which he recommended "a policy on Vietnam very similar to that we are now following." And there was certainly little to choose between the Johnson and Nixon policies on Southeast Asia.

Richard Nixon likes to contend that the United States won the dirty war in Vietnam when it achieved the successful withdrawal of its military forces there. This was accomplished under the umbrella of a threat that, if the Communist regime in Hanoi violated the conditions of South Vietnam's evident collapse, the United States would sharply punish such violations by massive and unlimited bombing while continuing to support the Saigon government. That this warning was ignored with impunity was not Nixon's fault. He was unable to gain the funds and commitments from Congress to which he looked for support. He was defeated by Watergate and his consequent loss of authority.

His position as a vigorous president quite obviously seeking to end the Vietnam conflict by simply pulling out was no longer even remotely strong enough to sustain his warnings to Hanoi. The Communist north overran all of South Vietnam and accomplished this assault with massive invasions of Laos and Cambodia.

Nixon was unable to do anything to halt this process because he had lost almost all backing in public opinion and in Congress as a consequence of the sour, spreading Watergate affair, which ended in his resignation to avoid impeachment. His successor, Gerald Ford, never even attempted to implement the menaces of which Nixon had warned, even though Ford kept Secretary of State Kissinger in office to ensure that U.S. foreign policy would continue along the lines of Nixon's presidency with as little alteration as possible.

As an ex-president, Nixon has sought to blame Congress and the American voting public for the disaster that overcame Vietnam once U.S. troops left. In this effort he is only technically correct. There was no longer any chance of Congress or public opinion maintaining a highly unpopular war once the Watergate mania took hold. Nixon was assuredly already aware of this at the time he elaborated this withdrawal policy backed up by the warning of heavy punishment if the accords were violated. Little was left for him but to assert that the United States had "won" the war and would guarantee that "victory" with its powerful air force.

No American president can promise such guarantees with any hope of their implementation if he so clearly lacks congressional authorization to finance any planned retribution. The sword Nixon dangled over the head of the North Vietnamese military machine was made of cardboard. Quite clearly no one knew this better than Nixon himself, an expert politician.

Although it fielded as much military strength in Vietnam as in a major conflict, the United States never had declared war against its enemy in Southeast Asia and, in fact, never dared to because the cause was too unpopular in Congress. From the time John F. Kennedy dispatched sixteen thousand men as "advisers" until the immense armies sent by Lyndon Johnson and backed by Richard Nixon, we were technically not at war.

This tactic may have avoided until far too late the test of congressional approval of a declaration. But it brought with it special and deleterious consequences of its own. Thus, for example, U.S. commanders in Vietnam were in no position to impose wartime military censorship on the media, although such a sensible restriction existed in two world conflicts and in Korea. In a Vietnam not "at war," news service reporters were able to hold open telephone lines to Hong Kong or Tokyo and describe from their start the takeoff and scale of U.S. Air Force raids bound northward from major air bases. This open conduit risked needless casualties from North Vietnam's defending antiaircraft installations. Television cameras could take ghastly pictures that were flashed back to the kitchens and living rooms of a horrified United States. But there was officially no "war" to justify military (not political) censorship.

On February 10, 1986, Kissinger wrote me from Washington:

> You are absolutely right on the linkage between Watergate and the collapse in Vietnam. There was, after all, a peace agreement in January 1973 and—in light of the force of the 1972 [U.S.] elections—at least the *prospect* of avoiding calamity. Its principal challenge was one of enforcement against North Vietnamese violations, elements of which

(such as continuing aid to South Vietnam) were in turn dependent on strong executive authority and Congressional support to stay the course. Watergate dissolved those conditions. With its acceleration and the onset of Congressional prohibitions, all reasonable options for enforcing the accord were foreclosed. The rest is history.

I made a point in a column I wrote on Vietnam last year of the difficulty of knowing for certain whether South Vietnam could have withstood even under the best of circumstances. But the impact of Watergate was crucial—it denied us the capability ever to test the alternatives.

Nixon has an obstinate character that he attributes in part to the never-say-die spirit of "Chief" Newman, his Whittier College football coach. According to Nixon, Newman told his athletes, "Show me a good loser and I'll show you a loser." Nixon insisted from the start of his first presidential term until after he was forced to resign from power because of Watergate that he not only could arrange a just settlement of the Vietnam War but, in fact, had done just that. In effect, he claimed to have won the war for the cause the United States supported.

There is something pathetically quixotic about the latter contention. It insists that the war was indeed won by the executive branch of the U.S. government but that victory was deliberately vitiated by the legislative branch, Congress. This is more or less like Gene Tunney claiming victory in his 1926 heavyweight title fight against Jack Dempsey because he knocked Dempsey clean out of the ring. The trouble was that Dempsey climbed back in and won by a knockout. Congress climbed back into the ring against Nixon and prevailed. The only trouble was that Nixon did not permit this possibility to play any role in his calculations. Thus he lost the title—although he still claimed to have won it.

Nixon was always a proclaimed optimist on Vietnam despite the failures of Kennedy and, above all, Johnson in that terrible mantrap. In April 1969 he sent a note drafted by Kissinger to Anatoly Dobrynin, the Soviet ambasssador, saying: "The President wishes to reiterate his conviction that a just peace is achievable" in Vietnam. Clearly in some doubt about that asseveration, he sent a personal letter to Ho Chi Minh through Jean Sainteny, the distinguished Frenchman who had helped the Americans greatly as a secret contact with the Vietnamese Communist leadership. This letter asked Ho for a breakthrough in the negotiations for peace and warned that otherwise "measures of great consequence and force could occur." That same July he warned Moscow that he expected more help in ending the Southeast Asian war.

Actually, the president's peacemaking initiative started in 1969 and may obviously be linked to the ideas suggested to him early that year by de Gaulle. On June 8, 1969, he met Saigon's President Thieu on Midway Island, and Thieu agreed to support Nixon's proposal. On July 16 he wrote Ho Chi Minh via Sainteny. On August 2 he asked his presidential acquaintance Ceauşescu to help, and the Rumanian agreed to use his influence in Hanoi to budge the North Vietnamese from dead center.

Although I had been in the habit of visiting Vietnam fairly frequently after 1950, when the French were slowly losing their war against the Vietminh—precursors of the Vietcong the United States fought and a cover name for the Vietnamese Communist patriots—I find to my surprise in my notes that I was only there three times during the 1972–1974 period, when the Watergate cancer undermined any remaining efforts by the United States to defeat the Marxist-nationalist enemy. In late March and early April 1973, I stayed in the U.S. ambassador's Saigon house and saw a good many Americans; yet there is no record in my notes of even the slightest mention of Watergate.

On April 1, 1973, I did talk with Ambassador Michel Gauvin, head of the Canadian delegation to the four-power International Commission of Control and Supervision, who made some astute observations. He said:

> Usually a war ends with one side exhausted and ready to make concessions. Here the situation is unusual. The powerful U.S.A. quit. It found its tremendous effort had grown beyond the conflict's worth. It went too far and not far enough.
>
> Its intentions were good—to prevent a country from succumbing to aggression—but the United States appears to be the loser. It wouldn't lose if South Vietnam's freedom could be assured. Maybe in the end it can. But it's difficult. Hanoi underestimated Nixon in October when it wanted him

> to leave and also lose face: a peace without honor. It linked the release of U.S. prisoners to Saigon's release of political prisoners. But Nixon decided to bomb again. This brought Hanoi to the real negotiating table.
>
> Nixon got his peace with honor. So he won't come back into this mess. But does Hanoi believe the Unites States won't use its air force on Hanoi and Haiphong?

What neither Gauvin nor I reckoned with was the sullen unwillingness of Congress to support Nixon on anything except surrender and the deleteriously weakening spread of the Watergate malady. Yet Gauvin acknowledged: "Hanoi's position today is that of a victor in a long and costly war. It is convinced of its righteous cause. The sole powers capable of restraining it are Russia and China. But neither is prepared to risk losing influence in North Vietnam by restraining it." He concluded: "In an emergency we can count only on the United States bombing of Hanoi and Haiphong—and that is very difficult to contemplate."

It is strange, looking back, to read my notes on talks with American officials stressing that the north had suffered a severe military defeat in their surprise Tet offensive, which severely shook the Americans and South Vietnamese even if it caused heavy losses to the north. One American leader said: "Kissinger, who wrote that if guerrillas don't lose, they win, was wrong. The 1972 offensive was a disaster for them. But they continued."

How right, alas, Kissinger indeed proved to be. And seemingly no one was yet prepared to assess the spreading effects of Watergate on a faltering American public and congressional opinion.

Kissinger was to write ruefully later on: "A Nixon reelected by one of the largest majorities in history [1972] might well have prevailed as he had so many times before. In the swamp of Watergate the President's political strength drained away and this option [mass bombing] did not exist."[1]

The Paris accord of January 27, 1973, theoretically put a formal end to the Vietnam War, but in fact all it accomplished was a means of swiftly withdrawing U.S. troops, abandoning to its own considerable resources a bewildered South Vietnamese government. The agreement followed a U.S. halt in bombing North Vietnam and mining its harbors (January 15, 1973). But even

Nixon was less obsessed by Vietnam at this stage. In May 1973 he wrote in his diary: "I think the most important thing now is to get the White House cleaned and cleaned fast." On April 30 he had already said in a speech: "The man at the top must bear the responsibility....I accept it."

Kissinger recalls that "Nixon was simply unable to concentrate his energies and mind on Vietnam. The records show that he was engaged in incessant meetings and telephone calls on Watergate."[2] And during the three months after the Paris cease-fire, the North Vietnamese refused to withdraw from Cambodia and sent thirty thousand more troops through Laos into South Vietnam.

On August 4, 1973, Kissinger told Lee Kuan Yew, prime minister of Singapore: "We have suffered a tragedy because of Watergate. When I saw you [in early April] we were going to bomb North Vietnam for a week, then go to Russia, then meet with Le Duc Tho [of North Vietnam]. Congress has made it impossible." And Kissinger concluded afterward: "Watergate destroyed the last vestiges of hope for a reasonable outcome. For the first time in the postwar period America abandoned to eventual Communist rule a friendly people who had relied on us. The pattern once established did not end soon. We will have to pay for a long time for the precedent into which we had stumbled that summer, now seemingly so distant."[3]

The most sardonic joke about the whole sad affair is that Kissinger and Le Duc Tho, the North Vietnamese Politburo member with whom he had negotiated, were *jointly* awarded the Nobel Peace Prize for 1973.

The fact that Vietcong and North Vietnamese forces suffered exceptionally heavy casualties in the 1972 Tet offensive meant nothing. A battlefield victory was outranked in importance by the political victory won in the United States by the surprise Communist attack. The Communist propaganda triumph in the U.S. political arena was joined to Watergate with disastrous effect.

Richard Helms, CIA director at the time, refused to allow Nixon's intimates to use the CIA in cover-up attempts to obscure Watergate and the ensuing scandals. Because of this, according to Helms's successor, William Colby, Helms was fired as CIA boss and sent to Iran as U.S. Ambassador, a splendid example of the frying pan–fire alternatives. Nixon then devised a strategic formula of producing an armistice agreement stimulated by U.S. bombing; but this failed to take into account the independent attitudes of the Vietnamese. And the CIA complained that Kissinger was withholding from it secret information from Soviet and North Vietnamese sources. Meanwhile, Graham Martin, who had succeeded Ellsworth Bunker as U.S. ambassador in Saigon, voiced fears that any mass American evacuation could trigger anarchy in South Vietnam.

Brezhnev had advised Nixon that the Soviet Union wanted an end to the war in Cambodia and Laos, and Nixon replied that 1974 would be a year of decision. But this became a negative decision after June 1973 when the House of Representatives terminated all funds appropriated to bomb Cambodia. Nixon complained sadly:

> *The effect of this bill was to deny me the means to enforce the Vietnam Peace Agreement.... The war and the peace in Indochina that America had won at such cost over 12 years of sacrifice and fighting were lost within a matter of months once Congress refused to fulfill our obligations.... This fatally undermined the peace we had won in Indochina.*

Peace might seem technically to have been "won" but in reality this was never true. It was like the 1926 fight; Dempsey did not in fact lose to Tunney.

It is a strange commentary on American political mores that a sordid political scandal involving the wiretapping of presidential conversations with others or of specifically designated American political figures should have been responsible for the first great military defeat of the United States. But such it was.

It is astounding how clumsily the whole issue of wiretapping has always been dealt with in the United States. It was well known that Franklin Roosevelt, John Kennedy, and Lyndon Johnson used technical devices without notifying subjects they were being recorded.

Nixon wrote to Senator Sam Ervin, whose committee investigated Watergate: "No president could function if the private papers of his office, prepared by his personal staff, were open to public scrutiny." The Ervin committee staff unraveled the White

House taping system, but Nixon argued that Presidents Johnson and Kennedy had "also used taping of telephone calls and conversations."

On July 19, 1973, Nixon wrote in his bedside diary: "Should have destroyed the tapes after April 30, 1973," adding:

> *From the time of the disclosure of the existence of the tapes and my decision not to destroy them, my presidency had little chance of surviving to the end of its term.*

The lacuna in his analysis came in not applying the same bitter logic to the conduct and prospects of the Vietnam War and its projected windup. With a doomed presidency and an irate Congress, there was no chance at all of support for a massive bombing program to ensure Hanoi's compliance with the Paris cease-fire accord. Nixon subsequently insisted:

> *We had won the war militarily and politically in Vietnam. But defeat was snatched from the jaws of victory because we lost the war politically in the United States. The peace that was finally won in January 1973 could have been enforced and South Vietnam could be a free nation today. But in a spasm of shortsightedness and spite, the United States threw away what it had gained at such enormous cost. . . .*
>
> *Our defeat in Vietnam can be blamed in part on the Soviets because they provided arms to Hanoi in violation of the peace agreement, giving the North an enormous advantage over the South in the final offensive in the spring of 1975. . . .*
>
> *By following the strategy I initiated in 1969, we and the South Vietnamese were able to win the war militarily by the time of the Paris accords of January 27, 1973. The 550,000 American troops that were in Vietnam when I came into office in 1969 had been withdrawn and South Vietnam was able to defend itself—if we supplied the arms the Paris accords allowed.*[4]

To claim that the war had been "won militarily" by the time of the January 1973 Paris accords represents a peculiar kind of historical shorthand. It soon became blazingly evident that Congress, representing American public and political opinion, had simply had enough of Vietnam in every way and wanted to get out and forget all the splendid promises we had enunciated along the road to disaster. Once our troops were out the South Vietnamese proved unwilling to defend themselves, and the Americans proved unable to supply the bombing, the heavy weapons, and the willpower to continue helping. The war had become a reflection of Watergate, and it, like the presidency, was lost.

On August 22, 1978, Nixon nominated Kissinger as secretary of state, ending his long role as just national security adviser to the president. A year later the president resigned his mandate, and his successor, Vice President Gerald Ford, issued a pardon covering Nixon's White House tenure.

Ford and Nixon had obviously discussed the advisability of giving Kissinger formal rank as chief of Ford's cabinet. I asked Ford on June 27, 1974, if he would retain Kissinger were he to succeed Nixon, and he replied that he didn't wish to discuss such contingencies but added: "There is no question but that I would keep him. I think he is a man of destiny. For all the world. He is the most successful srcretary of state we have had in my lifetime. He is indispensable."

Thus, Nixon, Ford, and Kissinger collaborated in the wise plan to retain continuity in U.S. foriegn policy amid the greatest Political upheaval to engulf America since the Civil War era. The arrangement was of vital importance and worked with success outside Indochina.

For a considerable time the impact of Watergate on U.S. foreign policy was not apparent. It had no effect at all prior to 1973, and even by then its cost to American power to negotiate was limited. There were no repercussions on Washington's attitude toward Chile. In China, although the Chinese leadership was very well informed, no concern or even interest in the affair was ever acknowledged, nor was the status of Nixon ever changed in the eyes of the leadership—especially Mao Tse-tung, who at no time gave the slightest hint he was aware of any change in Nixon's prestige or status at home.

But enormous harm to America's international position was later done by Americans to themselves, not by attempts (until late summer 1974, just before Nixon resigned) to help Congress cripple some of the president's key objectives. This was notably true in Indochina in 1974, when Nixon was deprived, by lack of congressional support, of the means of helping South Vietnam to protect itself after American troops were withdrawn, as had been guaranteed through the pledged use of U.S. air power.

Indeed, the Vietnam debacle was virtually the direct result of Watergate; what might have been a kind of passive victory by the evacuation of U.S. forces, like the French military evacuation of Algeria, became a shambles and not enough Americans bothered to think why. The word "Vietnam" itself had become as much of a curse as the word "Watergate," and the two were so linked in the U.S. public mind that they are almost synonymous in the history of that epoch.

Russia, while maintaining correct and even somewhat friendly relations with Washington, poured vast amounts of military equipment into North Vietnam and funneled this southward when they chose. By the spring of 1974, the north had more than 180,000 soldiers and almost 700 tanks in the south and was no longer bothered by American air superiority. Crippling U.S. air power was a thing of the past, and the Communists were able to move armies and supplies along newly built roads and pipelines. As U.S. aid to the south was pared down by congressional insistence, the north was being armed for the final deadly assault—which immutably came.

Hanoi's field commander charged with the final offensive observed that "the reduction of U.S. aid made it impossible for the puppet troops [Saigon's] to carry out their combat plans and build up their forces.... Thieu was then forced to fight a poor man's war. Enemy firepower had decreased by nearly 60 percent because of bomb and ammunition shortages. Its mobility was also reduced by half due to the lack of aircraft, vehicles and fuel."[5]

The atmosphere in the United States had been turning savagely against Nixon since word got out of his orders to secretly bomb Cambodia, where North Vietnamese sanctuaries were supplying their forces in neighboring South Vietnam. The bombing began March 18, 1969, and Nixon, following his talk with de Gaulle, started to withdraw U.S. troops gradually from South Vietnam. The term "Vietnamization" was invented to explain that the Vietnamese were to assume a greater portion of the burden of fighting and the Americans would reduce their own relative effect. That August, Kissinger contacted Xuan Thuy, Hanoi's negotiator, to arrange full negotiations.

On February 20, 1970, Kissinger met secretly in Paris for talks with Le Duc Tho, Hanoi's representative. On March 18 Prince Sihanouk's regime in Cambodia was overthrown by a military coup, and the following month U.S. troops invaded that country. In June 1971—to the horror and embarrassment of the Nixon administration—the *New York Times* started to publish the classified Pentagon papers. On July 15 the president disclosed that Kissinger had gone to China for secret talks.

January 25, 1972, Nixon revealed that Kissinger had been negotiating with the North Vietnamese. Four weeks later the president flew to Peking. On April 15 the president ordered the bombing of Hanoi, North Vietnam's capital, and Haiphong, its principal port. Five days afterward, in the wake of the bombing, Kissinger flew to Moscow to arrange a May 20 summit between Nixon and Brezhnev.

On June 17, 1972, five men were arrested for breaking into the offices of the Democratic National Committee in Washington D.C.'s Watergate complex. For the rest of the year the Vietnam negotiations were stalemated until, on December 8, Nixon ordered eleven days of heavy bombing of Hanoi and Haiphong. A cease-fire agreement was finally reached in Paris on January 8 and formally signed January 27, 1973. The last American troops left Vietnam on March 29, 1974. In accordance with a congressional ban, the U.S. also ceased bombing Cambodia.

As early as 1969, de Gaulle had counseled Nixon to end the Vietnam War by conducting simultaneous negotiations on political and military issues and by establishing a calendar for the departure of U.S. troops, which should not be withdrawn precipitously. The combined political impact of an unpopular Vietnam War, student rebellions in the United States (including the Kent State shootings), Watergate, and congressional handcuffing of the U.S. Southeast Asia position resulted in a helicopter evacuation of American diplomatic personnel. Nixon, rather foolishly, followed this with the statement: "We have finally achieved peace with honor."

Considering the fact that he knew Congress's mood on future Air Force aid to Saigon and that, without any more U.S. troops in

Vietnam, his hands were clearly tied, this statement was folly. "Peace with honor" is certainly not a phrase that can be applied to the Vietnamese situation after the long war. The United States had followed France into the ranks of the defeated in Indochina, no matter what words may have been chosen to disguise this bleak fact.

Nixon and his country had lost. The last American troops were out of Vietnam March 29, 1974, a day after the American Embassy closed and its personnel were evacuated. A month later four of Nixon's top Washington aides, headed by his attorney general, resigned. On May 9, 1974, the House of Representatives opened impeachment hearings on Nixon. August 9, 1974, Nixon resigned to avoid impeachment. On August 15, Congress put an end to air support of the Saigon government. On April 30, 1975, the Communists captured Saigon.

The effect of this disaster for the United States was not, however, as terrible as it at first seemed. The "domino theory," averring that all Southeast Asia would fall to the Hanoi-Moscow alliance if South Vietnam fell, proved exaggerated; only the Indochinese states of Laos and Cambodia were taken by the Communists after Vietnam; and China was openly at odds with both Hanoi and Moscow over the altered balance. Russia did gain significant trumps; the huge American naval base at Camranh Bay —of great importance to the defense of Singapore, Taiwan, and the Philippines—became a strong point for the Soviets between the Pacific and the Indian Ocean. And the hardy, capable North Vietnamese army was supportive of Russian policy along the southern frontier of China.

It is obviously wrong to blame Watergate for any of these disasters. Indeed, it is the other way around. Without the frenzied opposition this distant war inspired in the American public —above all in American youth—the Watergate break-in and its sordid consequences might have passed into history as a minor peccadillo hardly worthy of a crisis any worse than the Teapot Dome scandals under President Harding. But the atmosphere was so negative and so excitable that Nixon became an astonishing symbol for hatred in his own country, which paid him off in a morbid fascination and hysteria derived from the original break-in at the Democratic office. And this poisoned mass opinion visibly weakened Nixon's authority and inspired many foreign offices abroad to calculate arguments and decisions in terms of their estimate of the probable outcome of a harried American president hoist, as it were, by his own petard.

Nixon himself saw the direct impact of the Vietnam disaster on the pattern of U.S. diplomacy. He acknowledged:

The Vietnam war has grotesquely distorted the debate over American foreign policy. The willingness to use power to defend national interests is the foundation of any effective foreign policy but our ineptness in Vietnam led many Americans to question the wisdom of using our power at all....

Thus did our Vietnam defeat tarnish our ideals, weaken our spirit, cripple our will and turn us into a military giant and a diplomatic dwarf in the world in which the steadfast exercise of American power was needed more than ever before.... The American people, by then exhausted, discouraged, and confused, [had] tacitly accepted a congressional decision that led to a defeat for the United States for the first time in our history.... When we signed the Paris peace agreements in 1973, we had won the war. We then proceeded to lose the peace.[6]

On April 30, 1975, when North Vietnamese tanks rolled past demoralized South Vietnamese forces into the streets of Saigon, the war had truly ended—and in no sense with an American victory. Indeed, it was the first, and therefore obviously the greatest, military defeat in U.S. history. With not a little justice to his argument, Nixon concluded:

There were two underlying reasons for the mounting Congressional challenge to my Vietnam policy. In April 1973 Watergate had become the successor to the Vietnam war as the rallying cry for administration critics [and] some of my closest aides resigned under a darkening cloud of serious allegations and scurrilous innuendo. Watergate became an obsession in Washington. It not only began to consume much of my time and concentration, but also steadily chipped away at my executive authority to act in other areas as well....

Nor did the war's end produce a more peaceful world. Our defeat in Vietnam paralyzed America's will to act in other Third World trouble spots and therefore encouraged aggression on the part of those who had made them trouble spots to begin with. Over the next five years, Soviet clients and proxy forces unleashed a geopolitical offensive that led to stunning reversals for the United States in virtually every region of the world.... Terrorism today is an international challenge to international order, and it requires an international response.[7]

The United States gained nothing but a dubious reputation for keeping its word. China lost its Vietnam hopes. The Soviet Union won control of all Indochina and established a new naval balance in the Pacific, anchored on the vast American-built port of Vietnam's Camranh Bay.

The Watergate war was lost because of mistaken judgments by political leaders on the human condition of popular masses. When he came to power in the United States, Nixon soon showed that he was overconfident in assessing the degree of public and political opinion, and this optimistic misjudgment was clearly mirrored by Kissinger's assumption that insurance for peacekeeping had been built into a settlement by the emergency brake of the threat of massive bombardment. Their original miscalculations were reinforced by Nixon's thunderous reelection triumph in November 1972.

The search for peace rather than outright military victory in Vietnam was pursued from the start of his administration by Nixon, in contrast to Johnson, whose determined pursuit of a battlefield solution always evaded his grasp. And Nixon had a sufficient comprehension of diplomatic realities to work quietly toward a compromise solution to the Indochina conflict even though his generals were under instructions to overcome the enemy on the field of battle.

The search for a negotiated agreement was aided to some degree by Rumania but much more ably by France, whose president, Georges Pompidou, helped arrange secret contacts between Kissinger and the North Vietnamese. Jean Sainteny, a former delegate general from Paris to Hanoi, served as a conduit for messages to and from the Americans. Consequent diplomatic exchanges were irregular but persistent, until Nixon revealed in a speech that on May 31, 1971, the United States had proposed a deadline for the withdrawal of its troops but had been rebuffed by Hanoi.

Washington then offered a formula for internationally supervised free elections in the south coupled with the departure of President Nguyen Van Thieu as president of South Vietnam a month before the election date chosen. Hanoi also rejected this proposed formula. Nevertheless, the pattern for an inevitable overall defeat was being set by the relentless withdrawal of American forces from South Vietnam; by January 1972, 410,000 had gone.

In 1972, Hanoi launched a major offensive designed to defeat the Vietnamization program by which Washington sought to transfer the burden of South Vietnam's defense to Saigon. A U.S. invasion of Cambodia in 1970 and Laos in 1971 was designed to upset Hanoi's schedule. Despite the uproar in the United States, Prince Norodom Sihanouk of Cambodia accepted the American invasion as necessary because it was aimed at Vietcong and North Vietnamese concentrations, not Cambodians. I had toured the Cambodian–South Vietnam frontier by plane and helicopter northward to the Laotian border, visiting frontier posts of the U.S. Special Forces, and was wholly convinced that Hanoi had stationed strong forces at key points inside Cambodia. When I told this to President Johnson and his Defense Secretary McNamara at lunch in the White House, McNamara denied it!

On April 9, 1972, a force of twenty-eight B-52 heavy bombers was sent to the Western Pacific island of Guam, where these giant planes were based, to smash critical North Vietnam communications. Two aircraft carriers were then added to the four already off the North Vietnamese coast. One result of these moves was a moderation of Hanoi's negotiation proposals and a readiness to resume talks that had been suspended.

Kissinger described the air-naval maneuvers as a success for Nixon's policy, writing: "He had acted boldly and won a brilliant gamble. He challenged the Soviet Union and to a lesser extent China and in the end improved relations with both. He prevented the military collapse of South Vietnam."[8] Nixon was heartened by this tactical success and praised the effectiveness of air power in hurting the enemy, dictating in a memo to his security assistant:

> *We have the power to destroy this war-making capacity. The only question is whether we have the* will *to use that power. What distinguishes me from Johnson is that I have the* will *in spades. If we now fail it will be because the bureaucrats and the bureaucracy and particularly those in the Defense Department, who will of course be vigorously assisted by their allies in State, will find ways to erode the strong, decisive action that I have indicated we are going to take. For once, I want the military and I want the NSC staff to come up with some ideas on their own which will recommend* action *which is very* strong, threatening *and* effective.

Moscow's reaction to the American bombardments of the north was circumspect, and Peking's was negligible. Brezhnev refused to cancel his projected summit meeting with Nixon, and the official Soviet spokesman warned Hanoi that the USSR and the rest of the Communist world, including China, favored peaceful coexistence. As a consequence of these muted reactions, Hanoi conceded that the Saigon government need not be overthrown at the price of a cease-fire, as it had earlier insisted.

Kissinger was thus able to restart negotiations in Paris with the Communist emissary, Le Duc Tho, with whom he was to share a Nobel Prize for ending the war. By October 12, 1972, the outline of an accord had been reached, including a pledged U.S. withdrawal (which was well under way and had long been agreed), release of American prisoners in Communist hands, and a commitment to produce an armistice in Laos and Cambodia. Kissinger sent word to Nguyen Van Thieu, the South Vietnamese president, urging him to maximize efforts to seize as much territory as he could because of the impending freeze along cease-fire lines.

Kissinger, asserting that peace at last was "at hand," told Nixon the three major U.S. goals for 1972 had been reached: the President's visit to Peking, the Moscow Summit, and the Indochina armistice. Both the president and his national security assistant were confident that in the event of massive violations of the accord by Hanoi, the United States would enforce the agreement by heavy bombardment of the north and massive arms support of the south. As Kissinger recalled sadly: "We could not know that soon Watergate would nullify most of these assumptions.... We landed in Washington near joyous that we had brought home both peace and dignity."[9]

It took considerable time before the Americans realized that Thieu's acceptance of the cease-fire accord was at best dubious, no matter what he implied. As it developed, the thought of any compromise with his determination to achieve a complete victory over Hanoi would not be acceptable. Thieu insisted, it became clear, on absolute and undivided sovereignty and total control over the entire territory of South Vietnam.

I knew Thieu, if not well, and was inclined at first to underestimate the determination, fierce patriotism, and capacity for deceit of this small man with a slightly Chinese cast of features and a soft, quiet voice and manner. Jean Sainteny, the experienced Frenchman who had served as Kissinger's messenger to Hanoi, told me once that Thieu was the most effective chief of government Saigon had had, and I, who had encountered all of them starting with Emperor Bao Dai, certainly agreed.

Thieu told me in 1972, the last time I saw him:

> Nothing came of the so-called offensive that they [the Communists] were supposed to be mounting here during President Nixon's visit to Peking. I imagine they will try an all-out offensive later on to exploit political divisions in the United States and to press Nixon to yield more in negotiations [as a result of Watergate].
>
> What the Communists really want is to defeat Nixon. They know it will be very hard to impose their viewpoint if he is re-elected. Therefore they want to smash his Vietnamization program and they must also have a victory on the battlefield first if they are to get any great concessions....
>
> Moscow wants to demonstrate that it is impossible to negotiate over the head of Hanoi. Obviously the idea of such a Communist offensive at this time is favored by Moscow which wants to show Nixon the only way he could negotiate a settlement in Vietnam is with the Russians, not the Chinese. The Russians are trying to prove that the key to peace here can be found only in Moscow, not Peking. Moscow will do anything it can to block efforts by Washington and Peking to solve this war.
>
> Moscow is gaining increasing importance in North

> Vietnam by shipping in more and more armaments. And it gained considerably as a result of India's victory in the war with Pakistan last winter. Now it is strong in India and Bangladesh. It is strong in North Vietnam. Russia would like to contain China.
>
> Russia did not originally want North Vietnam to invade South Vietnam because it did not want to produce the U.S. intervention in this area which came. Moscow would like to establish neutral but pro-Soviet regimes in Laos and Cambodia to be sure those countries lean on Moscow and not on Washington.

This geopolitical analysis was not without a sharp logic of its own, one that did not wholly disagree with America reasoning. But when Washington evolved a more compromising attitude toward Hanoi and displayed readiness for compromises that would leave South Vietnam in an obviously weakened relative condition, Thieu was clearly not ready to yield, no matter how American diplomats and generals interpreted his subtle attitudes and apparently elliptical reasoning.

Thieu was a determined, tough man beneath his silken manner. He told Kissinger: "Ever since the U.S. asked me to resign and bargained with me on the time of my resignation, had I not been a soldier I would have resigned. Because I see that those whom I regard as friends have failed me. However great the personal humiliation for me I shall continue to fight."

Thus, although Kissinger had announced that the bloody and protracted Indochina war was ending, Thieu proved obdurate and unprepared to act accordingly. And when Washington wished to aid his last stand with aerial support, a congressional embargo on funds prevented this. Thieu's obstinacy encouraged Hanoi to pick up its sword and buckler again and slash at its weakened enemy.

Back in Washington Kissinger proclaimed on October 26, 1972, "We believe that peace is at hand." Between them, Thieu, the recalcitrant American ally, and Ho Chi Minh, the obdurate enemy, were to prove the statement false, and the White House was prevented from acting in this unexpected situation by new bonds fastened about executive power by Congress.

On November 7, 1972, Nixon won his greatest political victory in regaining the White House. Yet within two years both he and Thieu were out of office. When Hanoi resumed its attacks on the south, Nixon was still able to respond by ordering massive B-52 bombardments (since Congress had not yet enacted restraints canceling his ability to move accordingly). Negotiations for a new settlement were renewed January 2, 1973. But the damage had been done, and the arranged cease-fire of 1972 could never be resurrected. The denouement was gradual but complete. On April 30, 1975, after all troops had been withdrawn and there was a mad scramble by remaining American diplomats and others to clamber aboard helicopters, the massive U.S. presence vanished in an undignified bug-out. Nixon was to write:

> *The congressional bombing cut-off, coupled with the limitation placed on the President by the War Powers Resolution in November 1973, set off a string of events that led to the Communist takeover in Cambodia and on April 30, 1975, the North Vietnamese conquest of South Vietnam. . . .*
>
> *The war and the peace in Indochina that America had won at such cost over twelve years of sacrifice and fighting were lost within a matter of months once Congress refused to fulfill our obligations. And it is Congress that must bear the responsibility for the tragic results. Hundreds of thousands of anti-Communist South Vietnamese and Cambodians have been murdered or starved to death by their conquerors, and the bloodbath continues.*[10]

IX

Climaxes

The last fourteen months of Nixon's public life were crammed with climaxes of a personal and governmental nature crucially affecting both the president's career and the fate of his nation and of the world. At no time in the history of the United States have so many momentous events occurred so swiftly in the White House or been so directly connected with the decisions taken by its tenant. And it is quite impossible to separate from each other events that appear initially to be only politically American in their import and the repercussions abroad to which they may or may not be related in one or another degree.

Thus, for example, the ultimate unwinding of the Watergate affair had global effects that could seem to be connected with matters of war and peace in the Middle East or calculations by foreign powers with respect to the probability or improbability of the U.S. policy decisions under consideration at the time. And cruelly libelous rumors that one or another presidential diplomatic act may have been influenced by a desire to gain public backing for himself and for the office's reputation and efficacy continued to crop up for years, stimulated by prejudicial fiction rather than fact.

An arbitrary time frontier for this melodramatic era may be designated with the arrival in Washington of Leonid Brezhnev's plane on June 16, 1973, for a nine-day visit—second of the Soviet leader's three summit meetings with Nixon. Brezhnev, who showed himself especially amiable in a personal sense, assured his host that Moscow desired a speedy termination of the U.S. military campaigns in Laos and Cambodia and also that he would caution the North Vietnamese on their militancy, indicating that he was alarmed about Russia's relationship with China, a nation he saw as on the threshold of massive nuclear weapons power.

Despite this apparently helpful Soviet stance, internal American politics forced Nixon to accept an embargo on future U.S. bombing of Cambodia after August 15, 1973. Nixon recalled bitterly afterward:

> *I knew that since Congress had removed the possibility of military action I had only words with which to threaten. The Communists knew it too.... When Kissinger raised the question of the Communist violations of the cease-fire in Cambodia, the Soviet ambassador [Dobrynin] scornfully asked what we had expected, now that we had no negotiating leverage because of the bombing cutoff imposed by Congress.... The congressional bombing cutoff, coupled with the limitation placed on the President by the War Powers Resolution in November 1973, set off a string of events that led to the Communist takeover in Cambodia and, on April 30, 1975, the North Vietnamese conquest of South Vietnam....*
>
> *The war and the peace in Indochina that America had won at such cost over twelve years of sacrifice and fighting were lost within a matter of months once Congress refused to fulfill our obligations. And it is Congress that must bear the responsibility for the tragic results... Congress's tragic and irresponsible action... fatally undermined the peace we had won in Indochina.*[1]

Nixon was additionally afflicted by physical incapacity when, on July 12, he was hospitalized with a painful phlebitis. This host of insupportable burdens—mental, physical, internal, external, political, and diplomatic—produced a load that even his perplexed but courageous nature had difficulty in bearing. He said later:

> *It was my belief then, and it is still my belief today, that the Democratic majority in Congress used the Watergate scandal as an excuse for indulging in a purposeful policy of ignoring and actually overriding the landslide mandate that my programs and philosophy had received in the 1972 election. Unfortunately, by the way I handled Watergate, I helped them do it.*

The gloom that by then had embraced Nixon caused him to reflect on the problem of how to continue his policies, above all foreign, after his ultimate retirement. The thought that he might not be able to last the course, either for political or health reasons, had already entered his mind, and by July 1973 he became familiar with charges brewing against his vice president, Spiro Agnew, of illegally receiving money while in office. These allegations eventually forced Agnew's resignation on October 10, 1973, after he had pleaded *nolo contendere* in a federal court and been sentenced to three years' probation and a ten thousand dollar fine.

As if to demonstrate that there are no limits to negative pressures when a man is down on his luck, Nixon had just four days earlier received a cable from his ambassador in Israel reporting that Syria and Egypt had begun a final countdown for an attack against the Jewish state. Not only was Nixon horrified, but he was appalled by the failure in American and Israeli intelligence that prevented any faint signs of the assault from being detected. By nightfall on October 6, 1973, the Egyptians had driven an entire army across the Suez Canal into the Sinai desert, and the Syrians were hammering at Israeli positions in the north along the Golan Heights. And, just as the United States was struggling to build an air bridge of matériel to Israel, hindered by the refusal of our European allies to allow their bases to be used in the resupply effort, the Soviet Union was rushing equipment to Syria and Egypt and had alerted three of its parachute divisions for possible intervention. Even the reluctant King Hussein dispatched a small Jordanian contingent to help the Syrians.

Against these odds, both Israel—caught by surprise—and its American ally produced a remarkable effort. By October 13, thirty massive C-130 transports were flying from the United States to Israel and were soon bringing in a thousand tons a day, more than the far-shorter Berlin airlift had once managed. The tide soon turned in the Middle East, leaving Moscow with the unexpected problem of what to do about it. Nixon dispatched Kissinger to Brezhnev with a stern letter.

This urgent foreign crisis did nothing to ease the tension at home produced by the Watergate affair and the refusal of the special prosecutor appointed to handle it, Archibald Cox, or his boss, Attorney General Elliot Richardson, to withdraw or postpone resignations seeking to force the president's hand. The scandal spun onward. On November 15 the House of Representatives voted to allocate a million dollars for the purpose of starting impeachment proceedings against the president.

By then the Middle East war had passed its climax. Kissinger and Brezhnev produced a draft cease-fire agreement in Moscow, and, after the Arabs and Israelis had both grudgingly accepted its terms, the armistice began October 22. Within hours the two sides accused each other of not adhering to agreed terms, and the Israelis encircled the Egyptian Third Army on the east bank of the Suez Canal. October 24 a second cease-fire was agreed on, but the Russians increased to seven the number of their alerted airborne divisions and brought eighty-five ships including landing craft and helicopter carriers into the Mediterranean. On October 24 this inspired a global alert of all American conventional and nuclear forces. Nevertheless, the crisis wound down, and the Arabs, for a second time, lost most of the Soviet military equipment that had been sent to them to fight Israel.

Nixon told a White House press conference with some pride:

> *I should point out that even in this week, when many thought that the President was shell-shocked, unable to act, the President acted decisively in the interests of peace, in the interests of the country, and I can assure you that whatever shocks gentlemen of the press may have, or others, political people, these shocks will not affect me in my doing my job.*

Once the hopes of sudden victory faded from Arab minds, and the U.S. airlift replenished Israeli equipment losses, it was clear that the time for negotiations was ripe. But the situation was deeply complex and difficult. A dazzling Israeli drive across the Suez Canal and into Africa had cut off in isolation an Egyptian Army fighting on west Asia's Sinai peninsula in territory that had been recaptured from Israeli occupation. At the same time, the far smaller but more difficult northern front with Syria, along the Golan Heights, was deeply entangled, with the key Syrian frontier town of Quneitra threatened by Israeli artillery in its entirety where it was not already occupied by Israeli infantry. And from October 13, the seventh day of the war, a U.S. airlift had supplied Israel's arsenal.

The detailed armistice line of the Yom Kippur conflict arranged in October was nervously adhered to despite occasional hints of unilateral violation. Both Nixon personally and Kissinger sought to prepare an all-inclusive negotiation by conventional diplomacy and by recourse to Jordan's King Hussein, who had only played an indirect and minor role on the Arab side in the October offensive. Preparations for a final negotiation, by means of shuttle diplomacy, were all-embracing. With conjointed American cooperation and pressure, the nervous front lines around Suez (for Egypt) and Quneitra in the Golan (for Syria) were rejuggled. Nixon flew to Moscow, where he succeeded in persuading Brezhnev that his diplomatic position had by no means been totally eroded by Watergate, although Moscow intimated it had a negative view of his chances. Nixon also visited Syria. There he restored diplomatic relations between Damascus and Washington during the months of awaiting a final cease-fire arrangement.

The complicated and seemingly endless mobile negotiation bound up in the final strategic phase of the overall Middle East shuttle really began on March 30, 1974, in Washington after Kissinger's return from his trip to Moscow (on the eve of his wedding to the lovely Nancy Maginnes) and a visit to the U.S. capital by Moshe Dayan, the magnetic Israeli leader and the one perhaps most capable of arousing emotions for a cause. On his own subsequent way to Moscow and a meeting with Brezhnev, Nixon stopped off in Brussels to confer with leaders of the NATO alliance, among whom the American leader's reputation was still high and there was more than a little assumption that Watergate was more of a political coup by Nixon's enemies than a dereliction in the president's legal obligations.

There was immense confusion, varying from day to day and

from country to country, in the zigzag impressions produced by the seemingly endless Watergate imbroglio. On June 11, 1974, when Kissinger stopped off to join Nixon in Salzburg, Austria, where the two men caught a brief rest en route to the Middle East, he was so worn out physically from constant worry and travel and his nerves so eroded by the spreading strains of the scandal, which even seemed to be reaching out for him, that he threatened to resign as secretary of state. Nixon was scarcely pleased by this maneuver. But the problem soon evaporated when strong congressional support for Kissinger was evinced. Many opinions then expressed concluded that Nixon knew he could not survive the threatening debacle and resented the probability that Kissinger could, an idea that simply reflected the nervous tension embracing all the principal actors in the sad affair. In fact, the Soviet Union and Brezhnev showed Nixon a courteous respect at that moment, which indicated they reposed a certain confidence in his predictability, a quality they valued because it put them at their ease.

This somewhat allayed the suspicion of many of Nixon's entourage that the Soviets might have egged their Arab clients on to the surprise offensive, because the U.S. domestic crisis might deflect or deter the Americans from effectively aiding their Middle East ally. After his possible miscalculations had been borne in on Brezhnev, he showed by a letter to Nixon in mid-November 1973 that he was again prepared to pick up the dialogue of U.S.–Soviet détente where it had been left before the Middle East crisis. In the meantime, Nixon sent Kissinger through the Middle East in hopes of easing pressures by arranging to extricate the surrounded Egyptian army from the threat of an Israeli throttling and also to devise an acceptable settlement for the future of the Syrian town of Quneitra at the southern edge of the Golan Heights. Both procedures advanced perceptibly, and on November 7, 1973, after six years of severance, the United States and Egypt resumed diplomatic relations. Before November was over, Nixon's mind was again focused entirely on Watergate as he was forced to appoint a new attorney general following the departures of the incumbent, Elliot Richardson, and his Watergate prosecutor, Cox. Hardly had this been achieved than he swore in Gerald Ford as vice president on December 6, replacing the tarnished Agnew.

On January 30, 1974, Nixon delivered his regular State of the Union Address to Congress, stressing:

Tonight, for the first time in twelve years, a President of the United States can report to the Congress on the state of a Union at peace with every nation of the world.

This boast, still unreal factually in Vietnam, had been rendered meaningful by a magnificent piece of diplomacy achieved by Kissinger in his first venture of traveling statesmanship, to become generally known as "shuttle diplomacy" for its ceaseless weaving and bobbing without advance notice among the bellicose capitals of the Middle East. No other secretary of state, not even the peripatetic John Foster Dulles, was able to achieve so much in so short a time as did the bespectacled Harvard professor who turned the jet plane into a negotiating asset.

By January 17, after only a week of parleying, Kissinger was able to produce an Egyptian-Israeli troop disengagement, accomplished by his skill and energy, which in turn had brought admiration and friendship for Kissinger from both Egyptian president Sadat and Israeli prime minister Golda Meir. Nixon did not figure in the day-to-day maneuvers but served as the strategic guide for Kissinger's activity. Following the Cairo success, the next advance in Washington's parleying was securing an end to the Arab oil embargo enacted during the war. Seven of the nine Arab petroleum producers lifted their curb on March 18, 1974, after almost six months' prohibition that had seriously wounded American economic production.

The last specific problem to be settled was the stubborn Golan Heights row between Syria and Israel. By the end of May 1974, Kissinger had spent thirty-two days on a constant shuttle between Damascus and Jerusalem. On May 16 he was ready to throw in the sponge and alerted Washington that he was returning without a settlement. Nixon ordered him to give the shuttle process yet another try and wrote to Mrs. Meir urging a compromise that would enable the solution that seemed so near and yet so elusive. An accord was finally agreed and signed May 31, 1974. Nixon promptly decided to help firm up the gains made and to lay the groundwork for more progress in the future by visiting Egypt, Syria, Saudi Arabia, Jordan, and Israel in person.

The resulting trip produced a peculiar event that has never been explained in its entirety. Quite obviously Nixon, while masterminding the strategy behind Kissinger's flamboyant tactical maneuvers, must inevitably have felt removed from the glamorous headlines awarded the secretary of state's successes. It could not have been disagreeable for him to contemplate getting his own share of well-deserved kudos by a personal visit together with Kissinger to the scenes of the latter's success.

And Kissinger himself, despite his phenomenal energy, must have been worn out and nervous as a cat following his weeks in the Middle East pressure cooker. Against this background he bridled at reports that he had given false testimony to the Senate Foreign Relations Committee and sniffed: "I do not conduct my office as a conspiracy."

Nixon left the United States June 9 to meet Kissinger in Salzburg for a day's break in the protracted journey. The secretary called a press conference to answer charges in the press that he had dissembled in testifying about 1969 wiretaps connected with Watergate. Furious, Kissinger told the press he would resign if his character and credibility were not "cleared up."

Nixon issued a statement defending him, and the atmosphere of hysterical irritation subsided. But Nixon intimated he was indeed interested in the morale-boosting aspect of his trip to the Levant by writing in his diary: "I am going to devote myself over the next ten days to doing everything possible to restore some respect for the office as well as for the man." But he still felt physically debilitated, and his phlebitis returned painfully.

On June 12, Nixon was greeted in Cairo by Sadat. The two men took to each other in a mutual admiration society that endured even after Nixon's resignation from the presidency until, during Jimmy Carter's term, the Egyptian was assassinated by right-wing opponents who disliked his policy, especially with regard to Israel. Nixon found Sadat both subtle and sophisticated, a leader who avoided pressing his visitor in private about U.S.–Israeli ties but publicly urged Palestinian rights and return of all Arab territories occupied by Israel since 1967. However, he acknowledged to Nixon that he "just gave up on" the Russians who had failed to send promised military equipment prior to the Yom Kippur War.

Sadat succeeded in one big thing: convincing Nixon that

"Egypt is the key to the Arab world." Nixon urged him to pursue a moderate course, and the two leaders agreed on the text of a pledge of cooperation and a joint quest for Middle Eastern peace and economic cooperation. From Cairo, Nixon flew to Saudi Arabia where, in Jidda, King Faisal met him and soon gave him several versions of the favorite speech he reserved for foreigners: the unchanging theme that Moscow and the Jews were in cahoots. Nevertheless, he added: "Anybody who stands against you, Mr. President, in the United States of America or outside the United States of America, or stands against us, your friends in this part of the world, obviously has one aim in mind, namely, that of causing the splintering of the world, the wrong polarization of the world, the bringing about of mischief, which would not be conducive to tranquility and peace in the world."[2]

Nixon met President Assad of Syria for the first time on this trip. To his surprise, he found Assad even more impressive than he had been led to expect by the admiring Kissinger. He observed in his diary:

He was, as Henry had said, a tough negotiator, but he has a great deal of mystique, tremendous stamina and lots of charm. He laughs easily, and I can see he will be a dynamic leader if he can just maintain his judgment. . . . All in all he is a man of real substance, and at his age—forty-four—if he can avoid somebody shooting him or overthrowing him, he will be a leader to be reckoned with in this part of the world.[3]

Israel was the next-to-last country visited on Nixon's tour and the one that both he and Kissinger knew best from personal experience. Golda Meir had resigned as prime minister in favor of Yitzhak Rabin, but Mrs. Meir was still allowed to play an important personal role during the visit of her American friends and partners in previous conferences. At a state dinner she made a brief reply to a special toast from Nixon: "As President Nixon says, Presidents can do almost anything, and President Nixon has done many things that nobody would have thought of doing."[4]

The presidential tour ended in Jordan, where the brave little king, Hussein, said with impeccable courtesy: "Your coming to us at this time has been perfectly timed to preserve the momentum that American initiative had begun under your inspired and inspiring leadership."[5]

When the president, Kissinger, and their entourage got back to the United States, Nixon wrote in his diary:

With the congressional leaders I stepped out a little bit ahead of Henry in indicating that we would make Israel strong enough that they would not fear to negotiate, but not so strong that they felt they had no need to negotiate....

One thing the Mideast trip did was to put the whole Watergate business into perspective—to make us realize that all the terrible battering we have taken is really pygmy-sized when compared to what we have done and what we can do in the future not only for peace in the world but, indirectly, to effect the well-being of people everywhere. This, I suppose, is what we must always keep front and center regardless of what happens in the future.[6]

Two days later, on June 21, 1974, the House Judiciary committee finished hearing all the evidence on all the charges against Nixon (Watergate); it ran to more than 7,000 pages.

Nixon found there was no rest for the weary, ill, or harassed of this world. Hardly used to the Washington time zone again, Nixon flew to Brussels on June 25 to observe the twenty-fifth anniversary of NATO with his alliance partners. Two days later he was in Moscow, where Brezhnev received him promptly for a private talk opening their third summit meeting and said he was "convinced" Nixon would remain in office until the end of his second term in 1976. They then flew to Oreanda, near Yalta—a name they omitted from mention of their conference because of unfavorable connotations in many lands surrounding its earlier role as the seat of the famous Crimean meeting of Stalin, Roosevelt, and Churchill in February 1945.

Nixon wrote in his diary that he had told Brezhnev:

Don't let the Mideast become the Balkans for the U.S. and the Soviet Union. Don't let any place else, Southeast Asia, the Mideast, or the Caribbean, become a point of difference between us that draws us into conflict, when there are many more important issues that could draw us together.[7]

Nixon suggested to his host that they agree to meet again for a minisummit before the end of the year, at which they might be able to agree on an offensive-weapons limitation at some "halfway house" in Europe. He offered to send Kissinger back in September to arrange a date and venue. Brezhnev liked the thought. It was evident that neither party was yet ready for an important strategic arms limitation accord. While there was therefore no big deal at the Oreanda talk, Nixon observed:

In my judgment my Watergate problems and the impeachment hearings did not play a major part at Summit III. Our intelligence beforehand—and my distinct impression while in the Soviet Union —was that Brezhnev had decided to go all out for détente and place all his chips on my survival and my ultimate ability to deliver on what I promised. It was the American domestic political fluctuations, most of which had preceded Watergate, that cast the greatest doubt on my reliability; the failure to produce Most Favored Nation status and the agitation over Soviet Jews and emigration had made it difficult for Brezhnev to defend détente to his own conservatives. . . .

As it turned out, it's probably just as well that we were unable to reach any agreement with the Russians on the nuclear front, because to have to take this thing on now would mean that we would have to be opposed to some of our best friends prior to the impeachment vote.[8]

In early July Nixon was back in Washington.

On July 15, 1974, there was an abrupt coup d'état on Cyprus, with fighting beginning to erupt among Greek and Turkish Cypriot factions. Nixon told his diary:

The Cyprus thing brought home the thought that with the world in the situation it is, with the peace as fragile as it is in various parts of the world, a shake-up in the American presidency and a change would have a traumatic effect abroad and a traumatic effect at home.[9]

In fact, the very first crisis facing Gerald Ford the instant he was sworn in to replace Nixon was a Turkish invasion of Cyprus. From then until the denouement of each separate crisis, on a Mediterranean island and in the United States government, the two went hand in hand.

On July 29 a Supreme Court decision ordered that all the tapes of conversations Nixon had recorded among himself and advisers should be turned over to the congressional investigators of the Watergate affair. One tape, recording talks between Nixon and H. R. Haldeman, his principal White House officer for internal matters, was recognized by both the prosecution and the defense as a "smoking pistol" of evidence against Nixon. Nixon was recorded in a discussion as having favored the CIA limiting FBI investigations of the scandal for political rather than national security reasons, belying other testimony he had given. The House Judiciary Committee had already begun voting to impeach Nixon, article by article on the reasoning adduced. The first article was a plain defeat for the president. Two more impeachment articles were similarly passed by the Judiciary Committee in the wake of the Supreme Court's approval of the release of the June 23 tape. He was charged with abusing presidential powers. Even Nixon's closest advisers and defenders, such as General Alexander Haig, acknowledged to him that the long battle appeared to have been lost.

Nixon reluctantly decided that he had to resign, although he had until then resolved to fight every inch of his long retreat. He explained to his White House colleagues that Gerald Ford, who would now succeed him, was not experienced in foreign affairs but was a good and decent man. Likewise, Kissinger would be expected to stay on as secretary of state. Nixon told Ford he was right in deciding to remain silent on the impeachment and said no cabinet member should risk jeopardizing his ability to carry out his responsibilities after Nixon's replacement.

Kissinger acknowledged to the president that his decision was the best approach, because if he decided to fight an impeachment trial in the Senate he would be further dishonored and the national foreign policy might not be able to survive the resulting crisis. On August 7, Nixon told Kissinger he was resigning the next day, effective August 9. A schedule of messages to foreign nations was prepared, advising them that there would be no change in U.S. foreign policy.

Deeply moved, Kissinger, who owed so much to Nixon for his original national security adviser job, said he would resign as secretary of state if "they harass you after you leave office." Nixon told him he simply must stay on because his departure after Nixon's would be "the worst thing that could happen to America and to all our initiatives to build a more peaceful world." Nixon then took the secretary into the Lincoln bedroom, where the two men knelt and prayed in silence.

On August 8, Nixon's last full day in office, he vetoed an agricultural appropriations bill to avoid forcing Ford to have to make a difficult political decision on his first day in the White House. He also told Ford he considered Kissinger "absolutely indispensable" in the State Department and asked his successor to retain Haig as chief of staff at least for the transition period of the new presidency. Referring to his own resignation, he said bitterly to an associate: "How can you support a quitter?" And when he gathered forty-six close associates in the Cabinet Room to say farewell, he burst into tears when one of them started to weep. It was the first time he had cried publicly since President Eisenhower's death. At noon on August 9, 1974, Nixon ceased being president. He had signed a sheet of paper bearing one sentence, handed to him by Haig: "I hereby resign the Office of President of the United States."

X

The Infernal Triangle

Richard Nixon barely escaped direct involvement in another war and a major crisis by the accident of the date chosen for his resignation of the American presidency. He signed the paper relinquishing his high office on August 8, 1974, and this act took effect on August 9 when Gerald Ford moved into the White House to succeed him. August was the month selected by the Turkish high command to launch a major sea and air invasion of the Mediterranean island of Cyprus, which the Turks shared as a minority partner with their old enemies and unsteady newfound friends, the Greeks. A minor first Turkish landing had occurred July 19; the second ultimately came on August 14. Watergate was the political frontier for the U.S. involvement in the brief 1974 Cyprus war.

As a military operation, the first attack was uncoordinated and inept. One Turkish naval unit missed its scheduled landing place by miles. Dozens of Turkish paratroopers were dropped far from their mapped target zones. And as for the Greeks, who were fighting to defend the island so heavily populated by their kinsmen, their mobilization on the Hellenic mainland was a monument to inefficient confusion.

Because a 70 percent majority of the Cypriot population is Greek, Greece has always contended the entire island should be its territory. Turkey, which has a habit of opposing anything dreamed up in Athens, insists it will never accept such a solution. And the Western world, which desires peace and stability in the vital Mediterranean Sea, has never managed to invent an answer to the question.

Thus, it may have been fortunate for his personal history that Nixon was in retirement in California while the final scene was being played. Over the decades, few American presidents have managed to earn any popularity with either Greece or Turkey, and none since Cyprus was declared a bilingual republic in 1979, after tedious diplomatic negotiations. Moreover, American presidents have a particularly long casualty list on Cyprus.

Harry Truman and Dwight Eisenhower, whose White House terms preceded the creation of the island republic, were the luckiest recent U.S. chiefs of state with regard to Greco-Turkish relationships. Truman was wildly popular in both countries and, in cahoots with NATO, extended the shield of American protection over both rivals at a time when Russia was at least indirectly supporting a Communist insurrection in Greece and simultaneously pressing for territorial concessions from Turkey. Truman was more or less forced into the position of East European peacemaker when a bankrupt London, which had finally abandoned the precepts that "God is an Englishman" and that the road to India must be kept open, asked the United States to replace Britain as referee. Truman promptly accepted, although aware that the importance of India to the English-speaking world was decreasing in 1947 when he enunciated the Truman Doctrine. This was followed by the Marshall Plan and NATO. It might therefore be argued by a diplomat with forensic talent that thanks to Greek and Turkish jealousy, the two perforce became responsible for the protection of the Western world.

Truman backed up the new commitment he had assumed by shipping arms to both Greece and Turkey, helping them shore up their economies, and ultimately sending a military mission under General James Van Fleet to guide the wobbly Greek conservative government in squashing a bloody Communist rebellion. When the Turkish ambassador to Washington died, Truman made the grand, meaningful gesture (which delighted the Turks) of sending his body home aboard the massive U.S. battleship *Missouri*.

However, the apparently amiable relationship, under American guidance, between the two countries, disintegrated over feuding on Cyprus and a revival off mutual jealousies. These dated back to 1453, when Turkey destroyed the Greek Byzantine empire by capturing Constantinople, later changing its name to Istanbul, and then conquering all Greece. The Greeks ousted the Turks and proclaimed their independence in 1821. But the bad neighbors never really achieved any durable friendship. The Greeks kept up a running battle against Turkey through the nineteenth century and fought the Turks in the Crimean War, both the First Balkan and Second Balkan Wars, World War I, and finally launched a disastrous invasion of Turkish Anatolia in 1921.

As American leaders have successively found out, the Greeks and Turks have a vivid and long-enduring dislike for each other, even when they are members of the same North Atlantic alliance, a fact both often seem to forget. This was the long-smoldering background against which America inherited Britain's traditional guardian role in the eastern Mediterranean and South Balkans. When London gave up its suzerainty over Cyprus, America's diplomacy, unfamiliar with the emotional hatreds that had been nurtured for centuries by the peoples of the area, proved quite incapable of keeping them apart when the island both nations coveted was launched on a sea of questionable freedom. The Greeks, with their heavily preponderant population, had a clear geopolitical claim. The Turks had a clear geographic case with their evident proximity to Cyprus, only forty miles off the Anatolian coast.

The quandary of the United States was underscored at the very end of Nixon's presidency. All the possible formulas imagined by Washington as a means of settling the triangular hatreds of Greece, Turkey, and Cyprus had been attempted during Lyndon Johnson's administration. Although the Greeks had been flamboyantly favored in the United States and backed by an influential lobby that had flourished during Greece's heroic record in World War II, they were unable to persuade the American government that their Hellenic kinsmen were always right and their Turkish adversaries always wrong. Three retired U.S. cabinet members (Dean Acheson and Cyrus Vance—State—and Clark Clifford—Defense) had failed to cut the Gordian knot.

Neither Nixon nor Kissinger had had a great deal to do with Greek, Turkish, or Cypriot affairs until Nixon's resignation in

1974. They were not particularly well informed about developments in that tricky area. One faction kept complaining that American policy in Cyprus and also in Greece was elaborated by the CIA, not the State Department. I do not know if this was true, but I have little doubt that Henry Tasca, U.S. ambassador to Athens under Nixon, was both tactless and inadequate. (King Constantine told me with a sour smile that Tasca had complained to him because they had "promised me Italy and we had to go to Greece instead." Said Constantine: "A hell of a thing to tell a Greek.") But there is no doubt that CIA representatives were in touch with several officers' factions in the highly politicized Greek army.

The outcome of this unhappy affair almost coincided with the denouement of the Watergate mess in America. If anything, Nixon had cherished a sentimental affection for the Greeks; he had twice visited Athens. But Kissinger had no preconceived bias, and his realpolitik inclined him toward Turkey with its massive army, its military reputation, and its tough stand against threats on its long Soviet border.

And no matter where his emotional prejudices might have been, Nixon was enough of a realist to recognize that Turkey, whose armed forces received American supplies to the area on a ratio of ten to Greece's share of seven, must be favored if need be and if no other solution was possible.

Personally, I suspect that the CIA was more influential than it claims with regard to U.S. policy in Greece during the 1970s, and its agents were well connected at all levels of the Greek social structure. Certainly the CIA was close to a conspiratorial group of generals from the IDEA secret organization, which was planning a coup d'état in 1967. But the generals moved too slowly, and one of their number (in return for a cushy job afterward) informed on them to a lower-ranking colonels' junta, which seized power itself in April 1967. This junta crushed a countercoup mounted by King Constantine six months later, and he fled with his family to Rome.

Kissinger wrote of the uneasy situation prevailing in 1974:

> Only in the Aegean, where the primeval hatreds of Greeks and Turks flared again on Cyprus, did we have to endure an international crisis in those last weeks of Nixon's office, and it was not that they took advantage of Nixon's

plight or even calculated it in their decisions. It was an eruption of old frustrations and oppressions; but nonetheless it laid bare the vulnerabilities of a divided Administration with a President in no position to impose coherence....I touch on it here only to the extent that it illuminated the fragility of our policymaking process and because it showed that foreign policy claimed our energies even as we were steeling ourselves for the final act of Nixon's tragedy....

There was nothing we needed less than a crisis—especially one that would involve two NATO allies. Whomever we supported and whatever the outcome, the eastern flank of the Mediterranean would be in jeopardy. And our government was neither cohesive enough, nor did the President have sufficient authority, to sustain a prolonged period of tension.

The issue immediately became entangled in our domestic politics. Greece was a military dictatorship; hence, all groups critical of our approach to human rights urged us to turn on it as the instigator of the upheaval; failure in Cyprus would, it was hoped, produce the overthrow of the hated Greek colonels. This view was held passionately not only among traditional opponents of Nixon; it was the dominant conviction in the State Department; the Secretary of Defense moved toward it increasingly as the week progressed....

Turkey's demands left little doubt that it was planning to intervene. Explicit condemnation of the Greek junta by the United States would have turned a likelihood into a certainty. A Greek debacle was in my view probable; only a regime that had lost touch with reality would take on both Makarios and Turkey over the Cyprus question. My view, as I was to explain to a WSAG [Washington Special Action Group] meeting of July 21 [while Nixon was still president] was that the Greek government was unlikely to survive its follies. That made it all the more necessary that the United States not be seen in Greece as the agent of its humiliation.

We faced a strategic dilemma. We wanted to keep both Greece and Turkey in the Alliance; we sought to prevent unbridgeable fissures. The dominant view of the bureaucracy during the first week was expressed at the WSAG meeting of July 21. Two days after the Turkish invasion of Cyprus had started, Schlesinger [James Schlesinger, then secretary of defense] urged a conspicuous dissociation from the Greek government, a withdrawal of American nuclear weapons from Greece, and an end to home-porting arrangements in Greece for the US Sixth Fleet. To force my hand the proposal was helpfully leaked to the *Washington Post.*

For my part, I was convinced that the junta in Athens would not last out the week but I was certain that if we were perceived as the cause of Greece's debacle we would pay for it for years to come. Whatever one's view of the wisdom of our previous policy toward the Greek junta, a Greek-Turkish war was not the moment to dissociate ourselves. Our immediate task was to stop the war; to remove nuclear weapons from *Greece* while Turkey invaded Cyprus would eliminate all restraints on Turkish military action. I also feared that if we once withdrew nuclear weapons we might never be able to return them—setting a dangerous precedent.[1]

Kissinger, recalling that Nixon was in San Clemente, recollects:

During the night of July 21–22, we forced a cease-fire by threatening Turkey that we would move nuclear weapons from forward positions—especially where they might be involved in a war with Greece. It stopped Turkish military operations while Turkey was occupying only a small enclave on the island; this created conditions for new negotations slated to start two days hence, with the Turkish minority obviously in an improved bargaining position and with some hope of achieving more equitable internal arrangements.

On July 22, the junta in Athens was overthrown and replaced by a democratic government under the distinguished conservative leader Constantine Caramanlis. Within days, the mood in America changed. The very groups that had castigated us for our reluctance to assault Greece now wanted us to go into all-out opposition to Turkey. We were being asked to turn against Turkey over a crisis started by Greece, to gear our policies to the domestic structures of the governments in Athens and Ankara regardless of the origins or merits of the dispute on Cyprus, to take a one-sided position regardless of our interest in easing the conflict between two strategic allies in the eastern Mediterranean, and to do all this in the very weeks that the United States government was on the verge of collapse. For two weeks we maintained our tightrope act, but during the weekend following Nixon's

> resignation the crisis erupted again, culminating in a second Turkish invasion of the island. While Ford struggled to restore executive authority over the next months, a freewheeling Congress destroyed the equilibrium between the parties we had precariously maintained; it legislated a heavy-handed arms embargo against Turkey that destroyed all possibility of American mediation—at a cost from which we have not recovered to this day.[2]

It should be remembered that the Greek colonels and the Cyprus coup were very unpopular, and the combination presented the Turks with an unusual opportunity for an invasion that, in terms of worldwide popular opinion, would be, if not approved, at least understood. (On that, of course, they were right; popular opinion did support the Turks until the advent on the scene of the Caramanlis government.)

The basic American strategy was to try to hold back the Turks while seeking to get the Greek colonels to back down to a point that would avoid triggering the Turkish invasion. U.S. ambassador William Macomber's argument with the Turks all along was that the Turks could well afford to wait for a number of days to see whether the American effort with the Greeks would succeed. In the meantime, he pointed out, the balance of Turk-Greek power in the Cyprus region could not be altered significantly. The Greeks were too weak and too far away, and the Turks were too near and too strong for that.

Hours before August 14, 1974, when the Turks finally launched their major invasion, the prime minister received Macomber, who again argued for time. A U.S. special envoy, Joseph Sisco, had achieved nowhere near enough concessions from Greece to impress the Turks.

At the end of Macomber's last plea to Premier Bulent Eçevit for further delay, the ambassador noted that he was known in politics as a man of compassion, but that if he did not delay the invasion many Greek Cypriots and Turks would be dead within a few hours—and dead in an exercise that, if the Americans were given another week, might prove to be unnecessary. Eçevit turned to him, and the gist of his answer was that there was a moment when nations set out on a course and then reach a point where there is no turning back. Turkey had been on such a course, the critical point had been reached, the invasion would be launched, and there would be no turning back.

The August 14 invasion posed a far more critical problem for the new tenant of the White House, Gerald Ford, than the first had posed for Nixon during his last White House days. Not only was Ford wholly inexperienced in the realm of foreign policy, he had no basis for evaluating the information and recommendations of his principal advisers. Moreover, the new prime minister in Athens, Caramanlis, was known and highly regarded in the West as well as in his own country. And Caramanlis made the point that the second Turkish invasion "was against me and my government," not against the colonels' dictatorship. Both he and the heavy majority of Greece's population looked to Washington to intervene against the second Turkish invasion at least as strongly as it had done against the first tentative probe in July. Caramanlis was a refreshing democratic symbol to the NATO allies, and Turkey had suddenly become a pariah. Kissinger had warned Nixon not to get involved in the Cyprus incidents of July, but it was inescapable that the neophyte Ford should take a stand in August, now that he had suddenly assumed the vast power of the American presidency.

Indeed, late on August 9, the new president, Gerald Ford, who had replaced Nixon that day, sent a personal message to Turkey's President Korotürk and Prime Minister Ȩcevit urging Ankara to make an agreement on Cyprus that would not "humiliate" Greece. All U.S. efforts to forestall military action—including a threat to embargo arms deliveries to both NATO partners, Greece and Turkey—had failed. On August 9, when the Turks made their final decision to gamble on a more massive invasion than the first half-hearted flop (in July), Ȩcevit told me in Ankara: "The Greeks on Cyprus have even failed to govern themselves. The Turks have always feared large-scale massacre by the Greek majority because the Greeks have even been killing each other."

Oddly enough, an American political factor that might have had some repercussions in Greece was the disgrace and disappearance of Viçe President Spiro Agnew, whose ancestors had been Greek. He had been regarded by the colonels as a pro-Hellenic asset. But by the time the prolonged Cyprus crisis started, Agnew had resigned (October 10, 1973), and the colonels themselves were soon to vanish from the active scene.

They spoiled their last chance of gaining sympathy from abroad by seeking to murder Makarios in July 1974 in a Cypriot coup attempt designed to install a dummy government under a thug named Nikos Sampson. To my surprise, Kissinger implied to me (Washington, October 16, 1975) that the CIA might have encouraged the junta to stage this unsuccessful Cyprus coup. Kissinger indicated that Washington had instructed Tasca to caution the junta against this move, but that Tasca didn't follow instructions "all the way."

At that time Kissinger also claimed to me that he could have obtained a settlement of the entire Aegean mess—the infernal triangle—had Congress not intervened to impose an arms embargo on Turkey. The secretary had arranged to visit Ankara to see Prime Minister Bulent Ęcevit, a former Kissinger pupil at a Harvard seminar, in November 1974; but by then the fat was in the fire. Certainly there was no pro-Greek action by Washington in 1974 comparable to that by Johnson ten years earlier, when he rose in high dudgeon against the Turks.

Ford—clearly under Kissinger's strong influence because he had no previous diplomatic experience—initiated his own foreign policy by sending a message August 9, 1974, to Ęcevit seeking to calm him. On the night of August 9, the Turks told the seasoned U.S. ambasssador that they had "no immediate intention" of taking further military action in Cyprus. Yet, on August 14, Turkey launched a second and better-coordinated amphibious invasion on Ęcevit's instruction. The Turkish invaders drove to the center of Nicosia, the Cypriot capital. Caramanlis was furious and complained: "This was aimed against my democratic government."

Kissinger wound up as the symbolic goat for a long series of U.S. policy mistakes that commenced well over a decade before he ever started work in the Nixon-Ford administrations. He later admitted ruefully that the Greek-Turkish-Cypriot mess was the biggest failure of his career as a statesman. Nor was Kissinger's amour propre delighted when all the Athens kiosks that sold newspapers were decorated with "wanted" posters bearing his name and photograph and charging him with responsibility for the "murder" of 6,000 Greeks in Cyprus.

He argued less than a year afterward (May 30, 1975, Brussels): "Congress paralyzed us in Greece and Turkey. Turkey would have made concessions without the congressional embargo on arms aid." Caramanlis told me in October the same year: "The U.S. has neglected to do anything that would give the Greek people any psychological satisfaction. I mentioned this to President Ford and Kissinger in Brussels [at a NATO meeting]. I have great esteem and love for the Americans but the position of your government is a failure."

The upshot of this running sore in the Mediterranean's infernal triangle of equal unpopularity for the United States in Greece, Turkey, and Cyprus, is the best proof that our policy there has failed. That policy, which had been a bipartisan failure since the days of Truman and Eisenhower, was a consequence of both major U.S. parties' inability to estimate the situation correctly and to act in accordance with such judgments. And, although Kissinger was on hand for both presidents, Nixon escapes blame because he was helpless at the very end of his administration and Ford because he had just moved into the seat of power, without the experience to exercise it.

Nixon wrote:

Turkey is a time bomb that, if allowed to explode, could have a more devastating impact on NATO than even the upheaval in Iran.... Its 500,000 man armed forces are second in size in NATO only to those of the United States. For centuries it has been a target of Russian aggression.[3]

And in his autobiography he acknowledged:

The Cyprus thing brought home the fact that with the peace as fragile as it is in various parts of the world, a shake-up in the American presidency and a change would have a traumatic effect abroad and a traumatic effect at home.[4]

XI

Nixon and Gaullism

Richard Nixon was once asked if he enjoyed being president, and he answered:

I am not one of those who believe that there is any indispensable man for the presidency. I think any man who gets in this position will be up to the position. You grow into it. We have had very few poor presidents. Perhaps very few great ones.

But the point is that I have probably the most unusual opportunity of any president in history, due to the fact that in just the way the cards happen to fall I may be able to do things which can create a new structure of peace in the world. To the extent that I am able to make progress toward that goal, I would very thoroughly enjoy the job.

Despite his quiet and devout Quaker upbringing, Nixon showed early that he liked being projected into new experiences and broader fields. He still remembers the advice of "Chief" Newman, the Whittier College football coach who told the skinny, unathletic boy: "You must hate to lose." Nixon believes: "You must fight back in life, especially in politics and above all when the odds are against you." First in his small college, then in a wartime navy job, then as he took his first few strokes in the political swimming pool that began with California state campaigns and elections, he displayed a growing appetite for change and for adventure. And he continued to educate himself throughout life —especially in the field of foreign policy, for which he developed an enthusiastic fascination. In fact, he made himself into an international figure from a beginning as a quiet, small-town boy of limited means. At the end of his presidential career Henry Kissinger, who knew him well and retained both affection and admiration for him after six years of close and frequently tense collaboration, wrote of his boss after he had departed the White House: "Nixon had set himself a goal beyond human capacity: to make himself over entirely; to create a new personality as if alone among all mankind he could overcome his destiny."

Possibly this analysis was so unusually perceptive and shrewd because one might apply precisely the same words to Kissinger himself—a little German-Jewish boy, driven from home by Hitler's minions, who found his way to new careers and astonishing successes in the distant United States. He rose from a humble start to heights as a brilliant and much-honored Harvard professor; an adviser to Governor Nelson Rockefeller, the liberal Republican leader; and finally to the White House as Nixon's national security adviser and eventually secretary of state. When he was sworn into this, the highest-ranking cabinet position, keeper of the Great Seal of the United States, Kissinger said in a brief speech: "There is no country in the world where it is conceivable that a man of my origin could be standing here next to the President of the United States. And if my origin can contribute anything to the formulation of our policy, it is that at an early age I have seen what can happen in a society that is based on hatred and strength and distrust, and that I experienced then what America means to other people, its hope and its idealism."[1]

The extraordinary self-made pair, a Quaker of unassuming heritage and a German Jew who speaks English with a heavy accent, met on a peak both reached by a combination of ability, ambition, determination, and tenacity. And together they elaborated a complex U.S. foreign policy with global implications.

Nixon's principal attribute was insistent willpower. He would say: "You have to have the will and determination to go out and do what is right for America." Even though some sophisticates in the larger cities of the U.S. privately snickered at such homely sentiments, there was no doubting the sincerity of his beliefs, and they were widely appreciated.

Nixon insisted:

I would rather be a one-term President and do what I believe was right than to be a two-term President at the cost of seeing America become a second-rate power and to see this nation accept the first defeat in its proud 190-year history.[2]

The alternatives posed were incorrect, as history shows. The United States was ultimately defeated on all fronts in the Southeast Asian conflict. But the U.S. did not become a second-rate power; in fact, it bounced back with almost excessive vigor. And Nixon became neither a one-term nor a two-term but a one-and-a-half-term president, thanks to Watergate.

In his thoughtful study of presidential character, James David Barber concludes: "Nixon's appetite for crisis—for the dramatic excitement that, in his mind, lifts a man above vegetable existence—shows up in his military venture into Cambodia." Barber sees in the decision "prime evidence that the underlying Nixon character is still there. For Nixon as for other Presidents, the office channels character forces developed over a lifetime; it neither creates nor abolishes the fundamental equipment he brought to the White House."[3]

Kissinger, always perceptive, noted in his memoirs: "By 1973, a strong President serving a full term was needed to impose a re-examination of doctrine and weapons systems, and the expenditures for a new strategy. Nixon's heart was in the right place but the authority of the Presidency was declining."[4]

But the security adviser perceived the flaws in Nixon's character as well as the strength of his indomitable will. With scarcely disguised sarcasm he wrote of the president: "His Walter Mitty tendencies allowed him to perceive evasions as reality and endowed wishful thinking with the attributes of truth."[5] Yet, Kissinger generously added: "In Nixon's hierarchy of values, even at the height of his private suffering, the international position of the United States took precedence over his personal fortunes."

Nixon sought to analyze the character and personality attributes of leaders he encountered around the world, displaying particular interest for those who had clearly risen to global importance and displayed special traits of character. He concluded:

The public likes to glamorize its leaders and most leaders like to glamorize themselves.... The easiest period in a crisis situation is actually the battle itself. The most difficult is the period of indecision—whether to fight or run away.[6]

I know of no case in his foreign trips where he showed any disposition to follow the latter course, especially during his tense visits to Peru and Venezuela when Communist-led mobs demonstrated vigorously and angrily against him.

From difficult moments on his extensive foreign travels, when he more than once encountered hostile efforts to embarrass him, Nixon learned that:

A man who has never lost himself in a cause bigger than himself has missed one of life's mountaintop experiences. Only then does he discover all the latent strengths he never knew he had and which otherwise would have remained dormant.[7]

Nixon was almost obsessed with a study of "crises" and curiosity about how he himself would behave under duress of an unexpected sort. He resolved, on the basis of his experience, on

the necessity for thorough preparations for battle; the need for handling a crisis with coolness, confidence and decisiveness; the importance of guarding against a letdown in that most dangerous period of a crisis, after the battle is over.[8]

His axiom for behavior by a leader in the face of an angry mob was:

He must be as cold in his emotions as a mob is hot, and as controlled as a mob is uncontrolled.... In preparing for battle I have always found that plans are useless, but planning is indispensable.[9]

Nixon demonstrated during his career that he had a more successful intuitive feeling for foreign problems. And from his experiences overseas he derived certain prejudices and homilies that came to serve him well in his diplomatic approaches. The first of these—and it is something U.S. administrations and policy-makers often ignore to their subsequent regret—he counseled:

We should not appear to give dictators, of either the right or the left, the same moral approval that we give to leaders who were trying to build free and democratic institutions.[10]

I have long had the impression, both from conversations with Nixon and from perusal of his books, that the foreign statesman he most admired was Charles de Gaulle. There is something fascinating about the bond that developed between the arrogant, haughty, French professional officer, a devout Catholic whose intellectual father was acquainted with Henri Bergson and other leading thinkers of France, and the much younger American Quaker boy of humble antecedents. After Nixon was first received by the General he wrote of him:

He was stubborn, willful, supremely self-confident, a man of enormous ego and yet at the same time enormous selflessness; he was demanding not for himself but for France.[11]

Nixon was much taken by Churchill and also by Mao Tse-tung and Adenauer, but it is perfectly plain that the single figure who towered above the rest among his impressions of the world abroad was de Gaulle. And I haven't a doubt that the unabashed admiration of the young American pleased and touched the General. Nixon's very ostracism from the U.S. political picture for some years after he was barely defeated in his presidential race against Kennedy clearly appealed to de Gaulle, who recalled the years he had been forced to pass in political ostracism after he first resigned his post as French chief of state. Moreover, I believe one reason that Nixon is often viewed with particular respect and friendship among the French is that word of de Gaulle's sympathy got about, and even today there are many Gaullists in France.

After reading de Gaulle's fascinating early book, *The Edge of the Sword*, Nixon wrote that "a leader must not only decide correctly what should be done, but also persuade others and get them to do it."[12] De Gaulle recommended that leadership must enhance its power by mystery, character, grandeur, and "silence," but Nixon's personality eschewed this approach.

In July, 1986, I raised the subject of the human factor in formulating policy; how important to the resolution of issues were the individual men concerned with regulating them? I started the discussion off with the suggestion that of all the foreign statesmen with whom Nixon had dealt as a political leader the one who had most influenced him was General Charles de Gaulle. He acknowledged the suggestion readily, observing:

I think your conclusion is correct. However, I would like to qualify it by observing that I've been very fortunate over the past forty years. This is the fortieth year since I've entered politics. In that period I have had the opportunity of meeting and knowing on a personal basis most of the post–World War II great leaders. And in speaking so positively about de Gaulle, I wouldn't want to leave the impression that I did not also have respect for and in many cases affection for people like Italy's [Alcide] de Gasperi, who was the first foreign leader I met; Churchill; Adenauer; Yoshida of Japan; and a host of others in smaller countries whose advice and counsel I have profited from over the years and who impressed me as world leaders of the first rank.

De Gaulle, I think, has a special place because of a characteristic that he had that is very hard to describe. I was thinking of Bruce Catton, who has written some of the classics about Lincoln, and he said Lincoln was one of those unusual people who, when he looked out across the land, most ordinary people would say the sky meets the earth, but Lincoln could find the opening. He could see beyond where the sky meets the land. Lincoln could see beyond.

De Gaulle impressed one that way. He was farsighted. He was not just thinking about the immediate, the pragmatic, what do I do about this, but he was thinking about the events of the future, those that would shape the world ahead. He was not always right, nobody is always right. But he was more right than most. And anyone who met him, which was certainly the case with me, you sensed that in the man when you first met him, he had another-world quality. The word is usually "charisma" or "mystique." It's a quality that everybody knows but nobody can describe.

He had it in great amounts, but it wasn't simply his huge physical presence, his dignity, the way he conducted himself. He was a great actor, of course. I had the feel of that when I attended John Kennedy's funeral, and I remember how impressed I was. Mrs. Nixon and I were watching from a room in the Mayflower Hotel, and he was walking along with others behind the casket, and there was no question who was the major leader. It was de Gaulle, even though his wasn't the biggest country. Now I come to other things that impressed me about him. He treated me very well (of course we are all subject to flattery, I don't know why) from the time we first met when he came over on his state visit to meet Eisenhower in 1959.

I gave a dinner for him as vice-president. We had some talks and from that time on whenever I traveled, even when I was out of office, he always saw me when I came to Paris. Now that is a great compliment to a politican, particularly when he is out of office. And that is an interesting characteristic about him that I learned later from someone else. I remembered the magnificent reception that he gave me and my party when we visited France in 1969 on a state visit. It was done with splendor, real splendor, the red carpet and the honor guard and the canopy under which you stood. And Dick Walters who was military attaché there, for so many years in Paris, said to me later about that occasion, he said, "You know, the General does this for everybody. The smallest little African country leader who comes in to visit, he does it for." And it occurred to me, and this is another aspect of his character, that de Gaulle was probably having a reverse reaction. He looked back during the years of World War II when he was the odd man out.

Eisenhower told me this before I took my trip to see de Gaulle in 1969. Eisenhower was in Walter Reed hospital before he died, and he said, "You know we didn't treat de Gaulle very well during the war, but de Gaulle knew it." And he was very sensitive about that, and I think he must have developed this . . . feeling for the underdog. A feeling for the little leader as well as the big leader. I guess maybe that was one of the reasons he saw me when I was out of office. But above all about de Gaulle, I remember how impressive he was in conversation. How he would go to the heart of an issue. And how wise he was. I'm trying to sort out the major issues on which he did affect my thinking. I would say first China—he and Adenauer as well, on my trip in 1963—when I wasn't in office, independently these two senior men expressed the opinion that the United States should change its position toward the People's Republic. De Gaulle put it very directly then and later on in 1969 when I saw him as president and when I was able to tell him that we were moving in that direction.

He said it was better to recognize China now when she needs you because of her weakness rather than to wait later when you have to recognize her. Nobody said it better, and needless to say, it made an impression on me. That was very early.

Another area where he had influence on my thinking was with the Soviet Union. And here de Gaulle, whom many accused of being soft with the Communists, was very hard-headed. I mean no one could be more dedicated to ideals of freedom than de Gaulle. But he was one who knew the real world. He knew what was possible and what was not possible and when the argument was raging in Europe and in the United States about whether or not there should be some rapprochement, détente, call it what you will. Europeans were pressing it at that point, and Americans were resisting it. And de Gaulle said, "What are you going to do about this now? What are you going to do about the Russians? You are going to break down the Berlin Wall?" He answered his own question. He said, "If you are not prepared to make war, make peace." Now to many that would sound defeatist, but he was pointing out either you have to confront and take all the risks of confrontation or you must negotiate and not surrender, but negotiate to a live-and-let-live position. And that of course had its impact on me. I felt the same way, but it's always very reassuring and helpful to have somebody who follows up on that.

De Gaulle had a big influence on Nixon by stimulating ideas. Nixon said:

De Gaulle felt very strongly that the United States should withdraw from Vietnam. He used a word that you would find in French, it couldn't really be translated, but he said not in haste. I got the impression that he said not in a way that you appear to be accepting a defeat and so forth, but in a way that maintains your honor and dignity.

"In a measured way," he said. He knew that it was very difficult. We had good talks about that, in the sixties but also in 1969, when we had the long talks at Versailles. "Look," he said, "Algeria was very painful, but I did it. Now, you, I know it is very painful for you because I know that you have already taken a position of support for Saigon. But you must do it. Because this war is draining you. It is hurting you with your alliances, it is also making it impossible for you to move forward in other areas in your relationships with the Soviets and the Chinese, etcetera. And so you must do it."

Now, incidentally I am not saying this to be critical, but at least to indicate a reservation I might have with regard to his attitude. The French I found generally were very anti the U.S. position, because they had a very personal interest. They felt that we did not support them at Dien Bien Phu, which I think was a mistake. My feeling was always that it was best to support the French and lean on them to move forward in a measured way, with an independent status, or the associated states of Indochina, rather than to leave the French to be forced out and leave us only with the option of taking the responsibility ourselves.

But I think all French leaders having in effect failed, [they] did not really look with much favor on anybody else succeeding. A little of that may have entered into it. I think in de Gaulle's case, while that could have been part of it, his major concern was that the new administration, our administration, should succeed. He felt that Vietnam was very detrimental to an overall global foreign policy. He said, "If I can do Algeria, you can do Vietnam." Another point I should make, however; I did not say this to him directly, but I pointed out later in a conversation with Kissinger, this is in 1969; he did not do it immediately. It took him three years to get out of Algeria.

I think there are differences as well. What he did in Algeria affected really only France and Algeria. What we did in Vietnam affected, I felt, not only Vietnam, but it affected our relations with the Chinese and with the Russians and the surrounding states. So to answer your question directly, Did de Gaulle influence me in developing the policy of withdrawal trying to have what we call peace with honor, the answer is yes. Because I knew that it had to be done, but I felt it was very important that it be done in a way that the United States maintain the respect of the Chinese and the Russians and NATO, and our friends as well in the Asian area.

Well, there was still another area, too, which I think is of interest. De Gaulle I found was a very shrewd student of people in a way suitable to the American purpose. I'll never forget sitting by him at a dinner that was given at the Mayflower. I was vice-president. Mrs. Nixon had decorated the table beautifully and de Gaulle had great grace. He mentioned so gracefully the flowers, the food, all that sort of thing. It's all, of course, done with honor. He knew the American situation, and he said to me: "What you must do in order to win your election is you must stand for a new America." Now, he didn't describe what a new America was, but he said: "Now, you have been very loyal to President Eisenhower, and you should be. But on the other hand after a period in which he has been president for eight years, I sense that the country will respond to the concept of a new America." Well, of course, I was unable to do that. That is, I had initiatives and so forth, but it was made to order for John Kennedy, and that is one of the problems that any incumbent has, basically, who is running on their record, and so forth. But de Gaulle sensed that. I was also impressed by his effectiveness as a communicator. He was a great communicator. However, Churchill was a great communicator. Reagan is a great communicator. And de Gaulle was, but each in a different way. I'll never forget one time I was in Paris, and a mutual friend of ours, Chip Bohlen, was ambassador.

Chip was in his office and he said, "Say, you know, de Gaulle is going to have one of his semiannual press conferences today. Let's watch it on TV." Now, Bohlen didn't particularly like de Gaulle, but he respected him, and we sat there and we saw de Gaulle walk in with all of his majesty. He would have been impressed by what Reagan does at the White House, walk in on the red carpet into the East Room, and then walk back. He would very much favor that over the earlier days when Reagan would walk out and walk through the press, and after making all of his points, a gaggle of people shouting, questions, etcetera. De Gaulle didn't like that. He didn't think it was the right thing to do. Nevertheless, after he finished, then he pointed majestically to three or four people for questions. As Bohlen pointed out, he knew whom he was going to point to. Then he answered the questions, and then he went away. And Bohlen turned to me and said: "We know of course it was all a great act. What a great performance."

And de Gaulle was a great performer, no question about it. And another thing I would say briefly, read his Edge of the Sword. *It should be a handbook for anyone going into politics in the communication age, and his little book told you the story. Written beautifully. Written before he ever had power, political power, but its insight and so forth is fantastic. I never read the book until after I'd left office. But one thing he did, and incidentally people say why didn't I have more press conferences and so forth, one thing I learned from de Gaulle, I knew that his system was different. That we couldn't do it only twice a year, but I felt that it was important not to become too available, and that if you waited a while and had something to say, it had far greater impact than to be out there jawing with the press every time an issue came up. So he must take some of the blame, or maybe some of the credit, for whatever successes that I've had. So that's de Gaulle.*

I would say about de Gaulle, when it came to the world situation, he had great insight, and frankly it is really too bad in a way that France, despite everything he did to recover its spirit and so forth, that France was not a bigger major power. He was capable of working on a far bigger canvas than he had in his country.

But when I saw de Gaulle during the sixties there was a possibility I would return to office. Incidentally, Bohlen gave a small lunch for me, and de Gaulle proposed a toast. Bohlen told me later what he said, because he didn't translate it at the time. De Gaulle said: "I'm confident that your career has been cut short only temporarily and at the end you are going to be in a higher place." He was pretty smart.

Nixon was impressed by de Gaulle's theorem, "The setting up of one man over his fellows can be justified only if he can bring to the common task the drive and certainty which comes of character." Nixon felt de Gaulle lived up to his idea by the way he, by sheer willpower and astute maneuvering, more or less forced the French people (if with great reluctance and much opposition) to accept complete independence of Algeria under Arab rule, resulting in the forced emigration of about one million French who had spent years in that North African state. "Nothing great is done without great men," the General wrote, "and these are great because they willed it."

I have no doubt that de Gaulle's reflections had particular influence on the strategy Nixon followed on China recognition and on Vietnam and the tactics he encouraged in Kissinger with respect to both Asian problems. De Gaulle urged that the United States should not leave the Chinese isolated in their rage and he suggested the obvious that in his talks with Russia, Nixon might wish to keep an anchor to windward with respect to China. He also urged Nixon in 1969 to take steps to put an end to the Vietnam War as quickly as possible."

Nixon told de Gaulle he was in the process of initiating a withdrawal program and was already in secret contact with the North Vietnamese. Later he said:

In retrospect I believe this meeting [with de Gaulle] laid the groundwork for Kissinger's secret trips to Paris, which resulted four years later [1973] in the Paris Peace Agreement and the end of American involvement in Vietnam.

De Gaulle had urged that no withdrawal should be precipitate to avoid "catastrophe." However, Nixon was unable to prevail over Congress, which refused him the controlling power of possible retribution should Hanoi seek to produce "catastrophe" —which it did.

Nixon said:

Great leaders are the ones who first see what in retrospect, but only in retrospect, is obvious, and who have both the force of will and the authority to move their countries with them.

In this respect Nixon lacked the ability to win Congress over to his Paris Agreement formula, with its built-in aerial fire insurance against disaster. When the cataclysm came Nixon and Kissinger both justifiably blamed the refusal of Congress to back up the president's settlement formula; but this is equivalent to blaming de Gaulle had the Secret Army Organization of French professional officers forced the French government to hang on to its North African jewel, Algeria.

Barber stresses the importance of the Nixon quote on his

Cambodian policy, which was to backfire into a disastrous swing of congressional and public opinion on both the Cambodian invasion and the threat of aerial support to Saigon:

> *I knew the stakes that were involved. I knew the division that would be caused in this country. I also knew the problems internationally. I knew the military risks. . . . I made this decision. I believe it was the right decision. I believe it will work out. If it doesn't, then I'm to blame.*[13]

The blame, heated by the Watergate fire, was thrown back into Nixon's face by an emotionally hostile public.

Despite the furious French debate about both de Gaulle and Algeria, there was never more than an instant of doubt on whether the General would succeed in his gamble, far more audacious for his own country than even the immense Vietnam disaster had been for the United States. The French people and the French constitution are strikingly different from our own in many respects. But, while de Gaulle succeeded in overcoming his greatest crisis as France's president, Nixon was only able to bewail the fact that "the great silent majority of my fellow Americans" did not support him, for "North Vietnam cannot defeat or humiliate the United States; only Americans can do that."[14]

It strikes me that both Nixon and de Gaulle, endowed with formidable willpower, frequently considered resigning from high position. De Gaulle did resign in 1946, when he was chief of government, and he had to wait years in exile before he regained power. And in 1968, when his authority seemed to be tottering in face of thunderous student agitation in the streets of Paris, he flew to a French army base in West Germany and again contemplated voluntary departure. Finally, in 1969, envisioning the humiliating possibility of losing controlling power in the French political mixture, he called for a referendum that he knew in advance he would lose and thus stepped down from the presidency.

Nothing so dramatic plagued Nixon until his final "forced" resignation because of the uncontrollable Watergate scandal. In 1952, when he was attacked for accepting contributions to help pay for his vice-presidential campaign, he was represented as "ready to chuck the whole thing" but went on to win election as Eisenhower's vice-president. Two years later, he let it be known that he would retire from all politics when his vice-presidential term ended. He repeated this idea in 1956 and again in 1961. In 1962, following his defeat in a race for the California governorship, he told the press with no little sarcasm: "Gentlemen, this is my last press conference. You won't have Richard Nixon to kick around any more." On August 9, 1974, he finally yielded power.

It is not easily apparent what else, if anything, they had in common. They certainly both dreamed of achieving success for their countries in an internal and also an international sense, but psychologically, by heritage, and by upbringing they were immensely different. One obvious bond, however, that must have appealed to de Gaulle is that Nixon was the first and only president of his era who truly admired the great Frenchman and made note of all his thoughts and every word in their conversations.

Franklin Roosevelt had dismissed the General with more than a touch of a sneer and behaved toward him during World War II in a needlessly ill-mannered and offhand way. Truman had neither contact with nor knowledge of de Gaulle and was clearly preoccupied with fundamental war-end and postwar matters that tended to ignore the status of both France and its leader.

Eisenhower genuinely admired the Frenchman but was in a superior wartime position, thanks to his rank as Supreme Allied Commander. Nor did de Gaulle care for Eisenhower's original plan to bypass occupied Paris instead of liberating it. Kennedy looked up to de Gaulle and respected him but had little occasion to demonstrate his esteem, although the General clearly found the youthful president and his wife appealing. Lyndon Johnson was a zero in the Frenchman's book of records. However, Nixon was an avid courtier and sincerely respectful of the General's techniques and studied these with more than a little profit to his own ideas of governance.

While Nixon in no sense imitated the serene aplomb of de Gaulle in his personal behavior, he certainly took pains to discountenance any attempts at levity or excessive familiarity among his associates. Likewise, as did de Gaulle, he clearly believed in the management of information about his office, himself, his policies, and his objectives. As much as possible in the far more informal American system, which hallows the role of a free press, Nixon sought to guide the presentation of information as a prime presidential resource. While unable to isolate himself from the public eye as the General did in his magisterial manner, Nixon attempted, for a long time with some success, to limit the amount of information given to the press according to his own estimate of the national well-being or of his own convenience.

On matters of vital national importance, like Algeria's war of independence for de Gaulle and the Southeast Asian war for Nixon, both men behaved with great discretion. Each took care to husband his views and keep decisions quiet. But de Gaulle, in his monarchistic fashion, summoned his limited coterie of advisers and confided much to them, knowing there was no possibility of indiscretion.

Nixon maintained even tighter secrecy on coming events, actions, and reactions, but withheld from his associates, with rare exceptions, extremely important plans for such things as possible military retribution against North Korea for its attack on an unarmed U.S. reconnaissance aircraft or a massive, sudden plan for withdrawing large numbers of American troops from Vietnam between April 1970 and April 1971. Not even Secretary of Defense Melvin Laird was aware of this evacuation program in advance.

As the astute James David Barber noted in 1971, before the great Kent State–Vietnam–Watergate skein began to unravel: "Senior State Department officials had been suddenly cut off from key cablegrams.... Military orders were issuing directly from the White House, and especially the nearly complete isolation of the President from Congressional opinions as he stepped out beyond his most sanguine military advisers—the President's judgment came into question."[15]

There is no doubt that the crisis occasioned by the National Guard shooting of six students at Kent State University was mishandled by Nixon in his self-chosen isolation. This further poisoned a growing hostility toward him among a major element in the press. The undeclared war between the White House and the media was further nourished by surprise maneuvers and sudden announcements concerning foreign policy. However, his unexpected trip to Peking was clearly greeted with widespread favor.

In considering the implications of Nixon's behavior and methodology to his own foreign policy, it is essential not to be deflected from fact and achievement by the petulant, emotional attitude exemplified in many publications discussing these factors. His undoubted achievements must be considered with mature, sophisticated analysis. But Nixon often acted as his own enemy by choosing, and losing, needless battles.

He was surely proved right in the Hiss case, but many of his journalistic critics never admitted so much. On the whole, his record in internal affairs was nowhere near that of his record on international affairs. Thus, he might well have been able to survive the traumatic test of the Vietnam-Cambodian disaster had he not offended public opinion and Congress after the needlessly clumsy Kent State tragedy.

As I wrote earlier, the French used to say about the great crisis that overcame Nixon in the end: "Mais nous avons été Watergaté tant de fois [But we've been Watergated so many times]." It was the accumulation of Nixon's mistaken methods and awkward behavior that in the end destroyed him, not just one or two major events. One must view his career not simply as that of a political figure in the complex of American internal politics but, as this book seeks to do, as that of a statesman on the international horizon.

When Nixon first heard of the Kent State shootings of those he called "bums" he said: "When dissent turns to violence, it invites tragedy." And one might add: When tragedy got out of hand it invited disaster.

Indirectly, by exacerbating the relationships between Nixon and an increasing number of Americans, Kent State contributed to the political climate that allowed Watergate to grow from a sordid peccadillo into a crippling national issue. Thus Kent State, and the issue of undergraduates versus the armed authority of the state, exploded into something far, far worse than the serious student manifestations in France (May 1968) that ultimately resulted in de Gaulle's departure from the national scene.

The General had been deeply disturbed and infuriated at the way mass demonstrations in Paris's Latin Quarter turned into large-scale battles between the demonstrators and the police and security forces. When things had finally quieted down, the General resolved to put squarely to the country his program and prestige—in other words the question of his leadership and its popular approval. The referendum on which he decided was worded in such a way that this basic issue was not posed as such, but the implied meaning of the test vote was clear. The referendum showed an absence of the support on which he was resolved.

So he resigned and retired to his country house in Colombey-les-Deux-Eglises, disappearing from the public stage.

De Gaulle's retirement was clearly voluntary and deemed necessary only by his own proud self, unlike Nixon's resignation in 1974 to avoid an impeachment trial on the Watergate affair. As Nixon was to write:

He did not leave office because of a great issue, but because of what appeared to be a minor one: the defeat of his plebiscite involving senate and regional reforms. Malraux later asked him why he had resigned over such an "absurd" issue. His reply was what one would expect from General de Gaulle: "Because it was absurd."[16]

The General wrote to Nixon, who was still in office as president as the Watergate break-in had not even yet occurred:

> Your gracious official message and your very warm personal letter touched me deeply. Not only because you occupy the high office of President of the United States, but also they are from you, Richard Nixon, and I have for you—with good reason—esteem, confidence, and friendship as great and as sincere as it is possible to have.
>
> Perhaps one day I will have the occasion and the honor to see you again; in the meantime I send you from the bottom of my heart all my best wishes for the successful accomplishment of your immense national and international task.

De Gaulle wrote that a leader "must be able to create a spirit of confidence in those under him. He must be able to assert his authority."[17] The General decided that these conditions no longer prevailed when he tested the political climate in a deliberately obscure and artfully phrased referendum question. So he withdrew—his second resignation as chief in a remarkable career. Five years later Nixon resigned as president of the United States when it was blatantly evident to all including himself that such conditions no longer prevailed in America, and that, indeed, he would face the threat of disgrace and prison should he try to hang on any longer.

It is unfair and foolish to try to weigh the worth of the two men in a historical balance. De Gaulle, both physically and spiritually, was the larger, a bigger personality with a greater historical role for his country. But Nixon played his part on a much greater international scale. It was, one might say, a question of Superman and Superpower. And the quality of the two differed immensely. De Gaulle incarnated glory and a deliberate grandeur of personality. He could never be rude by error or omission, but like all infinitely courteous men he knew how to be magnificently rude when he deliberately chose. He would never have referred to the May 1968 student demonstrators as "bums," as Nixon did those tragically killed at Kent State. And he never allowed himself to be abrasive; only disdainful. And meticulously elegant to boot.

Yet despite their differences it is evident the two men attracted and respected each other. Perhaps, as Emily Dickinson observed, it is true that "opposites entice."

XII

White House versus State Department

Nixon had never been a great admirer of the U.S. career foreign service of professional diplomats. In part this may have derived from an echo of Truman's belief that these "striped pants boys" were part of the snobbish, eastern Establishment. Nixon had come to accept this view in his own mind and to resent it as supportive of causes he had successfully attacked during his political life: Mrs. Helen Gahagan Douglas's backers in 1950 and defenders and previous associates of Alger Hiss, trained by the mannered ambassadors he had encountered as he started his world travels. Nixon had always particularly distrusted the state department, which he considered both fuzzy minded and a nest of holdover liberal Democrats.

Henry Kissinger, who knew as much about this prejudice as any man, concluded that Nixon "had very little confidence in the State Department. Its personnel had no loyalty to him; the Foreign Service had disdained him as vice-president and ignored him the moment he was out of office. He was determined to run foreign policy from the White House."[1]

To this opinion he added that the president "came to deal

increasingly with key foreign leaders through channels that directly linked the White House Situation Room to the field without going through the State Department—the so-called backchannels. . . . Nixon increasingly moved sensitive negotiations into the White House where he could supervise them directly, get the credit personally, and avoid the bureaucratic disputes or inertia that he found so distasteful."[2]

Nixon selected Kissinger as his national security adviser in the White House before he named a secretary of state. He chose the estimable but inexperienced (in diplomatic affairs) William P. Rogers. When he discussed his thoughts with Kissinger, he said he was seeking a good negotiator, rather than a policymaker—a role he reserved for himself and his assistant for national security affairs. And because of his distrust of the foreign service, Nixon wanted a strong executive who would ensure state department support of the president's policies. Nixon left me with the impression that his first choice was Ambassador Robert Murphy, an outstanding retired diplomat and at that time chairman of the board of Corning Glass. Murphy had served with distinction in many senior posts and I grew to value his judgment and wit. Years later, Nixon told me that Murphy had turned down the position.

Rogers and Nixon had been good friends during the Eisenhower administration, when Rogers was attorney general, but their relationship under the Nixon presidency was strained by the chief executive's patent preference for Kissinger's advice. The latter wrote of Nixon and Rogers:

> This curious antiphonal relationship between the two men had the consequence of enhancing my position, but my own role was clearly a result of that relationship and not the cause of it. From the beginning Nixon was determined to dominate the most important negotiations. He excluded his secretary of state, for example, from his first meeting with Soviet Ambassador Anatoly Dobrynin on February 17, 1969, four weeks after Inauguration, at a time when it would have been inconceivable for me to suggest such a procedure. The practice, established before my own position was settled, continued. Throughout his term, when a State visitor was received in the Oval Office by Nixon for a lengthy discussion, I was the only other American present.[3]

Kissinger was convinced that Nixon wished to establish a relationship of primacy over his old mentor Rogers. The president seemed eager to prove that there were areas in which he was the more masterful; he had studied foreign policy all his life. Rogers came to it as a novice.

Whether Nixon planned it that way or simply permitted it—the relationship between Rogers and Kissinger soured. By the beginning of Nixon's second term, Rogers and Kissinger had no social contacts. Officially, they dealt with each other correctly without being cordial. Kissinger was the preeminent presidential adviser; Rogers controlled the machinery by which normal foreign policy had to be carried out. The stalemate deepened.

Partly because of this antiprejudice in his mind, which became a prejudice in its own right, and partly because he had confidence in his judgment on international matters, Nixon had never, from the start, wanted a decisive minister of foreign affairs in his cabinet. For this reason he chose as a trusted friend a previous attorney general who had no background of world affairs. The result was awkward. Kissinger had unique access to the president. His office passed on all vital cable traffic.

The tandem relationship between Nixon, the boss, the strategist, and his right-hand man Kissinger, the tactician and negotiator, attained its apogee of effectiveness in the crafty, visionary development of a new China relationship. It was as perfect an example as one can imagine of an unusual kind of exercise in an era of open diplomacy and total propaganda, a splendidly conceived and skillfully executed achievement. It remedied a foolish lacuna in normal connections between the world's most populous nation and the world's greatest economic and industrial power.

Looking back on the complicated process of creating a new relationship, it is obvious that Nixon and Kissinger employed Pakistan as the willing go-between because Pakistan was the only country allied to both Peking and Washington. Nixon and Kissinger were deeply impressed and fascinated by the Chinese leadership, mesmerized by the overpowering Mao Tse-tung and dazzled by the elegantly brilliant Chou En-lai. The acme of the successful partnership of the two American statesmen came with their trip to the Chinese capital to cement the new friendship. And, among other things, it clarified the dual relationship that had so remarkably established a novel methodology for U.S. policy, its conception and its implementation.

Kissinger fitted perfectly into the preconceived governance according to methods Nixon laid down at the start of his presidency. But by 1973 and 1974, as the Watergate crisis swelled and finally burst, this system proved fallible despite—and in some ways because of—the extraordinary aptitude Kissinger displayed in interpreting his role as national security adviser. Kissinger's vast influence and consequent ability to conceive and execute an intricate and brilliant diplomatic design was based on Nixon's strategic outline. It relied in the end on the strength of the chief executive whom he was advising but on whom he depended totally for his own influence.

Recognizing this increasingly as the Watergate cloud spread over the political horizon, Kissinger saw that:

> Watergate had made the hitherto preeminent position of the White House assistants untenable. My influence in the rest of the government depended on presidential authority, and this was palpably draining away in endless revelations of tawdry acts, some puerile, some illegal. Alexander Haig, recalled as presidential chief of staff in May [1973] had volunteered to me earlier in the summer that he saw no other solution than to appoint me secretary of state. . . . It was a painful decision for Nixon because it symbolized—perhaps more than any of the Watergate headlines—how wounded he was. He had never wanted a strong secretary of state; foreign policy, he had asserted in his 1968 campaign, would be run from the White House.[4]

Watergate left no doubt that the system could no longer be sustained. Melvin Laird, then serving his brief term as presidential counselor, told Kissinger his position as security assistant would soon become untenable. He would be ground down between the Congress and the increasingly assertive bureaucracy. He would have to become secretary of state or quit.

Thus a peculiar human and governmental situation developed at the top. Nixon correctly interpreted his constitutional responsibility for the conception and conduct of international policy and decided to operate along the lines of his immediate predecessors, who had influential expert advisers like Kennedy's Mac Bundy and Johnson's Walt Rostow. But he desired even more personal ascendancy in that position than his predecessors had devised. For this Kissinger was the perfect man: brilliant, knowledgeable, ambitious, thrusting, imaginative, and in no way competitive with Nixon himself, coming from an even more modest original background despite his latter years at Harvard and as a colt of the estimable Nelson Rockefeller.

Working in tandem during a comparably successful first term, the two (with Nixon at the helm) maneuvered around the Chile shoal, staged a remarkable improvement in U.S. relations with China, and also bettered the situation with Russia. By this double-jointed achievement they correctly adjudged that neither of the two earlier Communist allies would go too far in challenging the United States for fear of pushing it toward a closer friendship with the other. Meanwhile, in the Middle East, Egypt was showing hints of wishing to escape its previous embrace by the Soviet Union. And a start had been made toward a logical disengagement from Vietnam, without precipitating chaotic disaster. With the whole Watergate affair not yet a nightmare reality nobody could even imagine, a period of smooth sailing loomed.

In the absence of an unanticipated Watergate disaster and the consequent shudder of public opinion with regard to the slowness and deliberation of a Vietnam withdrawal, the global outlook seemed excellent for the kind of subtle games at which both Nixon and Kissinger were adept. As the latter described the outlook in his memoirs:

> We had to resist the temptation of playing the China card in our turn. To strengthen ties with China as a device to needle the Soviet Union would run the dual risk of tempting a Soviet preemptive attack on China—inviting the very disaster we sought to avoid—and of giving Peking the unnerving impression that, just as we tightened our bonds to respond to Soviet intransigence, we might relax them in response to Soviet conciliation. China would be transformed from a weight in the scale into an object of bargaining—an

> approach quite incompatible with the necessities that brought about the rapprochement in the first place....
>
> America had no interest in a policy of unremitting, undifferentiated confrontation with the USSR as China undoubtedly preferred. We saw no need to become a card that Peking could play. China had to be able to count on American support against direct Soviet pressures threatening its independence or territorial integrity; it must not be permitted to maneuver us into unnecessary showdowns. Complex as it might be to execute such a tactic, it was always better for us to be closer to either Moscow or Peking than either was to the other—except in the limiting case of a Soviet attack on China.[5]

Both Nixon and Kissinger were obviously unaware that any kind of internal U.S. political crisis might erupt, that a heart-rending, bloody confrontation like Kent State could lie over the horizon, or that the Vietnam withdrawal plan would be shattered by the diminishment of public support in the United States and the reckless mood of Congress that crippled Nixon's peaceful initiative. Kissinger recalled, years subsequently: "The vision of a new period of foreign policy, no longer overshadowed by a divisive war, was coupled with the conviction that an end had to be put to the Byzantine administrative procedures of Nixon's first term. No longer should power be centralized in the hands of Presidential assistants acting in secret from the rest of the government....If we had built well and true, the nation's foreign policy would have to be institutionalized."[6]

Not only had the balance of forces shifted so that the White House had lost much prestige and executive power, but the human balance also started to change. So many of Nixon's own adversaries were extolling Kissinger's achievements as a way of diminishing Nixon's that jealousies sprang up where none had existed before. The president's other advisers, who had always been envious of Kissinger's prestige and his proximity to the president, began a susurrous campaign to try to cut Kissinger down to size. There is no doubt that some of this mischievous malice took lodgment in Nixon's own increasingly irritated and irritable psyche. Despite this, Nixon sent Kissinger off on another flamboyant secret mission, a trip to Hanoi to try and consolidate the Paris Agreement on a Vietnam cease-fire.

By exalting Kissinger's unusual achievements, Nixon's critics succeeded in minimizing the major presidential role in foreign policy in a year (1973) that saw an alteration in the respective power position of the president and the dependent role of his chief lieutenant, a year that ended with Kissinger in the cabinet. He became secretary of state on September 22, 1973, while continuing to serve as assistant for national security affairs, a role he had played for four and a half years. Kissinger later philosophized: "Watergate had a severe impact on the conduct of diplomacy in almost all its dimensions, providing an object lesson, if one was needed, in how crucial a strong President is for the design and execution of a creative foreign policy."[7]

At the same time Nixon had had enough of the Kissinger-Rogers rivalry, for which he was largely responsible. He decided that Rogers must go. Everything but the date had been set. Kissinger believes that Nixon actually did not wish to promote him but realized the move had become inevitable. But until President Ford ultimately took the security adviser's role away, Kissinger had a dual function that he clearly relished.

His position with twin offices in charge of foreign policy was undoubtedly higher than anyone else's in the government save Nixon himself. But the president's power was now weakening at a perceptible rate as the Watergate affair spread darkly. In U.S. constitutional terms, without a strong president there cannot be a strong foreign policy. Thus Kissinger's increased personal importance could not offset the growing weakness in the executive authority.

In September 1973 the Watergate investigation began pressing hard for possession of tape recordings made in Nixon's office and hitherto held tightly by the White House. At the same time, Vice-President Agnew was teetering as the result of a scandal concerning electoral payoffs. In the middle of all this, Egypt and Syria attacked Israel in a surprise assault. The little Jewish state reeled on the brink of disaster. While Nixon and Kissinger were trying to rush emergency help to the Israelis, Agnew resigned. A few days later, Attorney General Elliot Richardson followed suit for reasons of conscience implicitly linked to Watergate and Nixon's role therein.

Precisely one week after Nixon finally named Kissinger secretary of state, on August 29, 1973, Judge John Sirica ruled that the president must turn over the embarrassing White House tapes he had hitherto refused to make available to the Watergate investigators. Seeing this as the beginning of the end, Nixon yielded, because he recognized political reality. This marked the start of a final destruction of his executive position, one that no triumph in foreign policy could avert.

Kissinger wrote in his memoirs: "Historians will misunderstand Watergate who neglect the destructive impact on American politics, spirit and unity of the war in Vietnam,"[8] where American troops were first dispatched by Kennedy, enormously reinforced by Johnson, and bolstered and then withdrawn by Nixon, who suffered the accumulated consequences of the misbegotten and misdirected adventure.

As Kissinger, who strove to terminate this unhappy affair, was later to reflect: "The Kennedy and Johnson administrations trapped themselves between their convictions and their inhibitions, making a commitment large enough to hazard our global position but then executing it with so much hesitation as to defeat their purpose. They engaged in Indochina for the objective of defeating a global conspiracy and then failed to press a military solution for fear of sparking a global conflict."[9]

From the start of the Nixon administration in 1969, the new president, supported by his approving right-hand man, wished to reduce and then withdraw U.S. forces in Indochina, a desire enhanced and accelerated after the meeting with General de Gaulle early in the new presidency. The paradoxical result was that a Republican chief of state strong enough to disengage from an ugly war without risking a revolt by conservatives who had backed him, was opposed by a Democratic opposition that detested Richard Nixon but privately hoped for an end to the war.

The consequent fact was that Nixon in the end terminated U.S. involvement, but an emotionally overwrought Congress, incited by an even more emotional public opinion that was "against" both the war and President Nixon, wrecked the carefully planned withdrawal operation by refusing the insurance of safeguards demanded. That Nixon should blame Congress for the resultant disaster is foolish, however; as a keenly perceptive politician who had shown much expertise in assaying political currents, he should have been aware of this possibility, if not probability, and better prepared to counter it.

Kissinger, whose summation of the tragedy is judicious, finally commented: "The ugliness of the domestic battles was a national tragedy. The issue was posed as to who was 'for' or 'against' the war—a phony question. Nixon was determined to end our involvement and in fact did so. What he refused to do was to doom millions who had relied upon us to [end] a bloody Communist tyranny. He believed that abject failure would vindicate the neo-isolationist trends at home, demoralize the American people, and make them fearful of foreign responsibilities."[10]

But while observing the increasing rise in the legislative power, as represented by Congress, and the judiciary, as represented by Sirica, it was impossible to imagine such a destruction of the normally ascendent executive power as represented by the president in such a way as to cripple, in one vital area, the foreign policy then being applied. Nixon and Kissinger constituted a virtuoso team never before attained in America since the days of James Monroe and John Quincy Adams.

Nevertheless, either Nixon himself or his internal affairs advisers, H. R. Haldeman and John Ehrlichman, should have assessed the congressional outlook much more accurately and in good time. At the end of April 1973 Nixon asked these two loyal henchmen to resign and sent word to Kissinger that he needed him more than ever. The infamous "plumbers unit" that had staged the inane raid that provoked the entire Watergate affair belonged to Ehrlichman's office in the White House.

Within a remarkably short time the machine that supervised American foreign policy was rattling. Nixon continued to govern according to his role while Kissinger sought to bind together a national consensus on our position and intentions overseas. The intimate contacts and discussions between the U.S. strategist and his tactical general simply evaporated as mere generalized principles replaced precise aims and methods. Kissinger generously recalls: "The worst punishment that befell Nixon was the knowledge that in the final analysis he had done it all himself. And in his extremity he acted with high purpose in the field of foreign policy; he seemed driven by the consciousness that even if his presidency could not be saved, the nation must be."[11]

• • •

Only one man is suited to judge the effect of the accumulated Vietnam–Kent State–Watergate crisis, better known as "Watergate"—a label for the entire malady—on the entire foreign policy mechanism and world position of the United States. That man is Henry Kissinger. From the start, before any hint of trouble appeared, Kissinger believed that the president should have demanded authorization from Congress to conduct the military "nonwar" being carried out in Vietnam, a struggle inherited together with the White House. But Nixon refused such a move in 1969, when he began his administration; and by 1973 he dismissed the possibility because he considered it incompatible with his executive responsibilities as chief of state.

When the crisis finally ripened and the hideous boil was about to be lanced, Kissinger found that the bad effects on America's world position had spread widely. The slightest relative impact was, curiously enough, on the most acute danger spot of the period, the Middle East. But even those Kissinger termed "the radical Arabs" needed the United States as an alibi, if nothing else, for facts they might be forced to accept; and also they exaggerated Nixon's influence to the point where they ignorantly thought him impervious to the stresses emanating from Washington.

Elsewhere abroad, there was an increasing if bewildered realization that what appeared as a minor criminal peccadillo was about to bleed a powerful world statesman to death. In Vietnam, Prime Minister Thieu seemed oblivious to thoughts of genuine compromise to terminate the war before the last invaders from the north had been expelled. He insisted that it wasn't his fault or affair that American public opinion couldn't wait so long, much like Nixon's and Kissinger's own insistence on blaming Congress for the falling structure in South Vietnam and the inability to prevent this. Finding scapegoats is a fruitless pursuit in diplomacy.

Meanwhile, as Saigon stalled, North Vietnam coldly and accurately based its strategy on the Watergate fever, concluding that Senate investigations had already "proved that the last U.S. presidential election was fraudulent and many members of the White House staff have submitted their resignations.... Therefore President Nixon must also resign because he no longer has enough prestige to lead."[12]

Kissinger later recalled that the Paris peace accords did not end the fevered Vietnam debate, now reinforced by Watergate. Congress voted in June 1973 to prohibit any American military action in or near Indochina and deeply cut the needed appropriations. "It launched an assault on détente at a time of maximum weakness of the executive branch. Thieu panicked. . . . America failed in Vietnam, but it gave the other nations of Southeast Asia time to deal with their own insurrections. And America's-very anguish testified to its moral scruples."[13]

The Chinese never wavered in their faith in Nixon, although they were fully aware of what was going on. Despite their ideological distance from the United States, their sense of geopolitical realism demonstrated that the interests of the United States and the People's Republic of China were virtually parallel in Vietnam. At least as much as Washington, Peking feared a unified Communist Vietnam dominating Indochina in close alliance with the Soviet Union—all of which came to pass.

Kissinger's ambition and self-esteem are equal to his extraordinary talents. Once when he was talking with Kenneth Keating, the amiable U.S. ambassador to Israel and former senator from New York, he asked him in all seriousness whether he thought the constitutional insistence that any candidate for the American presidency should have been born there would also apply to a vice-president. Keating claimed he dodged the answer (obviously yes, since a vice-president's primary function is to move to the White House if its tenant becomes *hors de combat* while in office), but the tale confirms the eager Kissinger's limitless ambition. While he personally found it easy to believe the best of himself, this was heightened by the constant company of admirers, including many who condemned Nixon.

Nixon was generous in his references to Kissinger almost until the very end. On May 29, 1974, he issued a statement crediting his secretary of state with the stiffly negotiated disengagement of Syrian and Israeli forces. But it had become less and less of a secret that the president, hard put to it on the home front, was becoming inclined to diminish the reputation of the man whose career he had made, first as national security adviser, then as secretary of state.

Yet Kissinger himself acknowledges in his memoirs that by the summer of 1973,

> Nixon reversed his attitude toward my growing celebrity. He no longer showed resentment at public attention to me (though he must have felt it); political calculation caused him to welcome it as a means of cementing the claim that Watergate was a trivial aberration from a Grand Design.... In the end Nixon had no choice but to fall in with the notion of *my* central role, however wounding to him—and however unfair....
>
> Since Nixon had not wanted a strong Secretary of State, it could never have crossed his mind that he would wind up with a Security Adviser having a constituency of his own.... Throughout 1972, the President and Haldeman missed few opportunities to reduce my visibility, to dissociate from me when I was involved in controversy, and to demonstrate my dependence on Presidential favor. It was one of the reasons... why I began Nixon's second term firmly determined to resign by the end of 1973.[14]

Yet, when Kissinger was enraged by innuendo in the press that he was associated with the Watergate scandal and—on June 11, 1974, in Salzburg, Austria—*did* offer to resign, the president (who met him there en route to Cairo) was furious. His secretary of state recalls: "The White House reaction was churlish; Nixon would not speak to me."

And, in an embarrassingly frank analysis, Kissinger summarizes:

> One of the more cruel torments of Nixon's Watergate purgatory was my emergence as the preeminent figure in foreign policy. Richard Nixon wanted nothing so much as to go down in history as peacemaker. He had organized his government so that he would be perceived as the fount of foreign policy, in conception and execution. To this end he had insisted on launching all major international initiatives from the White House; he had excluded the State Department and Secretary of State William P. Rogers relentlessly, and at times humiliatingly, from key decisions.
>
> I was his principal instrument because I seemed ideally suited for a role behind the scenes. As a Harvard professor, I

> was without a political base; as a naturalized citizen, speaking with an accent, I was thought incapable of attracting publicity; in any event, since I was a member of the President's entourage, my access to the media could be controlled by the White House.[15]

A misstatement, if ever there was one.

There is no doubt that the most important action taken by Nixon in connection with his foreign policy, although not in itself a direct diplomatic act, was the selection of Henry Kissinger as his principal agent and partner in elaborating U.S. positions and accomplishing U.S. objectives in world affairs. It is arguable that without the skill and brilliant negotiating ability of the bespectacled Harvard professor there might have been no successful opening to China, no armistice even of the existing uneasy sort in the Middle East, and no withdrawal agreement in Vietnam, disastrous as that accord proved to be when the American Congress tied Nixon's hands—an action that might conceivably have been foreseen but one for which Kissinger certainly cannot be blamed.

When I discussed his association with Kissinger, the former president told me (in 1986) that at first he scarcely knew anything about the man who was to become his effective right hand in global affairs. He recollected:

Now after the election while we were at the Pierre Hotel in New York preparing to take over, I was seeing numbers of people to kind of develop the administration team. And my recollection is that John Mitchell suggested that I should see Henry. He had been helpful during the campaign.

Between November 1968 and January 1969, in the transition after the election, Henry Kissinger came in one day while everything was still fluid. I had not yet named Rogers secretary of state. My first choice for secretary of state was Bob Murphy. I talked to Murphy and urged him to take it, but he declined on the basis of age. He said we needed a younger man, and eventually it was given to Rogers.

But in this case I had not yet made any decisions with regard to State, so I met Kissinger and we had about an hour's discussion. It was far-ranging but mostly about Vietnam. It was important to know what our options were, what we could do. And I knew Kissinger had done a lot of thinking on that subject, and as we talked I decided right then that this was the man to be the head of the NSC. My recollection is that I offered it to him at the end of the conversation.

Now, let me say also the first one I offered secretary of the treasury to was David Rockefeller. And David declined because he said he had too much to do at the bank. I was trying to bring together as many diverse people as possible, a lot of Rockefeller people, for example. We offered Defense to Scoop Jackson, a Democrat, and he would not take it; he said "I can help you more in the Senate."

At that time Kissinger and I did not discuss relations with China; Soviet-American relations, but not China. We were both on parallel tracks on China, and he was very pleased I supported the same concept. The first memorandum I wrote to the National Security Council was the week after I was president. I wrote a memorandum to Henry and I said, Please explore what we can do about China. And that is when he initially began. The China issue didn't start with his trip there, it began with that.

But he was aware, I'm sure, of the article I'd written in Foreign Affairs *on the Chinese issue. It is all petty to say who thought of it first. Some people say Kissinger thought of it and then he beat me over the head and dragged me into the position or I thought of it and Henry went along and then took credit. All that is beside the point. The critical part is that we both had the same conclusion. And in terms of implementing it, he was absolutely brilliant. There was nobody who could have done it as he did it.*

Before I became president I had very strong views as to the directions I wanted to go. I wanted to do something in Vietnam. I wanted to bring the war to an end. Peace with honor, so to speak. I wanted to do something on Russia, and that was included in my first inaugural. An era of negotiation rather than confrontation. I wanted to do something on China. Those were my three foreign policy goals. At a secondary level I also wanted to do something in the Middle East because I had been there and was concerned about it.

So once I had made the decision on Kissinger then I appointed Rogers secretary of state. I looked upon Rogers as being a superb negotiator, which he has demonstrated. I did not look upon him as a creative thinker.

I looked upon Kissinger as a creative thinker but I did not look upon him as a negotiator. The reason his role became so great, part of it, was because he is a very good bureaucratic infighter. He likes power, which is a compliment, and he knows how to use it.

But Kissinger also is a superb negotiator. So you had a situation here where he took over more and more of the negotiations on the major issues, but we shouldn't downplay Rogers's role. Rogers in the State Department did an excellent job in many of the other areas we couldn't spend enough time with, Latin America and so forth, which I also think are important.

So the job grew more in importance not because Henry was grasping for power but because I found in him a combination of a creative thinker and one also who was an excellent negotiator. When you had those two factors involved, he became indispensable in carrying out my three objectives. And incidentally, no one else, even if I had given them the authority, at that time could have carried out the China initiative, the Vietnam initiative, and the Russian initiative which Henry carried out.

In a subsequent conversation Nixon dealt at considerable length with the tactical relationship between himself and Kissinger, explaining how they worked together as a team, even if they occasionally disagreed on the best way of handling particular problems. Thus, for example, they were of two minds about the crisis following North Korean destruction of an unarmed American reconnaissance plane while it was flying over nonterritorial ocean waters and about certain political problems involving negotiations with North Vietnam. Nixon recalls that these were "basically differences that were not about policy, so much as about politics." Moreover, Nixon adds that by mutual agreement he and Kissinger worked out a tactical formula by which they pretended to disagree on complicated issues involved in negotiations in order to mislead and confuse those with whom the negotiations were taking place. He explained:

You know the common perception was during the Eisenhower and Dulles years that Eisenhower was a dove and Dulles was the hawk. Dulles was out there being tough and Eisenhower was really the conciliator. As a matter of fact, Eisenhower and Dulles saw each other, talked to each other all the time; they were on the same wave-

length. They didn't agree all the time but Eisenhower was no dove, I can assure you.

Now, in our period, as you know, the perception was that Henry was the reasonable one, that I was the hawk. As a matter of fact that is a complete misreading; they don't give either Henry or me enough credit for sophistication or subtlety. Henry will tell you that he often used me, as for instance saying: "I'm trying to do this but I'm not sure I can get the old man to do it."

And incidentally, the Russians also use this tactic. I noted recently something to the effect in an article that Gorbachev really was reasonable but that he had hard-liners in the Kremlin.

That goes back to Stalin. Stalin used to create the impression with Roosevelt, when Roosevelt was past his prime, that he was reasonable but that there were these hard-liners that he had to deal with. It was a false impression. Brezhnev used it with me. Brezhnev used to say, "I've got the Politbureau, and some of them are not going to go as far as we are." At the present time Gorbachev says, "Well, I've got my marshals."

Now, in their case it is a fiction, you see what I mean. They are all basically hawks, but they may differ as to the tactics, but the goal is the same. And, because we do have an open split in our country, Reagan can say very properly that the right wing will oppose something he does. But you must not assume that because we do have two different sets of opinions that they have. That's my point.

Henry and I saw the Soviet situation in the same way. We would disagree on occasion—on tactics but never on strategy. Now, let me give you some examples of where there was disagreement. The first one was very early in the administration—you remember the EC121 plane that was shot down by the Koreans in 1969? It was very early in the administration, in the spring of '69, this was an unarmed surveillance plane which was shot down by the North Koreans. There was a debate within the administration on what to do. Henry at that point was very hard line. He said it was important early in the administration to give a signal to the Koreans and through them to the Chinese and the Russians. And the North Vietnamese in particular. So he was in favor of going in and taking out a Korean airfield.

I felt the same way. I said, "I agree that's what we ought to do" because I wanted to put a shot across the bow at that point, particu-

larly because we had inherited the bombing halt from Johnson. In my view it was a great mistake that we continued to adhere to it as long as we did. It inhibited us more than we should have been.

I wanted the North Vietnamese to be under no illusions that we were going to continue to temporize with them. So Henry saw this as a good way to get that message across. I agreed. But within the administration Rogers, Laird, and virtually everybody else opposed us, because they thought that at that early stage in the administration it would cause demonstrations in the streets and so forth. You remember the country was in a pretty rough time then. So, much to Henry's disappointment, I decided against taking any military action.

All that we did was to order the fleet to police the area and I issued a warning and a press conference. That's when I said, "the President of the United States warns only once. If there are any other incidents of this type we will react." Well, many thought it was too soft; but the reason that I had to come down on this other side was at that early time the traffic politically wouldn't bear it. And that's an example of where Henry and I might disagree, when I had evaluated the political situation differently.

He, from the standpoint of strategy, was right and I agreed that way, but from the standpoint of politics you couldn't have a situation where a couple of cabinet officers might even resign over you. At that state it was too early. Now we come to another example. At the time of the secret negotiations in 1971 and 1972, Henry's twelve secret trips to Paris. He had more confidence in the negotiating track than I did. He proved eventually to be right, in my view, so on that score I think the record should be very clear. And Henry believed politically that it would be very helpful if we could get a peace agreement before the 1972 election.

I disagreed. I said, "No Henry, it is not to our advantage politically to make a deal unless it is the right deal. Don't let the North Vietnamese put time pressure on us." And then, of course, Henry made his famous statement, "Peace is at hand." I made the point that we would make peace whenever was the right time, but if it wasn't the right time we would not. We were not going to be forced into it because of political considerations. Let's come to a third point. The third point is not where we disagreed because he totally shared my view. In the 1973 war, the Yom Kippur war, Golda Meir had terrible problems and needed planes and arms. The Russians had a huge airlift; we had to match it. The Pentagon didn't come up with any kind of plan. They danced around. They wanted to use commercial airliners and we couldn't get insurance. Then they wanted to take Israeli airliners and pay off El Al. Well, that didn't work. Finally it was decided to use our own planes, and I remember one day Henry came in with what was the agreed position paper and that was that; we would send over an airlift using three C-5As. I said "Henry, how many do we have, C-5As?" He said twenty-five. I said, "Use them all; what is the Defense Department's objection?" He said it's political. I said, "Look, I'll decide the politics. They believe that twenty-five is more than the traffic will bear." And then I made this statement which is very important to bear in mind in terms of today: "You'll get just as much blame for three as for twenty-five. Do what is necessary. Do what will do the job." And that's when I called Schlesinger on the phone and I said, "Send everything that will fly." Now Henry totally agreed with the decision; he wanted to do that, too, but he was concerned then about the political objections that would be raised in the Pentagon. But I, as the political leader, said, "I will decide the politics; just give me the options."

Another thing that I should point out about Henry; he was a great teacher. In the early days we used to walk the sands at San Clemente, and he would just talk. I would talk on the basis of my experience and world travels, and he talked about how he evaluated the Soviets and others.

After the most dramatic accomplishments of his administration and the obvious success of Kissinger as a diplomatic agent far superior in importance to Secretary of State Rogers, Nixon with apparent suddenness named Kissinger to the principal cabinet post while at the same time retaining him as the president's national security assistant.

At the end of the first term I made a mistake asking everybody to submit resignations. It was not my intention not to express appreciation, but I wanted to have an opportunity to bring in new people, and so forth. I think one of the worst things that happens is for people to stay on too long in jobs. They get tired, they get bored, and yet they feel they can't leave because they think it will be a personal affront or admission of failure.

Bill Rogers was ready to leave. Now the relationship between

Rogers and Henry as we know was a very fiery one. It was very difficult. I did not want that to happen again. I felt that if Henry were to be secretary of state he had to continue as my top adviser here, and saw no way I could put somebody in the White House without having another fiery relationship. And that's why it was done. And of course Ford and Henry were on very good terms.

Henry is better when he is running an operation. Henry's mind is all-encompassing. He must be in charge. It is difficult to have a situation where somebody else is an equal with Henry in his area, because he towers over them. And there is the personality problem. Henry does not tolerate competition, which is the mark of a very great leader.

Nixon is quite clearly prepared to share before history Kissinger's role in gaining the greatest foreign policy achievement of his administration, but he does not allot to him any significant share in responsibility for its failure.

The biggest success, historically, and Clare Luce is my witness on this, was China. Clare said, "You know, in history books a hundred years from now, a thousand years from now, there will be one line on your administration—'He went to China.' " I think most people would say that. China made a difference. If we had not made China an issue, look at the situation we would be confronted with in the world today. It did not just happen because we were balancing the Chinese with the Russians. I felt it had to happen for other reasons. If there had been no Russians, we still had to go to China. But I would say I rate three things about equally.

I would say our greatest successes were China, the development of a new relationship with the Russians (it did not hold, but I think had we not had the Jackson-Vannik amendment, had I been able to survive, we could have made what I call hard-headed détente). "Competition without war" is the best phrase. We could have made it work. And the third area, which was the most difficult of all, and I think had our administration survived would have been the greatest achievement, was the disengagement of Vietnam. In a way we kept not just our honor—you don't fight wars for honor—but kept the compliments of our friends in the area and respect of our potential adversaries. And the deterring, for example, of the Russians, as a result of the failure in Vietnam and the enormous impact it had on American self-confidence.

What I am saying is had we survived, our self-confidence would not have gone down. The Soviets would have had a greater stake and interest in the relationship had we survived. They wouldn't have moved into Angola and Ethiopia and Nicaragua, etc. I think all of those things were part of the Vietnam syndrome.

Our greatest failure as I look back was the Middle East. I am just looking, for example, at this 1986 budget for worldwide foreign aid. Everybody's now trying to cut that. It is twelve billion dollars; six billion goes to two countries—Israel and Egypt. Now that's a total distortion of American priorities.

I bore it because, after all, that's part of the cost of Camp David and the rest. As long as you keep Egypt out of the game there isn't going to be war there. But on the other hand, I felt had we survived—that with Henry's brilliant negotiating capabilities and disengagements—he really set the stage for what I think was a great achievement by Jimmy Carter. Camp David was a great achievement.

But I felt at the time I had to leave office that I had established a very interesting relationship. I had the confidence of the Israelis, because Golda Meir knew that when the chips were down we would send in the planes and call the alert. So the Israelis trusted me. I also, however, had the respect of Sadat and even the Saudis, another element in the area, who felt that I would be fair. And I felt that we were in a very good position. Had I been able, together with Henry's negotiating and my personal involvement, we might have made progress in the Middle East which would have obviated most of the problems we now have.

The toughest decision by far was the May 8, 1972, decision to bomb the dikes at Haiphong, North Vietnam, because it came three weeks before the summit with Brezhnev. It was the danger that we had to consider that it might blow the summit, which many experts thought, and which both Henry and I thought, was possible. But it worked. And don't get the impression that the experts were wrong totally in worrying about it, because we worried about it too. But it did work, and that was the toughest decision.

Now the greatest mistake. The question that is often asked is: Why didn't you bomb Cambodia earlier? And here is the greatest mistake, in my opinion: when we went into Cambodia. Not that we went in—but at the same time we did not bomb and mine Haiphong at that point.

I think at that time we could have broken their backs and we were already negotiating. We could have broken their backs and gotten the agreement then that we got later, and then be able to police it.

Henry and I considered it. There we both felt that it was more than the traffic would bear, because there there was very honest disagreement about going into Cambodia in both Defense and State.

So there was the mistake. Prince Sihanouk of Cambodia wanted us to come in, and in fact invited us in. He said, "Just so you don't kill any Cambodians. All we have got is a bunch of buffaloes and so forth in here." Sihanouk wanted us in.

Looking backward, Nixon reflects that Secretary of State William Rogers and Henry Kissinger were a useful team, even if they didn't get on at all personally. He remembers:

They used to argue with each other, but in the end if the decision were made they would both support it. Rogers and Kissinger never really got on, there wasn't any overwhelming sentimental attachment ever. But it's useful. You can't have sparks unless sticks are rubbed together. It is important for the leader to decide at some point. If you continue to ride two horses going in different directions, they'll eventually split you apart. So at some point you have got to decide I'm going to ride one or the other.

Nixon says Chou En-lai and Kissinger were principally to be credited for the Sino-American accord, not Mao Tse-tung and himself.

Chou was the one primarily responsible for the American-Chinese rapprochement in 1972. Mao approved it but Chou En-lai took the leadership; without his skill and Henry's skill we would not have got the Shanghai communiqué, one of the greatest diplomatic achievements of the century. Henry and Chou did it together. And the Chinese still refer to it as the charter for the relations between us two. Rather than for example glossing over differences it said we have these views, they had their views, we agree on this, we disagree on that.

A brilliant solution. Usually communiqués are so bland. They are made for one day's headline. The Shanghai communiqué was made for history. But Chou after my visit developed cancer, as you know. And then Mao's widow and [the] so-called Gang of Four, they probably ganged up against him. I don't think he was in disgrace, but he didn't have the preeminent position that he had had previously. But then after he died, shortly after my second visit, he was elevated again.

I talked with Kissinger (June 1986) about his personal relationship with and opinion of Nixon. He says without hesitation: "I respect Nixon as a fine statesman. In foreign affairs he was first class." Kissinger believes de Gaulle was "certainly the most influential Western statesman for Nixon; Adenauer was next, a splendid man but not as important as de Gaulle. In China, Chou En-lai was outstanding. Nixon himself was a man of vision and strength in foreign policy."

Kissinger's memory coincides with Nixon's:

> He recalled that he had read my book on *Nuclear Power and Foreign Policy*. At that time I was still a Harvard professor, and Nixon was regarded as the great enemy by such people.
>
> At the end of November 1968 he offered me the job of national security assistant at the White House. I was still a close friend of Nelson Rockefeller and asked him and others of his advisers who had gathered to discuss with Nelson what he should to if Nixon offered him the job of Defense Secretary. Nixon didn't offer it, but Nelson was a very good sport and never gave any sign of disappointment.
>
> From the start I got on well with Nixon. In 1973, in the fall, the president saw he could not run anything from the White House any more, because of the weakening of his position on account of Watergate. He couldn't just run foreign policy from the White House. He had to make me secretary of state or put in someone else and lose me. He couldn't run things the Nixon way with me simply as security assistant. He wanted to keep some control on foreign policy. But the system didn't really work out.
>
> I chaired meetings of the cabinet as secretary of state, but also continued as White House adviser. The State De-

partment had to be represented by a deputy secretary to speak its collective mind. It was impossible for me to act in a dual position without either having to overrule the attitude of the secretary of state or, in effect, overrule myself as security adviser.

That was why Ford had let Kissinger go as security adviser while keeping him as secretary of state. Kissinger regards Nixon as "a very important president."

He had the most sophisticated view of foreign policy of any American I have known. He made a major contribution. All the major policies we are still practicing today were designed originally during the Nixon presidency.

Without Watergate there could have been a satisfactory Vietnam settlement based on the agreement that was later negotiated with Hanoi. This would have seen the war over and settled before the end of Nixon's term.

XIII

Supersummits

America and Russia are two of the rare great powers that have never been at war with each other. Indeed, they were partners in the two world conflicts and, although frequently at odds with Russia both under the imperial czars of Saint Petersburg and the empire-building commissars of Moscow, the United States has never thrown down a gage, and peace has been a permanent feature of their mutual history.

There is of course a vast difference between real war and what has come to be known as cold war. The United States has been at odds with the Soviet Union most of the time since 1917, the year Lenin took power from the brief postczarist Russian regime of Alexander Kerensky, and made a separate peace in World War I.

Since then Washington's attitude toward Moscow was one of distrust, with the exception of the anti-Hitler war, when the White House and the Kremlin symbolized a brotherhood in arms. But, apart from that interlude, the relationship has varied between cold disdain and cold warfare. There have been several grave crises over Czechoslovakia, Berlin and the Wall, Cuba, the Middle East, Korea, and Afghanistan.

And both superpowers seem particularly concerned about the territories to the south of them that lead down respectively to the Suez Canal and to the Panama Canal. Moscow is deeply concerned about the entrance-exit to the Mediterranean–Arabian Sea waterway that links European Russia to its great Asian ally, India. And Washington has a morbid fear of trouble arising in Central America and the Panama link between the Atlantic and the Pacific. Since the Soviets have attained the huge blue-water navy of Admiral Gorshkov, who carried out Stalin's command to build such a fleet, the Soviet Union is seen in America as an even more formidable threat to both the East and West coasts of the United States. The perceived Communist threat of the 1950s in Guatemala was far less insidious than the subsequent perceived Communist threat in Nicaragua. In between came the Cuban missile crisis when the Russians, still with a serious naval vulnerability, were forced to back down. The first good talk I had with Richard Nixon, when he was vice-president, came in Washington, July 25, 1958, and already Russia was much on his mind.

Until the time when the imperialist Communist movement began to be effective—since the latter part of World War II, I think—[U.S. foreign] policy was relatively adequate to protect our security. But now we find that the Communists have developed to a degree never before reached the tactics of indirect aggression. Therefore we must expand our concepts. . . .

The people of this country and perhaps its policymakers cannot stress too much that we are devoted to peace at almost any price. And there is an important ingredient of our foreign policy which we have not adequately conveyed abroad: We are not wedded to the status quo. We recognize that the world, above all the world outside the West, is in a process of change and that the popular masses want a better way of life. Unfortunately, the image we present to many people abroad is precisely the opposite of this desire on our part. We are not for change merely for the sake of change as Russia is, but we do not oppose change. . . .

We must get across to other nations that ours is the true revolution. We should talk more about the promise *of the American revolution and less of the* menace *of the Communist revolution. But we must make it plain that we do not expect other peoples to share all our views and to imitate us in all their action.*

A year after this conversation, Nixon showed he meant what he said when he was sent to Moscow by President Eisenhower in July 1959 to represent the United States at the opening of its exhibition in a Moscow international fair. There he met Khrushchev, then the Communist boss, and had his widely reported "kitchen debate" in the American exhibit. Before his departure from the United States, he consulted John Foster Dulles at his bedside in the hospital where the secretary of state was dying of cancer. Dulles said: "Khrushchev does not need to be convinced of our good intentions. He knows we are not aggressors and do not threaten the security of the Soviet Union. He understands us. But what he needs to know is that we also understand him. In saying he is for peaceful competition, he really means competition between his system and ours only in our world, not in his. He must be made to understand that he cannot have it both ways."[1]

On July 23, Nixon was received by Khrushchev in the Kremlin. At first their conversation was amicable. Khrushchev praised a speech Nixon had made and said that he, too, welcomed the kind of peaceful competition Nixon had described. But then the atmosphere changed and the Soviet leader attacked the Captive Nations resolution Congress had passed just before Nixon's departure, a routine resolution voted each year with reference to the Soviet Baltic states in particular. After a barren exchange the two men drove together to the American exhibit and their "kitchen debate."

To his credit, despite the plague of other problems whether in the American Congress or public opinion, whether in the swamp of Vietnam or the burning deserts of the Middle East, Nixon never lost sight of the salient problem of his presidency, relations with Soviet Russia. The Khrushchev "kitchen debate" was but a slight foretaste.

Before he began direct presidential negotiations with Moscow, he had been thoroughly briefed by his White House experts, who reinforced his own view that the Soviets respected power and understood military strength best. They could not comprehend restraint, which perplexed them, and allowed them to conclude there was room for them to advance their interests.

As Kissinger analyzed the view from the Kremlin for his boss:

> The problem with U.S.–Soviet relations is not only that there are two competing bureaucracies with their assumptions and guesses; there are also conflicting conceptions of negotiation. Americans tend to believe that each has its own logic, that its outcome depends importantly on bargaining skill, good will, and facility for compromise. But if one side in a negotiation has only a vague mandate coupled with a general desire for agreement, negotiability—an elegant phrase meaning what one knows the other side will accept—becomes an end in itself and the outcome is foreordained: The negotiation will see the constant retreat of the party that is committed to it. Persistence in a negotiating position is disparaged domestically as "rigid," "stubborn," or "unimaginative." No position is ever final. Critics demand greater flexibility; soon the proposition is advanced that the United States has an obligation to overcome the stalemate by offering concessions. The other side, aware that we are in effect bidding against ourselves, has the maximum inducement to stand rigid to discover what else we may offer.[2]

The White House security assistant observed later:

> Soviet diplomacy has one great asset. It is extraordinarily persevering; it substitutes persistence for imagination. It has no domestic pressures impelling it constantly to put forward new ideas to break deadlocks. It is not accused of rigidity if it advances variations of the same proposals year after year. There are no rewards in the Politburo for the exploration of ever-new schemes, which turns so much of American diplomacy into a negotiation with ourselves. Like drops of water on a stone, Soviet repetitiveness has the tendency sooner or later to erode the resistance of the restless democracies.[3]

Nixon did not return to Moscow until May 1972, when, as president of the United States, he had the first of three summit meetings with Leonid Brezhnev, the Soviet chief. He was clearly excited by this first supersummit. His romantic streak was aroused by the Kremlin's history and the fact that he was the first

American president to be received there. And, both participants in the tête-à-tête were keenly aware that their confrontation was of unusual importance. Brezhnev later observed with self-satisfaction that Nixon went to Peking for banquets but to Moscow in order to do business.

The primordial subject had already been examined by Soviet and American diplomats and military experts working in prolonged bilateral conferences at Helsinki for months on end in what came to be known as SALT (Strategic Arms Limitation Talks). Nixon had announced a year earlier (May 20, 1971):

> *The Governments of the United States and the Soviet Union, after reviewing the course of their talks on the limitation of strategic armaments, have agreed to concentrate this year on working out an agreement for the limitation of the deployment of anti-ballistic missile systems (ABMs). They have also agreed that, together with concluding an agreement to limit ABMs, they will agree on certain measures with respect to the limitation of offensive strategic weapons.*

The president arrived in Moscow on the crest of a wave, having ordered the mining of North Vietnam's supply lines from Russia by rail and by sea without having the irritated Soviet regime cancel the scheduled meeting. As he left Washington, Nixon stressed that the initial SALT accord reached in Helsinki, the Finnish capital, by U.S. and Soviet delegations, represented "concrete results, not atmospherics [such as] would be our criterion for meetings at the highest level." The latter signified "the first step toward a new era of mutually agreed restraint and arms limitations between the two principal nuclear powers."

The summit dialogues were on a high level and saw the exchange of some serious ideas. They were marked by an ambience of some friendship as the two leaders rapidly got to know each other. Brezhnev talked bluntly but, unlike Khrushchev, his tone bespoke cordiality. And, after a stilted welcoming statement, he began to talk of the need and advantages of a personal relationship between the two men as leaders of their countries.

Following a plenary session with their chief advisers the next day, Brezhnev, with his expert on U.S. affairs, Andrei Alexandrov, met Nixon, flanked by Kissinger. Brezhnev showed himself to be impressively briefed, above all on such military aspects as missiles. They agreed that the sole antiballistic missile system permitted the USSR under an American accord with a similar limitation should endure for five years. The two later that day signed an ABM treaty and an interim agreement on offensive weapons.

Much to Nixon's surprise, after a long subsequent talk about Vietnam, Brezhnev offered to send a high official to Hanoi to seek a basis for peace. Nixon agreed to the desirability of such a move and promised to suspend bombing of the North Vietnamese capital while the Soviet negotiator was there.

This first Brezhnev-Nixon summit was useful and serious as well as laying the basis for an improved personal relationship between the two heads of state. Apart from this important feature, the meeting produced the accord on strategic arms limitation, and the ABM agreement halted a trend toward a defensive arms race. It also signaled the acceptance by both superpowers of a permanent concept of deterrence through "mutual terror." As Nixon put it, "the Interim Agreement on strategic missiles marked the first step toward arms control in the thermonuclear age." It was a great move forward. Nixon wrote of the dialogue:

These summit agreements began the establishment of a pattern of inter-relationships and cooperation in a number of different areas. This was the first stage of détente: to involve Soviet interests in ways that would increase their stake in international stability and the status quo.[4]

Nixon confided his impression of Brezhnev to his personal diary.

Anybody who gets to the top in the Communist hierarchy and stays at the top has to have a great deal of political ability and a great deal of toughness. All three of the Soviet leaders [the others being Kosygin and Podgorny] have this in spades, and Brezhnev in particular. His Russian may not be as elegant, and his manners not as fine, as that of some of his sophisticated European and Asian colleagues, but like an American labor leader, he has what it takes....

There is no question that the Russian leaders do not have as much of an inferiority complex as was the case in Khrushchev's pe-

riod. They do not have to brag about everything in Russia being better than anything anywhere else in the world. But they still crave to be respected as equals, and on this point I think we made a good impression.

He noticed that all three Soviet bosses were well dressed and wore cuff links. Brezhnev "was even somewhat of a fashion plate in his own way." In human terms Nixon found Brezhnev

very warm and friendly. As we were riding in the car out to the dacha *[Brezhnev's country house in Zavidovo] he put his hand on my knee and said he hoped we had developed a good personal relationship.... At one point he said to me, "God be with you."*[5]

The president was impressed by Brezhnev's "overall strength."

He has a strong, deep voice—a great deal of animal magnetism and drive which comes through whenever you meet him.... While he sometimes talks too much and is not too precise, he always comes through forcefully, and he has a very great shrewdness. He also has the ability to move off of a point in the event that he is not winning it....

Brezhnev at one point said to me, "I am an emotional man, particularly about death in war." I told him that while my reputation was for being unemotional, I was just as emotional as he was about this issue.[6]

Kissinger thought very highly of this 1972 Moscow summit. He wrote:

> A strong, confident American President should be able to use occasional summit meetings to impress the Soviet leaders with his determination to reduce the risk of miscalculation, to keep open the possibility, however slim, of an ultimately constructive dialogue....
>
> From this point of view, Nixon's 1972 summit in Moscow took place under nearly ideal circumstances. Two weeks before, Nixon had ordered the resumption of bombing of North Vietnam and the mining of its harbors. When Mos-

cow maintained its invitation nevertheless, the Kremlin showed that it would subordinate some of the concerns of its friends to Soviet-American relations.[7]

Presidential euphoria after the meeting was soon disappointed by erosion of Nixon's shaky domestic position as, to his surprise, both liberals and conservatives attacked him for "overselling" America, although this negative line was puzzled by Soviet behavior. The Kremlin cracked down on dissidents and the Middle East war broke out anew in the autumn of 1973, further confusing efforts at détente.

The next meeting between the two superpower leaders was in Washington in June 1973. The circumstances were by no means so favorable. The Watergate tumor had turned into an inoperable cancer and a highly visible one, at that. Senator Sam Ervin's televised committee hearings were becoming increasingly explosive. Indeed, Senator "Scoop" Jackson proposed a week before Brezhnev's arrival that the summit be postponed. This could, in some ways, have been wise, but it was bound to reduce the position and reputation of the U.S. government while wrecking its negotiating status for at least some time to come.

No extraordinary business was transacted either in Washington or at Nixon's house in San Clemente, California, where he returned Brezhnev's dacha hospitality. But on a personal level it seemed to have been a success. Brezhnev clearly relished the idea of an American trip, and he even embraced Nixon when he arrived at the presidential rest house at Camp David. And he assured the Americans that all East-West problems were soluble if both sides were willing to compromise. But Nixon subsequently reminded his guest politely that no superpower condominium could ignore the rights of other nations.

Nixon gave a cocktail party for Brezhnev but few of the Hollywood stars invited for the impressionable Soviet chief arrived in nearby San Clemente, choosing the Watergate mess as an excuse to boycott the president. That night, after everyone had retired, Brezhnev sent a surprise request to Nixon that they meet immediately to discuss the Middle East. He then proposed that a settlement could be arranged on the basis of an end to belligerency following Israel's withdrawal to its 1967 borders. Brezhnev coyly suggested that this should be a secret deal between the superpowers. Clearly, Nixon could not be interested in such a suggestion. According to Kissinger, the 1973 summit laid bare the ambiguities of East-West relations in the nuclear age. But the two chief summiteers seemed if anything to have improved their personal relationship.

Nixon acknowledged a human rapport with Brezhnev and had some extraordinarily interesting observations to make. In July 1986 he told me he had had very private conversations with the Soviet leader both at Camp David, the presidential country hideaway near Washington, and at San Clemente, where Nixon had his private house. Kissinger had confessed to me that he didn't know anything about these conversations, and I asked Nixon what they dealt with.

The subject was the same both places. He went over at great length the Chinese threat. You have to understand that in the first summit in 1972 they never mentioned the Chinese thing, the initiative that we had undertaken. They didn't want to indicate that it worried them, but in this one they went over and over it again.

It was Brezhnev's goal to have a condominium between the United States and the Soviet Union. And a personal relationship between me and him, such as Stalin had with Roosevelt. He often spoke nostalgically of how Roosevelt and Stalin at Yalta and in other places had a personal understanding that overrode all these other (what he called) less important considerations. He said, "Now, it is important that you and I have the same kind of personal relationship." And then he went on and said, "Look at the Chinese." He talked about how bloodthirsty they were and didn't care about human life and all that sort of thing, and, "We Europeans must unite to control them, because in the future," he said, "in ten years they are going to be a superpower."

He spoke of "we Europeans." He called us Europeans. He also said "white." And "we the whites" and "we the Europeans." There was a racist implication, no question about it. Oh yes, absolutely. The Chinese were not white, they were not European, they had a different background than we had. But then he made the interesting comment. He said, "Now you talk about your allies," speaking of NATO, and we talked about ours. He said, "You and I both know that these allies really don't matter." He said, "What really matters is what you and I do." I said, "Well, now, it's very important for us to bear in mind that our allies are—they represent—great peoples, and we cannot make deals and so forth behind their backs." But that was *the essence of the conversation.*

What he was suggesting was a condominium not only between governments, but between the two leaders of government against the Chinese and without regard to the sensitivities of allies. That's what it was all about. Now some of that, only some, they repeated to Henry.

In other words, Brezhnev proposed that the two superpowers divide the world and rule it. Nixon recalled sagely:

All this gives you a feeling of the foreign statesmen you deal with, and what some of them are like, and when and how you have to reckon with their personal characteristics.

Nixon's recollections of Brezhnev's hope for a cynical deal to carve up the globe between the two superpowers as leaders of specified blocs gives an interesting insight into the Soviet leader, whose affable personal behavior (well described in Nixon's memoirs) masked a purely Stalinist conception of foreign policy. Indeed, Brezhnev may have been thinking he could emulate what is a widely believed but inaccurate interpretation of the Yalta agreements entered into by Stalin and Franklin Roosevelt in early 1945. But the compacts agreed to by the two wartime partners, and approved by the third man at Yalta, Winston Churchill, were designed only to facilitate political arrangements in the period leading to the termination of World War II and the immediate postwar era, when the armies of the USSR and of the West would be facing each other across a liberated continent, divided in two by the victors but in no sense occupied by them.

Stalin broke his pledged word when he imposed his monolithic political system in Poland, which had been occupied by his army. Had Stalin lived up to his pledged word, as specified in the Yalta accords, and granted democratic forms and liberty to Poland, the conflict would have had a reasonably satisfactory ending in Europe.

But Stalin ignored his own pledges, and the effect was Europe's political partition into two essentially differing ideological systems. What Brezhnev was proposing with ill-disguised intent was a partition, on a global basis, similar to the deal to follow

World War II's end, brutally imposed by Stalin on Roosevelt and Churchill in violation of his own pledged word. Nixon, quite patently, was not interested in any ideas that were so immoral, impossible, unfeasible, and wholly unacceptable. And Brezhnev, carefully discreet, never ventured to mention the topic at any of the conferences he had when others than Nixon were present, nor, as far as is known, before any of his own Soviet colleagues. It remained his own dark secret.

Brezhnev's idea of world partition, if indeed he was serious, derived basically from two notions. First, there was the fear of China with its huge population and rich resources, a country clearly destined to become a superpower on the Soviet Union's borders. Second, there was the demographic concern of a racially white Russia faced with the alarming growth of the Asiatic racial minorities among Soviet citizens, the Uzbeks, the Tadzhiks, the Turcomens, the Azerbaijanis, and so on. It was the same kind of racism that was once prevalent among Southerners in the United States, who feared domination by a black majority that claimed and had obtained equal rights and opportunities during the postbellum period of speedy evolution and education. Brezhnev wanted a free hand to keep his Asian minorities away from their racial neighbors and subject to Moscow's rule.

The 1972 and 1973 summits certainly improved the apparent personal relationships of the two leaders—but little else. The improvement of personal relationships was to a degree sham on the Soviet part. Brezhnev by now clearly realized that Watergate was deeply serious and might indeed mean the end of Nixon's authority. He therefore seemed deliberately to remove himself from the direct line of fire in negotiations. It would have been folly if the Soviet leader's prestige should in the slightest way be involved with that of the American president. The net effect was, as Kissinger analyzed: "Watergate did not permit us the luxury of a confrontational foreign policy, and it deprived conciliatory policies of their significance."[8]

On October 24, 1973, Washington learned through its espionage that, although the second Mideast cease-fire, ending the latest Arab-Israeli war, had just gone into effect, restraining a sudden brief spasm of fighting after the first accord was violated, heavy Soviet air and sea forces were being sent into the western

Mediterranean area. Nothing occurred, and it eventually became clear that Moscow was simply trying to show that its interest in the Arab world had not abated.

In late November, Brezhnev concluded a letter to Nixon, easing the strain in the Middle East, with the following reassuring words, in the light of the Watergate disaster looming:

We would like, so to say, to wish you in a personal, human way energy and success in overcoming all sorts of complexities, the causes of which are not too easy to understand at a distance.[9]

On March 24, 1974, Kissinger flew to Moscow to arrange the agenda for a third Nixon-Brezhnev summit. Both leaders had apparently encountered trouble from their armed forces chiefs opposing any retreat from the prevailing hard line on armaments. And that spring the Russians seemed to be carefully weighing the diplomatic effect of Watergate. Walter Stoessel, the able and careful American ambassador in Moscow, reported of a meeting he had had with Brezhnev: "Brezhnev said he respected the President for fighting back, calling this one characteristic of a statesman, and expressed amazement that the United States had reached a point where the President could be bothered about his taxes [as had crept into the affair]. He viewed the President's opponents as 'senseless.' "[10] When Foreign Minister Gromyko saw Nixon on April 11, he said he admired the President for standing up "despite certain known difficulties," adding: "We admire you for it on the human plane."[11]

The third summit was a washout, what Kissinger called a pale "imitation of the first two."[12] There was no longer in the White House a decisive president either able to resist Moscow's expansionist tendencies or to negotiate in earnest and the assurance of authority. When Nixon arrived Brezhnev met him at the airport and soon afterward received his guest in his Kremlin office. He told the president he had been following the political situation in the United States and was convinced Nixon would still be there until his second term expired in 1976.

In the formal meetings Brezhnev urged acceptance of a comprehensive nuclear testing ban Nixon proposed, saying: "Speaking quite candidly, we have an ironic situation in the United States, as 1976 approaches, with respect to détente. Those who applaud our efforts toward détente over the past two years now, for reasons that are more partisan than philosophical, would like to see our efforts fail. So, I would not make any enemies if I were intractable here today."[13] He continued in an odd bit of logic for a negotiation with an adversary: "I am in a unique position of being able to bring the American public along in support of détente. I can handle our so-called hawks—but only one step at a time, and I do not want this process to be interrupted. I want it to continue."[14] To make matters still more difficult for the president, he began suffering an attack of the painful phlebitis that affected him on several occasions.

Brezhnev wound up the business of the summit by flying his guests down to the Crimea and at Oreanda, near the seat of the famous Yalta conference of 1945, continued the discussion at an unimportant meeting where he abstractly doodled hearts shot through with arrows. He advised Nixon that he had done all he could to bring peace to the Middle East but feared he could not indefinitely restrain the Arabs from another round of war. But a measure of agreement was reached on progress toward disarmament. And Foreign Minister Gromyko, the dour, capable professional diplomat who had served as ambassador in Washington for years, told the president at Oreanda that his reports said Nixon was doing considerably better politically and added: "It's really about nothing."[15]

How much in earnest Brezhnev was is open to question. At one point, when discussing Jewish emigration from Russia, he said: "What the hell difference does it make what God Americans pray to—we recognize all religions. All we care about is whether they are for peace.... As far as I'm concerned I say let all the Jews go and let God go with them."[16]

On the ride to the airport Nixon suggested the two men meet again before the end of 1974 for a minisummit at some place midway between Moscow and Washington. Brezhnev liked the idea and speculated about Switzerland. Nixon stressed that the minisummit should agree in principle on specific arms reductions and proposed that Kissinger return to Moscow in September to arrange an agenda for this meeting in the autumn or early winter. Brezhnev agreed.

Nixon considered that in normal conditions Summit III would have been considered a great success because it produced a threshold test ban and further ABM restrictions. He did not think Watergate had played a major part and reckoned that:

Brezhnev had decided to go all out for détente and place all his chips on my survival and my ultimate ability to deliver on what I promised.[17]

He confided to the diary in which he wrote rather than dictated, to avoid Soviet eavesdropping techniques:

It's probably just as well that we were unable to reach any agreement with the Russians on the nuclear front, because to have to take this thing on now would mean that we would have to be opposed to some of our best friends prior to the impeachment vote.

This is a pretty shaky confession for a president to make on the rationale and prospects of his foreign policy.

The human relationship of Nixon with Brezhnev seemed to continue to warm up. Personally I had met Khrushchev (twice) and liked him, although it is evident that Nixon did not. But he clearly took to Brezhnev. He seemed to enjoy his little foibles, like a passion for automobiles and fast driving and his gimmick cigarette holder that automatically rationed him to one smoke an hour (except that he cheated gleefully like a mischievous boy, using a reserve pack).

Nixon observed that the Soviet boss was much more forthcoming at informal conversations, as in his car, than in groups with others present. And a kind of sympathy developed between the two. When the president was driven to Moscow Airport for his departure, Brezhnev climbed in and sat on the jump seat in front of his guest. Nixon later confessed: "I really think he had a feeling of loss and felt sad that the trip was over."[18]

There is no doubt that Nixon appreciated Brezhnev's apparent support for him during the unfolding Watergate disaster. In 1973, at the time of the Washington–San Clemente summit, Brezhnev was in poor health, but he insisted on flying out to California despite his doctors' negative counsel. He sent a message to the president saying: "The President knows full well that from the outset we have unhesitatingly followed a consistent line in relations with him and our respect and my personal respect has not diminished a bit."

Doubtless this indication of personal warmth struck a chord in Nixon's tormented personality. And doubtless this helped bring about certain adjustments in the clearly opposing views of the two chiefs of state who saw the requirements of their nations through such contrasting optics. But Nixon, first unconsciously and then consciously, weakened his own dominant role in the formulation and execution of foreign policy as the Watergate juggernaut rolled ruthlessly on.

Following the resignations of Haldeman and Ehrlichman in 1973, the president explicitly told Kissinger to follow his own judgment in choosing among the options considered on the immense subject of Strategic Arms Limitation (SALT). Kissinger said nothing but continued his past role of submitting options to his boss. It was clear, however, that Watergate worries deprived the president "of the attention span he needed to give intellectual impetus to SALT."[19]

The scandal undermining the U.S. internal political structure had an invisible but sadly debilitating effect on the remarkably effective U.S. foreign policy mechanism that conceived and executed a role in world problems that would achieve the goals and further the interests of the United States. Kissinger wrote sadly in his remarkable memoirs:

> But early in his second term Nixon was no longer a normal President. And the damage was nearly irreparable. Between the Moscow summit of 1972 and Vladivostok in 1974 [Brezhnev and Gerald Ford] the chances for stable long-term coexistence between the United States and the Soviet Union were the best they have ever been in the postwar period. The U.S.S.R. suffered a major setback in the Middle East and accepted it; the conflicts between us, while real, were managed. We had laid extensive foundations through a network of agreements. We had assembled incentives and penalties that seemed to moderate Soviet behavior. Never were conditions better to test the full possibilities of a subtle combination of firmness and flexibility.
>
> We will never know what might have been possible had America not consumed its authority in that melancholy pe-

> riod. Congressional assaults on a weakened President robbed him of both the means of containment and the incentives for Soviet moderation, rendering resistance impotent and at the same time driving us toward a confrontation without a strategy or the means to back it up.... Partly as a result of our domestic weakness and Soviet power, for many of our allies détente became what conservatives had feared: an escape from the realities of the balance of power, a substitution of atmospherics for substance.... Thus America sacrificed a great deal to its domestic divisions.[20]

There was no minisummit for Nixon in the autumn of 1974. He was no longer president of the United States. Instead, Ford met Brezhnev at Vladivostok.

Nixon and Brezhnev knew each other sufficiently well to make personal impressions on which they could base policy assumptions. It is noteworthy that as an ex-president, Nixon visited Moscow during July 1986 and talked at length with Gorbachev, the current Soviet leader, of whom he formed a vivid impression. He wrote to me (September 2, 1986):

As you know, Gorbachev is the third General Secretary I have met. I had long conversations with Khrushchev in 1959 and with Brezhnev in 1972, 1973, and 1974. In addition, I have had extended conversations with other Russian leaders like Mikoyan, Gromyko, and Kosygin. Of all of those I have met over the past twenty-seven years, I would rate Gorbachev as the ablest.

This is not to suggest that he is stronger than the others. I have met some weak leaders in my travels around the world, but never in a Communist country. I vividly recall a National Security Council meeting in 1954 where some of the State Department's experts were discounting Khrushchev because he was allegedly poorly educated, drank too much, wore ill-fitting clothes, and spoke bad Russian. Foster Dulles interrupted them and said, "I disagree, Mr. President. Anyone who claws his way to the top in the jungle warfare of the Soviet hierarchy is bound to be a strong, ruthless and able leader." Gorbachev, like the others I have met, fits that description.

Khrushchev had the quickest reaction time of any leader I have met. Gorbachev is not quite as quick but is just as smart as Khru-

shchev and much smoother. Brezhnev was as tough as any leader I have met, but Gorbachev is just as tough and far more subtle.

Based on my conversation with him, I would rate Gorbachev very high in terms of intelligence. It was also obvious that he is one who does his homework. He was able to discuss the intricacies of arms control without consulting an aide or a note.

But even more impressive than his toughness and his intelligence [are] his leadership qualities. You cannot talk with him for ten minutes without recognizing that he has political charisma—a quality that everyone recognizes and no one can describe.

While he has had no training as an actor, I would say that he is a born actor. He wants those who talk to him to be convinced of his sincerity and of his reasonableness and invariably is able to make that impression.

Does this mean that as Margaret Thatcher put it, "We can do business with him"? The answer is yes, provided we understand what kind of business he is prepared to do with us. The fact that he is better educated, smoother, and appears more reasonable than his predecessors does not mean that he will be easier to deal with, but that he will be far more formidable. He, for example, has the same goals of expanding the Soviet empire which Khrushchev had, but he will not make the mistake of being rash in attempting to achieve those goals. He has the best understanding of public relations of any Soviet leader since the Russian revolution in 1918. He is a modern man in every respect, but this does not mean that he has abandoned the old ideas he inherited from his predecessors. He will try to make the old system run better. But we must never forget that he is a dedicated Communist and a product of the communist system.

He will try to improve it, but he will not make fundamental changes as Deng appears to be making in China. In view of his age and his obvious excellent health, he could be in power for twenty-five years. The intriguing question is whether he eventually will face up to the fact that in order to compete with the Europeans, the Americans, the Japanese, and even the Chinese, he will have to change the system rather than just tinker with its parts. He certainly has the intelligence to make such changes. If he is bold enough and strong enough to do so, he will go down in history as the greatest of all Soviet leaders.

XIV

No Year of Europe

The "Year of Europe" was an idea elaborated by Nixon and Kissinger to grab the particular attention of that portion of American politics and public opinion concerned with foreign affairs. Among other aims it had were the refocusing from China, Vietnam, and the Soviet Union onto the Western European community and the NATO alliance, the original and fundamental postwar primary interest of American policy abroad.

That policy, starting with the Truman Doctrine, had produced the Marshall Plan and NATO. Also, as far as Nixon was concerned, certainly, it was hoped that the progress of the idea of 1973 as the Year of Europe first enunciated under that label in a speech by Kissinger, might relegate to the inside columns of the press some of the front-page newspaper space occupied by the expanding Watergate scandal.

Nixon had been intrigued by Europe since his early days in the House of Representatives. It betokened the most important and most glamorous part of the foreign world the young congressman, always interested in other countries since his college days, was eager to become personally acquainted with. And thus, to his delighted surprise, he read in a newspaper on July 30, 1947, that he was one of nineteen members of a congressional committee chosen by Representative Christian Herter of Massachusetts, to visit Europe and prepare a report on U.S. foreign aid as developed by Secretary of State George C. Marshall. And Nixon, the budding statesman, happily accepted the assignment despite letters addressed to him as a politician, warning him not to back a dangerously unworkable and profoundly inflationary foreign policy.

The young Californian was fascinated by the experience and impressed by disturbing discoveries. He found Communist leaders in Europe "usually more vigorous and impressive" than their democratic counterparts. He saw that the Communists were making clever propaganda use of nationalist sentiments. But he concluded that economic aid from the United States was vital to avoid the "twin specters of starvation and Communism." He also noted an absence of strong leadership among the majority of non-Communists.

American devotion to Europe was well reciprocated during the 1950s and 1960s but began to run into trouble shortly after Nixon's arrival in the White House. This was in no sense due to the president's lack of interest or energetic concern or that of his brilliant policy adviser, Kissinger, who was himself a European by birth and instinctively devoted to the concept of a vast transatlantic family. But with the departure from the scene of men like Italy's Alcide de Gasperi and France's Jean Monnet and Robert Schuman, as well as Germany's Konrad Adenauer, a certain lassitude became detectable among the succeeding generation of political leaders. They had suffered less during World War II and therefore, probably, were less inclined to dream of new and unprecedented futures.

At the time Nixon and Kissinger were trying to construct their Year of Europe the French president, suffering from an incurable disease, was the courageous Georges Pompidou, and the West German chancellor was the impressionable Willy Brandt, who was deeply eager to arrange a détente with East Germany and Russia even at the risk of loosening ties with NATO and the West. Moreover, the principal agents of each man, Michel Jobert for France and Egon Bahr for Germany, both serving in a Kissingerlike capacity for their bosses, were less than anxious to abet any closer connections with the United States and worked quietly to thwart such moves. Thus, although Pompidou himself took the

American project seriously and viewed it favorably, his efforts were undermined by a combination of his own bad health and the wily blocking efforts of the exceedingly intelligent but shifty Jobert.

Egged on by Kissinger, Nixon, who was anxious to broaden his political base by the success of a moderate but firm Allied policy in Europe, agreed to a summit meeting with Pompidou in Reykjavik, Iceland, from May 31 to June 1, 1973. Unfortunately, this was far less productive than the Americans had hoped. Kissinger later wrote of it: "Jobert was turning the Year of Europe into a wrestling match.... We had put forward the Year of Europe precisely to transcend the obsession with East-West relations. We were convinced that without such an effort the democracies would lose their sense of direction and cohesion."[1] But Jobert thought there was a danger for France, which had (under de Gaulle) weakened its tight bonds with the western alliance, that Nixon might be using the "year" as a device to bring France back into NATO as a full participant or, on the other hand, might be hoping to undercut France's leading role in the European Economic Community (Common Market).

Nixon sought to head off these somewhat contrived objections. In his presentation he started by brushing aside implications that he was driven by a desire to outflank Watergate discussion in American newspapers and television or to help prepare the U.S. position for further Soviet summits.

First of all, the timing of our initiative for Europe has nothing to do with the Russian summit or with U.S. political institutions. If we proclaim this year of 1973 the Year of Europe, it is because I feel that during this year of so-called détente with Russia, in this year when Europe is flexing its muscles, we would face a very great danger if Europe were beginning to disintegrate politically.

He warned against

each country in the West and in Europe going to Moscow to negotiate and make deals [an obvious hint directed at Bonn]. Of course there must be individual meetings, but there must be some underlying philosophy that animates all of us. Otherwise, those shrewd and determined men in the Kremlin will eat us one by one. They cannot digest us all together but they can pick at us one by one.

He recommended that the United States, Britain, Germany, and France should have frank talks to decide on their future course.

It is worth quoting Jobert at some length exposing his proclaimed reasons for blocking the Nixon-Kissinger European project. In explaining his views, he summoned to his aid all the old French suspicions of the Yalta meeting among Stalin, Churchill, and Roosevelt in early 1945, a meeting to which General de Gaulle was not invited. From that moment on the general and all Gaullists took pains to depict the conference as a secret deal partitioning Europe into Soviet and U.S. zones or spheres of influence. The legend is still current in France, and Jobert did his best to contribute to it. As any cursory student knows, had Stalin lived up to the promises he gave at Yalta, Poland would not have been satellitized by Russia and even Hungary might have had a different fate. The trouble was that Stalin firmly believed (and rightly, as it turned out) that an army brought with it its own political system, and the Red Army, in full control of all Poland by the time of Yalta, brought with it the Soviet dictatorial system and ideology. Jobert wrote:

> Kissinger later told me that, due to the course of events that this difficult business had taken (the deviations known only too well to both himself and the president), he had been obliged quickly to introduce an important international announcement to create a diversion [from Watergate]. This was a way of making excuses for a proposal, which could be regarded as aggressive or clumsy, for a "new Atlantic Charter." Japan, which was considered "a partner of prime importance," would participate in the negotiation of the charter....
>
> The "Year of Europe," as envisaged by Henry Kissinger, surprised the Europeans, who had hardly been consulted on the evolution and the direction of their destiny....What determination...in organizing his faction, in apportioning tasks, and in assigning places; what brutality also in demanding of Europe, regarding economic organization and

defense, subordination and a contribution in exchange for the right of suzerainty.... The relentlessness of Kissinger, for a year, in obtaining from the Europeans one or several texts assigning American preeminence in the countries of the Atlantic Alliance and of the Common Market shows only too well that the pursuit of success in foreign policy was important for Nixon, who was already in a dangerous position. But it also showed the stamp of a fundamental determination in American policy to organize the Western camp in a perspective of planetary strategy....

Once again the two great powers, who had divided up the world at Yalta in 1945, were not reluctant to acknowledge the freedom of each to organize their own side. After the American-Soviet summit of June 1973, it became evident to everyone that the "Year of Europe," for the United States, was only a sequel to the accords made with the Soviets....

It is surprising that Henry Kissinger, to whom realism excluded rashness, should have believed that he could impose on the Europeans plans so crassly requiring them to become dependent on the United States, and also could manage to control the progress of European unification conducted in "a spirit of reciprocity" with respect to the United States....

Regarding the frailty of Nixon's position, the strange conclusion was drawn in European capitals that Kissinger must not be upset by opposition to his plans—which were of no importance as the presidency was about to collapse—and, moreover, that such pressures only meant a change in domestic policy....

Europe and Japan were invited to join an "energy action group" to which various tasks were assigned, on condition that Western consumers assembled around the United States. Regarding détente and defense, Henry Kissinger wanted to appear reassuring: "The United States will not sacrifice the defense of Europe on the altar of condominium [U.S.–Soviet]." Soon would come the proposition of a conference in Washington, designed to assemble the countries in the sphere of American influence under the topical theme of energy....

Right from the first meeting the conference was blocked. Of course, there were private conversations and luncheon meetings. I met Henry Kissinger in his office, surrounded by a barrage of photographers and reporters. I sug-

> gested to him several ways to save appearances. But he was looking for brilliance rather than compromise, determined ...to put an end to [what he believed was] this French obstinacy that didn't stop fostering indiscipline in the Western camp. Persuaded to take the Europeans in hand, he deliberately subjected us to the test of isolation.[2]

Jobert's arguments were typical of a certain French chauvinist spirit that featured classical Gaullist theories. I don't believe that even Pompidou shared such vigorously antipathetic views. But Jobert was a skilled logician and exceedingly clever, serving as a kind of gadfly to the thoughtful, inventive, but more lumbering Kissinger, who was unable to rescue his idea from the French foreign minister's stings. And even though Pompidou himself was not so frantically inimical to the Washington approach, he allowed his chief diplomat a free hand.

But Pompidou was not optimistic. He did not believe 1973 was slated to be marked by the "advent of Europe." He said the transatlantic dialogue lacked a clear-cut partner in Europe, which could only constitute an economic, not a political, entity. He worried about Bonn's intentions and thought Heath, the British prime minister, represented only a small minority of Britain's "Europeans." He concluded that Americans alone could invoke *a* Year of Europe; for France every year was *the* Year of Europe. No united European body existed in a political sense. Some NATO members were not in the European Economic Community, which for its part included some not in NATO, and the functions of the two bodies differed.

Moreover, despite the inherent good will of Nixon and Pompidou, they showed themselves less capable of mutual understanding. The American took pains to elegize the great Charles de Gaulle, apparently quite unaware of the bitterness Pompidou felt for his former mentor—a result of difficulties in the final years. And Pompidou could not resist the elegant wit of the French intellectual when he described their meeting: "I am convinced that this conference has not given birth to anything, but it bears a seed for the future, and conception is more fun than delivering." The only "seed" in sight was somewhat disguised rancor among the French, who turned the screw later by advising American diplomats that the existence of the European Community blocked consultation by the Western Big Four, as proposed by Nixon.

The only European leader who seemed really to welcome the Nixon initiative and understand the genuineness of its intention was Joseph Luns, the tall Dutchman who was secretary general of NATO; and Luns didn't even speak for his own government, which regarded him as no longer in tune with the times. Thus, as Kissinger was to write: "By the end of June 1973, we were treading water. Two months after our initiative, no one had put forward any concrete idea of what the Year of Europe should contain."[3]

Nixon was reminded by a few perceptive, loyal European statesmen that the American tendency to humor the French with bilateral dealings was weakening the position of the eight non-French members of the Community in trying to nudge Paris toward a conciliatory position. As if to confirm this, Nixon received Jobert, the biggest problem child of Western unity, in San Clemente at the very end of June—a reward for the prodigal son.

Washington had become more or less accustomed, since the days of the haughty chauvinist de Gaulle, to difficulties with France as an ally, but from the days of Adenauer it had counted on West German support in its political aims. However, the handsome Willy Brandt, Social Democratic leader, was a new and puzzling experience. He saw as his historical mission the discovery of a means for amicable coexistence with the other half of a partitioned Germany, and that meant primarily with Moscow. Brandt's "Kissinger," Egon Bahr, an astute operator, spoke of achieving German unity by cementing relations with the Communist East and using the Federal Republic as a lodestone to attract trade and influence from all of Eastern Europe, Germany's traditional commercial and economic larder. But Nixon worried whether the Federal Republic would be the magnet of the West or magnetized iron filing to be drawn eastward.

Nixon made many efforts to cultivate traditional special ties with Britain and sought to harmonize the two nations' strategic concepts. Prime Minister Edward Heath seemed to go along with this approach but avoided any thought of Anglo-American study groups, which Nixon had suggested. Heath wished to put off until the indefinite future any intimate partnership until the eventual institutions required by the new Europe had been established by the European Community. Heath was known to favor the Community more than most British politicians did. Indeed, he appeared to favor that policy over the traditional mid-twentieth-century concept of a "special relationship" with Washington. He was clearly more indifferent than his predecessors to an American connection. And he was aware that Macmillan's Britain had been regarded by the French as a U.S. "Trojan horse" in Europe.

It was Jean Monnet, the remarkable "Father of Europe," who had first urged cooperation between the Community and the United States in a coherent arrangement governing political leadership, security, and economic development. Monnet first urged Nixon to visit Europe to meet with the Council of Ministers of the European Community, a visit that never occurred. Nixon wanted the Community first to develop along its own indigenous lines without any American pressure.

Hoping to gain some credit from the disdainful Brandt, Nixon cabled him in Bonn to report on his own conversations with Jobert and invited the German chancellor to send a representative (presumably Bahr) to the United States for bilateral talks. Brandt replied without enthusiasm. Shortly afterward, the foreign ministers of the European Community met in Copenhagen and agreed to draft "principles" on the transatlantic bond. Kissinger assessed this move: "We begin to understand what had happened in Copenhagen was not only to put the Year of Europe on ice for two months and to cold-shoulder a Presidential visit [which the Americans had hinted at]—two unprecedented events in Atlantic relations—but also to turn the European-American dialogue into an adversary proceeding. . . . Europe had responded to the Year of Europe initiative with a procedure in which those who talked with us were not to be empowered to negotiate while those who could have negotiated with us no longer had the authority to talk."[4]

The Americans felt that more than any other man Jobert had cleverly obstructed progress on this momentarily favored proposal. But two other causes were clearly playing their part. One was Nixon's growing and increasingly perceptible political problem. The other was Pompidou's painful and incurable illness. Some believed Jobert was hoping to succeed the stricken president as the candidate of an anti-American faction. (This seems a highly improbable analysis and a mistaken view of such currents in France as well as of Jobert's political significance.)

But the idea of celebrating an American "rediscovery" of Europe's importance received less than enthusiastic support in other quarters, too. Heath, the cultivated British premier who had distinguished himself among the English for staunch backing of Britain's association with "Europe," received a clearly distant letter from Nixon as a consequence of his frosty view of the American president's program. Nixon wrote in part:

Although I accept your view that a certain amount of progress was made in the general direction of what we hope to achieve, I must tell you frankly that I am quite concerned about the situation in which we seem to find ourselves. I thought we had agreed when we discussed what became known later as the Year of Europe initiative in our January meeting that this was a major enterprise in the common interest at a critical time. In that meeting and in numerous subsequent exchanges in this channel and in conversations with your representatives, it was common ground that the revitalization of Atlantic relationships is at least as much in Europe's interest as in our own and that extraordinary efforts with strong public impact were required....

If we have sought to preserve the privacy of our bilateral exchanges it was largely at European request and because we agreed that under the circumstances it was the best way to make progress. I find puzzling what you say about the exploitation of our private bilateral contacts by the country that had initially insisted on them.

And the whole process of warming up transatlantic cooperation was clearly ended for the time being when Nixon wrote Brandt terminating all thought of his own project to visit Europe at the time. On July 20 he told the German chancellor:

I must in all candor express to you my surprise at the approach that has emerged from the European deliberations. Three months after our initiative, and after numerous discussions which at European request we conducted on a bilateral basis, we now find that the Europeans are unwilling to discuss substantive issues with us until mid-September....

In these circumstances, you should know that we will take no further initiative in either bilateral or multilateral forums but will await the product of the Nine [European Community members] in September and then decide whether and how to proceed. . . . I will not come to Europe unless there is a result commensurate with the need for strengthening Atlantic relationships.[5]

Heath sent his discreet civil servant adviser, Sir Burke Trend, to Washington the day of Nixon's letter to Brandt. They found nothing to talk about. Kissinger later observed: "Atlantic—and especially Anglo-American—relations had thrived on intangibles of trust and consultation. They were now being put into a straitjacket of legalistic formalisms."[6]

Calling it "the Year that never was," Kissinger mournfully summed up the failure of the Year of Europe. He made several points, including: (1) History cannot be repeated on command, and a self-conscious emulation of the Marshall speech that resulted in a great economic plan named for him was impossible to recreate; (2) Washington, seeking to get away from Southeast Asian preoccupations, was seduced by its own nostalgia for historic initiatives; and (3) the proposed Atlantic Declaration of 1973 conferred no immediate benefits.

I might add to these some comments of my own. Washington was not yet aware how deeply its position as a Western standard-bearer had been eroded by Watergate. Marshall had spoken up at a moment when he was a pure Sir Galahad who had commanded victorious liberation forces in a desperate war, and the United States then was a welcome Santa Claus to the stricken, bitter nations of Europe. Also, Western reactions to Vietnam were in no sense so supportive of the United States as Washington assumed; in addition to much questioning of the wisdom of our intervention in that distant former colony already lost by France, there was acute awareness of the fact that we were failing in our objectives. Most of our Western European allies had lost colonies and thought of our Indochina conflict accordingly. And there is little doubt that the Nixon administration—while displaying brilliance in its handling of policy regarding the Soviet Union, China, and the Middle East—had lost touch with the Europe of just a few years earlier—the time of de Gaulle, Adenauer, de Gasperi, and Macmillan. The 1973 Year of Europe turned sadly into an adversary procedure.

The misconceptions, the grinding of the gear wheels, the political uncertainties that contributed to a stillborn Year of Europe tended perforce to press U.S. policymakers more in the direction of better relationships with the Soviet Union, relationships that had been slowly and gradually improving under their own twin momentum. But an obvious failure in Europe, continued failure to achieve real peace in Vietnam despite the Paris Agreement on troop withdrawals, and the gnawing and voracious destruction of Watergate helped push foreign policy toward the illusory but optimistic dream of détente with Moscow.

The Nixon Administration had already managed the difficult trick of introducing "détente" into the current American political vocabulary while at the same time heavily increasing the budget for national defense. And, with or without a harmonious working arrangement with Western Europe, the United States was keenly aware that despite ideological divisions, the dangers of the nuclear missile age condemned us as much as any nation to coexistence with our adversaries. Kissinger defined Washington's conception of this status in a speech at a Washington conference on October 8, 1973:

> Coexistence to us continues to have a very precise meaning:
>
> —We will oppose the attempt by any country to achieve a position of predominance either globally or regionally.
>
> —We will resist any attempt to exploit a policy of détente to weaken our alliances.
>
> —We will react if relaxation of tensions is used as a cover to exacerbate conflicts in international trouble spots.
>
> The Soviet Union cannot disregard these principles in any area of the world without imperiling its entire relationship with the United States.[7]

But the same forces—the looming changes in Vietnam and the cooling off of the project to revive relations with Europe, all mixed together with the ravages of Watergate as they were at last being appreciated abroad—served to dampen the prospects of progress in the relationships of détente with Moscow. As Kissinger was to write: "No East-West policy can abolish crises altogether. This is especially true if both the carrot and stick are removed, as occurred in the attack on executive discretion from 1973 onward."[8]

To facilitate the renewed drive for détente, Kissinger sent a clarifying memorandum to Nixon, saying (just prior to his 1973 Brezhnev summit):

> Like all Soviet postwar leaders, Brezhnev *sees the U.S. at once as rival, mortal threat, model, source of assistance and partner in physical survival.* These conflicting impulses make the motivations of Brezhnev's policy toward us ambivalent. On the one hand, he no doubt wants *to go down in history as the leader who brought peace and a better life to Russia.* This *requires conciliatory and cooperative policies* toward us. *Yet, he remains a convinced Communist* who sees *politics as a struggle with an ultimate winner;* he intends the Soviet Union to *be that winner.* His recurrent efforts to draw us into condominium-type arrangements—most notably his proposal for a nuclear non-aggression pact—are intended both to safeguard peace and to undermine our alliances and other associations.
>
> Almost certainly, Brezhnev continues to defend his détente policies in Politburo debates in terms of a historic conflict with us as the main capitalist country and of the ultimate advantages that will accrue to the USSR in this conflict. Brezhnev's *gamble* is that as these policies gather momentum and longevity, their effects will not undermine the very system from which Brezhnev draws his power and legitimacy. Our goal on the other hand is to achieve precisely such effects over the long run. . . .
>
> The major, *long term question is whether the Soviets can hold their own bloc together while waiting for the West to succumb to a long period of relaxation* and to the temptations of economic competition. Certainly, our chances are as good as Brezhnev's, given the history of dissent in East Europe.[9]

Disappointed by the failure of the European "Year" project and increasingly worried about the voracity of the political scandal that was destroying the authority of the president, on which both U.S. foreign policy and Kissinger himself depended, the security adviser concluded in his subsequent memoirs:

> I believe that a normal Nixon Presidency would have managed to attain symmetry between the twin pillars of containment and coexistence. Nixon would have been able to demonstrate to the conservatives that détente was a means to conduct the ideological contest, not a resignation from it. And he could have handled the liberal pressures by rallying a majority of moderates behind his policy of settling concrete issues. He could then have used his demonstrated commitment to peace to marshal the free peoples of the Alliance behind a new approach to defense.
>
> But early in his second term Nixon was no longer a normal President. And the damage was nearly irreparable....
>
> We will never know what might have been possible had America not consumed its authority in that melancholy period. Congressional assaults on a weakened President robbed him of both the means of containment and the incentives for Soviet moderation, rendering resistance impotent and at the same time driving us toward a confrontation without a strategy or the means to back it up. The domestic base for our approach to East-West relations eroded. We lost the carrot in the debate over Jewish emigration that undercut the 1972 trade agreement with the Soviet Union. And the stick became ineffective as a result of progressive restrictions on executive authority from 1973 to 1976 that doomed Indochina to destruction, hamstrung the President's powers as Commander-in-Chief, blocked military assistance to key allies, and nearly devastated our intelligence agencies. In time the Soviets could not resist the opportunity presented by a weakened President and a divided America abdicating from foreign responsibilities. By 1975 Soviet adventurism had returned, reinforced by an unprecedented panoply of modern arms.[10]

And, I would add, with the fresh weight and vigor that could have been joined to the American position had the Year of Europe achieved anything like the goals envisioned for it by its Washington promulgators, there still might have been a chance to bolster a position overseas that had begun to show signs of debility.

A harassed President Nixon himself appends a sad, bitter note to this entire zigzag search for a policy of Western alliance and, when that failed, accommodation with the Russians:

> *It was the Soviets who put the nails in the coffin of détente. They destroyed détente by their support of the North Vietnamese offensive in South Vietnam that violated the Paris peace agreements and by their expansionism throughout the Third World.*[11]

The year 1973, although marked by brilliant U.S. diplomacy in the Middle East and by seemingly affable summits with Russia, in fact achieved for America a sour balance of a disconcerted, dissatisfied Europe and a distempered Soviet Union.

XV

Swan Song

Richard Nixon's career as a world statesman ended abruptly on August 9, 1974, when he resigned as president, received a pardon from his successor, Gerald Ford, for Watergate transgressions, and retired to private life. Looking back, the windup of his public life, which had occupied the international stage for six momentous years, seems to have occurred in such a fashion that one is surprised it had no more momentous effects on global affairs than appears to have been the case.

Both Nixon and Kissinger, as the latter confirmed to me over lunch in the White House, April 3, 1972, were aware that: "All modern governments have seen foreign policy move from the ministries of foreign affairs to the office of the prime minister or president—in France, West Germany, Britain, China, Russia. This is clearly happening in the United States; it is part of the same process and the need for the policymaking authority to drive the bureaucracy against its inclinations." (This had always, to a degree, been a truism in the United States, where the Constitution charges the president with that role and, since the Fifth Republic was installed by de Gaulle, in France.)

For Nixon, the moment when he was squeezed out of the public eye came at a time of involved diplomatic relationships. Had he been able to remain in office he would no doubt have been pleased to see a change in the kaleidoscopic pattern of leadership in key allied countries. Poor French president Pompidou, with whom Nixon had gotten on quite well and whom he respected for his courage in the face of a dolorous terminal illness, finally died that summer. He was replaced by Valéry Giscard d'Estaing, but the big news, from Nixon's viewpoint, must have been the disappearance from French policymaking of Michel Jobert, who was replaced as foreign minister.

Likewise, Nixon must have welcomed the substitution of the crisp, efficient, pro-NATO Helmut Schmidt for Willy Brandt as West German chancellor, and with Brandt's departure the decline in the importance of Egon Bahr, the would-be peacemaker with East Germany and skeptic on the Western alliance. Finally, Edward Heath, who never tended to overvalue the "special" Anglo-American relationship, was out as British prime minister, and the veteran Labor party leader Harold Wilson came in. U.S. relations with Wilson had traditionally been steady and with no suspicion of mistrust or absence of helpful understanding.

For Nixon there was a deep personal disappointment that Britain, France, and West Germany had all, each for its own reasons, failed to join to support his dream of revitalizing transatlantic relationships. Heath's foreign secretary, Sir Alec Douglas-Home, was personally favorable to the idea but obviously could not disagree with his prime minister.

On May 23, 1973, I breakfasted with Kissinger in Paris and asked about the effect of Watergate on foreign policy. Optimistically (as it turned out) he said: "So far it isn't important. We are able still to continue running on momentum." He added that the "basic point" of Nixon's foreign policy was a deal with Moscow, and its prospects had not (yet) been affected by the scandal. "As things are right now, we can continue along this course. But that will depend on how long this period of national masochism [over Watergate] lasts. It will depend on a change in the existing mood. Certainly these Vietnam negotiations right now [prior to the Paris accords] have been made more difficult because of this."

The Year of Europe idea was not to bear fruit after Nixon's retirement or after the new governments took over in the three leading Western European lands. But Nixon's activity during his last months in office was feverish and extraordinarily productive, considering the shakiness of his position in Washington. He made a strikingly successful tour of the Middle East the June of his last presidential summer and even managed a last summit with Brezhnev in Moscow and Oreanda at the very end of the month.

That meeting, which was supposed to produce a consequent minisummit that had to be aborted because of Nixon's departure, nevertheless bore fruit in the Vladivostok summit between Brezhnev and the new American president, Gerald Ford. This took a measured step toward arms limitation and détente, the goals for which the Nixon administration had labored so hard. Fortunately Ford was able to avail himself of the counsel of Henry Kissinger, whom he kept on as secretary of state, as arranged with Nixon.

Nixon, who had been deeply influenced by his conversations with de Gaulle, had sought détente for the reasons outlined by the General: "To work toward détente is a matter of good sense; if you are not ready to make war, make peace." It had been a source of assurance and comfort for Nixon to deal with de Gaulle, and he recalled regretfully, when thinking of Jobert, the words of the late French president:

> As I am learning to know you better—and by this visit [1969] you have given me that opportunity which I consider historic—I appreciate more the statesman and the man that you are.[1]

Nixon had chosen 1973 to be the "Year of Europe" because he felt it was a propitious moment: Things were going quite well with Moscow; the Paris Agreement that was supposed to lead to peace in Vietnam and U.S. troop withdrawal had been signed; the Middle East appeared quiescent; the summitry game with Brezhnev was well under way; and Jean Monnet, the inspirator of European unity, was urging a Nixon Atlantic initiative.

But the effect of British, French, and German wavering and the disinclination of certain key statesmen in those three countries doomed all chance of success. This caused keen disappointment to Nixon, who had been increasingly Europe-minded since his first visit to that continent with the Herter Committee. He deeply hoped that he could crown the efforts started by Herter, and this was the inner meaning of the Year of Europe speech given by Kissinger on April 23, 1973. Ruefully Kissinger acknowledged in his memoirs later: "Perhaps we should have sensed from the lack of precise response to our approaches that our allies, who had urged us for years to give higher priority to Atlantic relations, were going to disappoint us."[2]

Kissinger had addressed his words to a meeting of American newspaper editors—a surefire audience—and spoke of a "dramatic transformation of the psychological climate in the West—a change which is the most profound current challenge to Western statesmanship." He proposed that "by the time the President travels to Europe toward the end of the year... we and our allies should work out a 'new Atlantic Charter,' or declaration of common purpose."

Nevertheless, less than a fortnight after Kissinger's speech, Nixon doggedly warned in his annual foreign policy report that "We must close ranks and chart our course together for the decade ahead."[3]

The pressure of Watergate and the need for a positive achievement perhaps made Nixon imprudent in his determination, but he was a firm believer in a strong Atlantic bond and was determined to leave progress in such an aim as a major part of his legacy. But, as Kissinger noted sadly, the Watergate crisis, in this respect, "became both a major cause of deadlock and the obstacle to its resolution."[4] And, before the year had ended, it even stimulated new recriminations with France.

The damage had been done, but so much dramatic news was soon to flood the American media that the negative impact of a great failed project was soon forgotten among the dramas that accompanied Nixon's last twelve months in office. First came the October Arab-Israeli war. Washington never fully analyzed the Soviet aspect of the Egyptian-Syrian surprise attack on their Jewish neighbor: Did Moscow have advance information, and did it support the offensive? Cairo and Damascus complained afterward of insufficient Soviet logistical backing.

But, although swift and massive United States aid saved Israel from disaster, the entire showdown in the Middle East was considerably mitigated in the U.S. press by the building Watergate drama. Vice-President Spiro Agnew resigned and Attorney General Elliot Richardson left the cabinet at the same time.

Nixon was suddenly so distracted by the political tragedy that he could no longer deal with the complexities of an entangled military stalemate along the Israeli-Egyptian front.

Although an emotional and Manichaean strain was observed by Kissinger as a traditional factor in the American view of international affairs, the tendency to assume successive pragmatic analyses and take separate steps on a discrete basis was heightened by the influence of Watergate—the most discrete factor of all and the one that came to outweigh all the others.

Already (March 15, 1973) Nixon had personally warned:

> *The Europeans cannot have it both ways. They cannot have United States participation and cooperation on the security front and then proceed to have confrontation and even hostility on the economic and political front.*[5]

And the Middle East war exacerbated these irritated feelings. As Kissinger observed: "The accumulated tensions in our alliances suddenly erupted with the outbreak of the Middle East war."

He continued, "Europe showed no greater wisdom than we had nearly two decades earlier"[6] (over Suez in 1956). Britain and France failed to support the American idea of a UN cease-fire resolution. Turkey and Greece banned the use of American bases to support Israel's equipment needs. Spain also closed U.S. bases against an air bridge. The Soviet air force was thus able to use NATO airspace over Turkey to resupply Syria and Egypt while U.S. airbases were closed to U.S. planes. West Germany refused U.S. shipments of supplies for Israel via German ports. And France declined to associate itself with American diplomatic efforts to end the fighting.

Despite this painful awareness of alliance ties being snipped around him, Nixon retained his courage. When it became clear the Russians were thinking of flying troops and reinforcements to the Middle East, the president ordered an alert for all American forces, showing a determination to risk the existing world equilibrium to protect U.S. commitments and interests despite Allied backsliding. When Moscow recognized the dangers it was courting it cooled its intervention plans. Our NATO partners almost unanimously then urged the United States to press Israel to withdraw its troops and establish new boundaries at the 1967 frontiers—what the Arabs had been requesting since 1967 despite truculent Israeli refusal.

Pompidou called for an independent European Middle Eastern policy, with an Israeli withdrawal to the 1967 frontiers. Heath bemoaned the lack of a joint understanding between Europe and the United States and added: "I don't want to raise the issue of Suez [the 1956 war when Washington opposed an Anglo-French-Israeli attack on Egypt] but it's there for many people.... The U.S. had ample opportunity to bring pressure on Israel to negotiate and has done nothing."[7]

It was comforting—but not sufficiently—to have Douglas-Home, the British foreign secretary, confirm that he did not favor Heath's desire for Britain to play a role in Europe as necessitating the loosening of its transatlantic ties with the United States. And Kissinger sought to reaffirm that idea when he addressed the renowned Pilgrims Society in London, stressing that "the United States is committed to making the Atlantic community a vital positive force for the future as it was for the past. What has recently been taken for granted must now be renewed. This is not an American challenge to Europe; it is history's challenge to us all."[8]

Kissinger summarized the administration's disappointment accordingly: "We were much more deeply committed to the Year of Europe than to any initiative toward the Communist world. That is why we turned the other cheek to so many rebuffs."[9] And for Nixon, personally, it was obviously a double disappointment. For almost thirty years, since his introduction to Europe and its problems as a member of the Herter Committee, he had been deeply interested in and concerned with Europe. It must surely have hurt him to see benevolent American intentions disdained and discountenanced.

Kissinger analyzed the affair sourly: "The opposition to us was led by France in the person of Michel Jobert, supported by Heath and tolerated by Brandt for their own reasons.... We were serious about a reaffirmation of Atlantic solidarity. We were prepared to subordinate détente policy to the consensus of our allies. But not all our allies were ready for similar undertakings.... Some of our partners wanted us to slow down our détente efforts so that they could accelerate their own. France and Germany, eager as they were to circumscribe *our* freedom of action, were not prepared to pay in the coin of a coordinated Western policy."[10]

The first major diplomatic event of 1974 was the Washington Energy Conference in February. This saw yet another attempt, whose spokesman was again Jobert, to create a European club under French leadership in undisguised opposition to the United States. This effort by France confused most other North Atlantic allies and the American attempts to continue pressing for collaboration with Paris even alienated some friends of the U.S. And Jobert pursued his offensive by circulating a warning against "U.S.-Soviet condominium" (a steady phobia of the French ever since the Yalta conference of February 1945), and he sought to pursue a European-Arab dialogue in a way that Washington considered aimed at its own diplomacy.

The atmosphere, as far as Washington was concerned, changed in early spring 1974. First poor Pompidou died and Jobert was discarded. Then Brandt was replaced as German chancellor by Helmut Schmidt. And suddenly, that May, not three months before Nixon's disappearance from the scene, a brand new vibrant phase of Atlantic cooperation began.

Lacking a superpower accord on how to bring real peace to the Middle East, an apparently workable modus vivendi was put into effect after the 1973 Arab attack was thwarted by swift, massive, solitary reinforcement of Israel by U.S. weapons. And a new American strategy seemed to develop, acknowledging that the aims and methods of the two superpowers in that area were inherently opposed and recognizing as a basic fact that there could be no compromise with Moscow so long as it encouraged its Arab clients to seek maximal aims.

One embarrassment to the Nixon administration in connection with the Soviets was the congressional enactment of the Jackson-Vannik amendment refusing to accord most-favored-nation trading status with Russia until Moscow allowed more liberal emigration of its Jewish citizens. Nixon clearly saw the dangers of linking trade relationships, which had their own raison d'être, to the emigration question that, while humanitarian and accepted in the UN and Helsinki obligations, did without doubt impinge on the internal policy of a foreign country.

For reasons not entirely clear, as the Watergate maelstrom gathered fury in the spring of 1974, Moscow seemed to reduce its interest in East-West negotiations. On April 11, however, Gromyko, on a visit to Washington, told Nixon: "We in the Soviet leadership are most satisfied that you hold true to the line you have taken despite certain known difficulties [the polite phrase for Watergate]—which I don't want to go into—and we admire you on the human plane."[11]

It is strange for Americans to realize that apart from such reassuring personal messages from Moscow, Nixon's reputation in Western Europe also remained high, despite the failure of his Year of Europe gesture, because most leading European personalities tended to regard the Watergate affair as an effort by the president's adversaries to achieve a political coup, not an attempt to cripple the legal basis of the administration. Nixon derived some satisfaction from the knowledge of this sign of personal confidence in himself, above all by the Russians. In Moscow late that June the president told Brezhnev that the two superpowers had accomplished several improvements since the Mideast War:

> *They were possible because of a personal relationship that was established between the General Secretary and the President of the United States. And that personal relationship extends to the top officials in both of our governments. It has been said that any agreement is only as good as the will of the parties to keep it. Because of our personal relationship, there is no question about our will to keep these agreements and to make more where they are in our mutual interests.*[12]

This was a logical and respectable assurance, postulated on evident fact, but in the perfervid atmosphere of American public opinion and the political jungle, it had no effect whatsoever. Indeed, there were indications from the United States that many elements would have been worried by any dramatic achievement in the Soviet Union that might even slightly have glamorized Nixon and his evident diplomatic qualities.

Indeed, there is perhaps some suspicion that Nixon may have been more interested at that time in the appearance of more détente rather than its reality because of an obsessive desire by the Soviet leadership to isolate China and jointly to force it to accept a unilateral disarmament program.

The June–July 1974 Soviet-American summit appeared to be

the last occasion Nixon considered as possibly opportune in reversing his political decline. He had still proposed—and Brezhnev had accepted—a minisummit for later that same year. It was his hope that a dramatic new advance on disarmament could be achieved there, something that could have almost certainly improved his standing as a statesman. But he never had a chance. President Gerald Ford, his successor, abetted by Kissinger, whom he had inherited from Nixon, was able to register some success in arms limitation when he met Brezhnev for the first time in the autumn of 1974.

By that time, Nixon could but rest in the background of retirement on hard-won laurels garnered from a foreign policy that had proved brilliant in its own right but even more so during its last year and a half. During that final chapter of swan song, anything gained or saved for the United States position was achieved against the usual difficult odds abroad and against the passionate dislike of the president as a person by the nation which had voted him into office.

The fact that the electorate, feeling he had traduced its faith, now withheld its support had little effect on his astute and energetic efforts in foreign policy during a difficult period. This period included the extremely dangerous Middle Eastern war of 1973; Soviet attempts to gain control of the entire Arab world; and endeavors to withdraw U.S. forces from Indochina although unable to do so honorably and effectively because of congressional refusal to sustain protective and retributive threats against betrayal.

The endeavor to improve relations with Europe in 1973 was a flop, but it paved the way for a success not long thereafter. And relations with the USSR, never good, were if anything a bit better when Nixon was forced to resign than when he took office in 1969. On the whole, as the sound of his swan song faded away, he could look back on an administration whose successes in the foreign field had been striking and whose failures had been successfully limited.

And when he departed he had wisely added the role of secretary of state to Kissinger's responsibility, thus ensuring that the diplomatic neophyte Ford could carry on with a sage, experienced statesman at his right hand.

XVI

What Watergate Did to the World

By early 1973 the Watergate scandal had grown to such immense proportions that Nixon's position as an international statesman had been seriously weakened. A U.S. president whose term in office began to appear shaky was in no position to negotiate from strength and with confidence or even to devote as much time to foreign policy as was his desire and natural bent. Moreover there were rippling side effects, such as a temporary weakening of Kissinger's position.

By the time the first dismal shadows of the Watergate break-in and cover-up had started to darken the White House walls, Nixon had demonstrated a striking ability in the global cockpit of statesmanship. He had learned how to envision diverse long-range trends and problems and how to link them in a pattern so he could pragmatically encourage their development in ways favorable to peace and to the United States. He had also demonstrated his ability to get along with foreign leaders and to express his own views with clarity if not always with elegance. He was the first American president who had an activist *world* outlook that was based on demonstrative realities.

Wilson, another activist in the White House, failed to achieve his aim of American participation in the League of Nations he had envisioned and helped promote. His feeling for and concept of United States internal politics misled him. Also, his views were not nearly so global as those of Franklin Roosevelt and Nixon. He showed limited interest in Latin America or mainland Asia, apart from the Turkish Empire.

FDR's views were extended over a broader horizon. But he needlessly irked the French by refusing to deal with their resistance symbol, Charles de Gaulle, and his concept of the realities in China was deeply flawed, at least in part because of his admiration for Madame Chiang Kai-shek. Roosevelt never showed himself able to envision complexities of the interlinked destinies of peoples on the six inhabited continents, as did Nixon, and he often chose to follow bad advisers such as Joseph Davies on Soviet Russia and Patrick J. Hurley on China. But his support of China as such, not just one political faction, was amply justified in the end.

Nixon's more modest approach proved more successful. He chose excellent advisers on foreign policy, and he listened to them with receptive sagacity. In the latter respect he honored (although not consciously) the wise advice of Callières: "In diplomacy ... the best minds, the most sagacious and instructed of public servants should be appointed to the principal foreign posts regardless of the ... party attachments of the chosen ambassadors"—men like David Bruce and Ellsworth Bunker.

On May 23, 1973, I saw Kissinger in Paris, and he felt

> that Watergate would stimulate miscalculations in the Middle East and thus create an unexpected crisis there. The United States intended to conduct a "strong" foreign policy. Everything that will come up with Brezhnev has been discussed back and forth for a year. The deal with Moscow is the basic point of Nixon's foreign policy. The bias against India has served as a milestone on the way to Peking which, in turn, was necessary to get to Moscow with enough authority. That was the most important thing. But now relations with India are improving again. By autumn they should be good.
>
> Our foreign policy has been painfully built up so that now all the pieces are in place. We are at last in a position to reap the fruits. Now everything may be wrecked. There is

a masochistic effort to dismantle the executive power and this is being led by those very same liberals who used to wish to strengthen it under other presidents. This runs counter to the tide of current history and it will hurt our policy and world position more than Watergate.

Kissinger was exceedingly bitter about Watergate and seemed to think of it as some kind of demonic plot to destroy the foreign policy skein he had been so carefully weaving with his harassed boss, Nixon. At a dinner party my wife and I gave for Henry and the émigré Greek prime minister (later president) Constantine Caramanlis, Kissinger talked a great deal in front of all the guests (none of them American). He claimed the people being exposed (like Haldeman, Ehrlichman, and Dean, White House functionaries) were "small-town, middle-class politicians who were used to fixing municipal elections and thought they could do the same thing in the White House." "He failed," I noted in my diary, "to mention that Nixon had, after all, brought them in and let them run wild. Kissinger also said it was all right to lie for 'a great cause' but not for a small one."

I doubt if Nixon would have sent American troops to Vietnam had he been president instead of John F. Kennedy, when the first small detachments were dispatched; and I suspect he would never have built up their strength to the startling levels achieved under Lyndon B. Johnson. Nixon was keenly aware of the dangers to American power and prestige when small countries not contiguous or directly involved with the United States collapsed because he, like Truman and Eisenhower, thought it necessary to "contain" communist advances throughout the world. But, like Eisenhower and his secretary of state, John F. Dulles, he considered that financial and diplomatic aid to the French, when they were fighting the Vietminh (later Vietcong) Communists, was necessary to U.S. interests.

However, Eisenhower was firmly convinced that no American ground troops should be sent to help France out, and he vetoed all thought of a heavy air strike or nuclear bombardment in help of the French position when it first was desperately challenged at Dien Bien Phu. Nixon had great respect for Eisenhower and his military prestige.

Yet Nixon was never faced with the decision of whether to

send troops to Southeast Asia; they were already there in quantity by the time he entered the White House. He made it clear from the start that he wanted to withdraw as soon as conveniently possible, but he hoped to pull out American forces in stages while developing protective safeguards for them in "Vietnamization" of the war. And Vietnam, as an issue, proved its deadliness by becoming hopelessly entangled in Watergate, the cancer that ultimately destroyed the Nixon presidency. Vietnam was an inherited problem, but Watergate was wholly originated and conceived by Nixon's own White House, and the one became ultimately entangled with the other. Vietnam was not Nixon's fault and was essentially a foreign policy problem. Watergate, an internal affair, was his fault and before the illness had been fumigated after destroying its creator, it had intruded into diplomatic matters that should have had nothing to do with dirty, politically motivated crime.

The president had expanded the Southeast Asian war by ordering a bloody and unsuccessful ground and air invasion of Cambodia. Vietnam was in no sense Nixon's fault; Watergate was—entirely. As Stanley Karnow wrote:

> Nixon...was largely responsible for his own doom. The domestic opposition to the [Vietnam] conflict that grew during his first term in office exacerbated his sense of beleaguered isolation, prompting him to sanction the accumulation of offenses that became Watergate. His White House chief of staff, H. R. Haldeman, later wrote that "without the Vietnam war there would have been no Watergate"—asserting that Nixon might be "revered today" as a brilliant President had the scandal remained submerged. Given his record, however, Nixon seemed to be destined for disrepute. His political career began as it ended, with deliberate duplicity designed for one purpose: to win. "If you can't lie," he once confided to a friend, "you'll never go anywhere."[1]

I cannot, for one, vouch for the accuracy of the above statement, despite my respect for Karnow and his painstaking research. Another Karnow citation of Kissinger rings more true: "Vietnam is still with us. It had created doubts about American judgment, about American credibility, about American power—not only at home, but throughout the world. It has poisoned our domestic debate. So we paid an exorbitant price for the decisions that were made in good faith and for good purpose."[2]

In June and July 1986 both Nixon and Kissinger assured me that, had there been no Watergate affair, the U.S. cause in Vietnam would have triumphed. Apart from the fact that there *was* a Watergate affair and that the president misjudged its development in the United States as well as its impact on his foreign policy, I personally do not think the American and South Vietnamese cause could have won in the end. This is a pity, because it was not an evil cause, although many of those supporting it were far from admirable men, like the Diem brothers and Air Marshal Ky, for example.

Nevertheless, the U.S. program was not well conceived. Its political basis was weakly founded and led, and the military strategy, largely imposed by Washington, was outdated and not suited to a mass guerrilla conflict. American generals had too much confidence in modern weaponry and insufficient knowledge of a people's war of the sort originally codified by Mao Tse-tung. The combination of errors dependent on these facts would, I believe, have collapsed ultimately, even without a Watergate. Moreover, one cannot ignore the mounting popular discontent with the war in the United States long before Watergate assumed anything like the proportions it was to develop in the end. The mood generated by Kent State underlay and combined with the mood developed by a Watergate; in terms of popular opinion, the two were like a nuclear explosion.

Nixon asserted to me July 1, 1986:

Now, in terms of Vietnam I have always felt that had we survived, the peace agreement would have been carried out, because the North Vietnamese, after I had not only bombed them in May of 1972 but after the bombing of December 1972, knew I would not tolerate their continuing to violate the agreement.

The December bombing of 1972, they called it Christmas bombing, was the one that broke the deadlock and got them to agree. After, as a result of the Watergate business and the restrictions that the Congress imposed in the summer of '73, the War Powers Act meant that we could talk and warn them, but on the other hand not back up warnings.

The former president now insists:

It is significant to note that when I left office in August 1974 (we have to realize that the peace agreement was signed in '73 and for all the balance of '73 until August of '74 it held), the North Vietnamese had not taken a single provincial capital, but after that it collapsed. I am confident and I think Henry Kissinger has made this point. I would agree with him. Had Watergate not occurred, the peace agreement could have been sustained. In order to sustain it you had to have both public backing and the state. Now, incidentally, when I say both public support and the state, we were prepared to provide economic assistance to the North, Hanoi. But we couldn't get that through the Congress either. But, even more important, they didn't have any fear after I left office, they had no fear that there would be a reaction whatever they did. We paid a great price.

The Watergate scandal wrecked Nixon's very successful and brilliantly executed foreign policy in the Far East, although it seemed to have no effect on China where, thanks largely to Chou En-lai's wisdom, it was simply ignored. All Vietnam, Laos, and Cambodia were gobbled up by the Communist machine led by Hanoi. But the forecast of a successful "domino theory" dating back to the Eisenhower days fortunately proved illusory. Russia, which had strongly backed Hanoi even while negotiating with Washington, gained massive influence in the area south of China and west of the Philippines, where it developed the huge ex-American naval base at Camranh Bay. But so far this has not greatly shifted the balance of power existing in the Orient. The new Chinese-American friendship, for which history will credit Nixon's diplomacy, more than made up for the losses in Indochina.

In the Mediterranean another extremely important problem was surely exacerbated by Watergate. This involved Cyprus and its two belligerent allied neighbors, Turkey and Greece. The Turks invaded Cyprus and carved out a satellite state in its northeastern area, just at the very moment in August 1974 when Nixon was resigning and the inexperienced, unproved Gerald Ford was moving into the White House. Given the record of successful diplomacy the United States had displayed in the area since the Truman Doctrine of 1947 and including the forcible peacemaking of Lyndon Johnson, I believe it highly unlikely that the Greco-Turkish quarrel over Cyprus would have become so savage and enduring had a crisis not paralyzed the American government. Nixon said in 1986:

> *It happened, you recall, just before I left the White House. We were in Los Angeles at the time. I can remember a message came in. Henry was working on it at the time. We thought that we had cooled it to an extent. Here we had two allies, the Greeks and the Turks, and it was terribly difficult for us to line up for one against the other. And in the United States from a political standpoint you line up with Greeks because there are a lot more Greek-Americans than there are Turkish-Americans.*
>
> *But we had also to do what was right and have in mind the fact that Turkey has more divisions than any other country in NATO, and therefore it is a very important ally of the United States. I think I'd sum it up this way.*
>
> *Had I not at that time been involved in the last days of the Watergate situation, had I not been so involved I think that I would have been able, particularly with Henry Kissinger's brilliance as a negotiator, to exert the authority to make clear to our two allies that we were going to be honest brokers; and we would have played that role. I was unable to do it then and I think that it was very difficult for Ford to do it later because that was a time when, as Henry has put it, the executive authority was weakened. But I can't add to that.*
>
> *I would say Cyprus could have been handled more effectively if I had not been weakened by Watergate, but it came at the wrong time. It was too late in 1974. Henry did as much as he could, but we didn't have the leverage and it would have required great leverage, political leverage from the highest level. The Turks might have deliberately taken all this into account in their invasion. I wouldn't be surprised.*

Cyprus as an issue has not loomed large on the diplomatic horizon in recent years, although it is a constant sore spot. But if one could imagine a quiescent Cyprus, there would surely be a stronger NATO position, were Greece and Turkey to cool their quarrel. And Cyprus could be removed from its undesired role as a geographical fulcrum in the Middle East dispute and a route connecting terrorists from that area with chosen targets outside it.

Thus, although the Watergate scandal was essentially a purely American affair, linked by emotional fervor with the rising level of anti-Vietnam sentiment, it had important overseas effects in terms of Nixon's foreign policy. In China, Russia, and the Arab-Israeli conflict, this policy was however sufficiently effective and soundly based to shrug off the emotional syndromes caused by the presidental misdemeanor.

I've known Nixon for almost thirty years and took notes on many conversations I had with him during this period. I am surprised by his persistence and continuity on several basic themes and how some, like his emphasis on morality, bely Nixon's public reputation in the United States. He believes he strove to emulate the morality of his Quaker forebears and thought he was succeeding. The emotional American public thought differently.

Famous last words (Nixon to the author, Washington, March 8, 1971, in the White House):

I work here as if every day was going to be my last day. My theory is that you should never leave undone something that you will regret not having done when you had the power to do it.

Nothing is so remote as regret.

I have little doubt that North Vietnam's primary consideration in elaborating its crucial political and military strategy was postulated on a Watergate crisis in America. From the years of the Lyndon Johnson administration right through the Nixon years, Hanoi had shown diabolical cleverness in its ability to influence U.S. public opinion and congressional reliance on it to favor its military tactics in South Vietnam. It is arguable that even without Watergate, the Communists would have managed to seize control of the area Saigon ruled, but the contrary is also arguable, as by both Nixon and Kissinger. In the absence of a Hanoi triumph, the balance in Southeast Asia would be different from what it is today, with Laos, Cambodia, and all Vietnam firmly under Hanoi's domination. Moreover, the most valuable piece of Vietnamese real estate, Camranh Bay, would be in American, not Russian, hands.

But these are dubious assertions, and history is not written by "ifs." There is no gainsaying that Watergate seriously damaged the U.S. position abroad, and it was not until subsequent administrations took over the reins in Washington that foreign belief in American self-confidence returned.

The instant that Watergate became an irrevocable and disgraceful malady at the heart of Nixon's presidential power, Kissinger recognized the disastrous effect this was likely to have on U.S. foreign policy. He recalls that when Singapore's prime minister, the astute Lee Kuan Yew, came to Washington, it was solely to estimate the effect of Watergate. Lee observed: "You [America] are the anchor of the whole non-Communist world and because of righteous indignation this anchor is slithering in the mud."

Kissinger added the reflection: "This was the issue precisely. With every passing day Watergate was circumscribing our freedom of action. We were losing the ability to make credible commitments for we could no longer guarantee Congressional approval."[3]

It is difficult to assess the immediate and long-term effects of Watergate in terms of world affairs. Its immediate impact was puzzling and negative in many allied capitals, which feared the diminished strength of the United States as a global political factor; nor could most of them understand what seemed a minor peccadillo. The scandal's impact on our Vietnam position and its ultimate effect on Southeast Asia have been disastrous.

Nevertheless, the global repercussions of Watergate were surprisingly minimal. Nixon's great successes in foreign policy—the China relationship, the first strategic arms treaty, and the antiballistic missile pact with Russia—long outlasted the Watergate swamp. And the accomplishment of bringing an end to the 1973 Arab-Israeli war has continued uneasily into the present.

Watergate was thus a far less significant milestone in international history than in the United States itself. And the American system of constitutional democracy ultimately showed its powerful vigor in the way it shrugged off its anger and its embarrassment, recovering the vitality of its world position . . . for a time.

XVII

Summing Up

Roman doorways were guarded by the god Janus, who was given two faces to perform his duties, so he could look in two directions at once. Richard Nixon may be said to have a pair of faces. One peered at the outside world that had fascinated him since his youth. The other focused on the inner world of politics and its associated chicanery. The two belonged to the same man but presented contrasting outlooks.

It is difficult to think of the face representing the inner man whose personality appealed so much to the aloof General de Gaulle or the deeply suspicious Leonid Brezhnev and then, examining him from another angle, to see the man who became so vividly disliked by his own people, the Americans, within two years after they had overwhelmingly reelected him.

The extraordinary paradox of Nixon as a statesman is that his greatest success was in establishing a solid U.S. world position *despite* Watergate, perhaps the outstanding internal policy failure of any U.S. president. For as long as possible he avoided his own destruction by that affair, and while so doing he managed to impress himself and his country by favorable reactions overseas. In the terrible adversity he had produced, he thus, in a sense, triumphed in the field he most coveted, foreign policy.

Of all the important diplomatic areas covered by U.S. policy during the period of the rapidly growing scandal, it was in Europe that the U.S. was most hurt by Watergate and least in China. Yet now, thirteen years after his resignation from the presidency, Nixon's name is still widely respected abroad and, perhaps strangely, most of all in China and Russia. The wisest psychological explanation of this phenomenon is possibly that of Henry Kissinger, Nixon's closest associate because he was the expert on overseas relationships. The former secretary of state and national security adviser wrote in his memoirs:

> Nixon had set himself a goal beyond human capacity: to make himself over entirely; to create a new personality as if alone among all of mankind he could overcome his destiny. But the gods exacted a fearful price for this presumption. Nixon paid, first, the price of congenital insecurity. And ultimately he learned what the Greeks had known: that the worst punishment can be having one's wishes fulfilled too completely. Nixon had three goals: to win by the biggest electoral landslide in history; to be remembered as a peacemaker; and to be accepted by the "Establishment" as an equal. He achieved all these objectives at the end of 1972 and the beginning of 1973. And he lost them all two months later—partly because he had turned a dream into an obsession. On his way to success he had traveled on many roads, but he had found no place to stand, no haven, no solace, no inner peace. He never learned where his home was.[1]

It seems clear to me that Nixon applied more practical realism to his foreign policy, which was founded on traditional concepts of realpolitik than to his practice of internal politics. Both he and Kissinger had a tendency to blame Congress whenever anything went wrong with U.S. diplomatic plans. This was especially true with respect to Indochina. But a shrewder politician, for example Franklin Roosevelt, would have had a more perceptive finger on the national political pulse and almost certainly might have managed the potential conflicts between national political and international diplomatic affairs with a more adroit hand.

Nixon indeed displayed great skill on particular projects, for example his clever handling of China and its relationships with Russia; and he gained respect in both Peking and Moscow for his manner of doing this. He succeeded in employing the new U.S. relationship with the Chinese to establish a true balance of power of the sort first envisioned by the Medici prince, Lorenzo il Magnifico, to keep peace among rival Italian principalities in the fifteenth century. But Nixon's balance, which outlasted his own term as a statesman, was global and among superpowers and their coteries of supporters.

Having seen the way to dodging major wars, although unable to produce an acceptable peace in Indochina, Nixon had a logical and perceptive vision of the meaning of peace when it came to avoiding holocaust:

> *While war has become obsolete as an instrument of policy the tools of war must continue to play a role in keeping the peace. Military deterrence, including nuclear forces, is an essential component of any lasting peace. When each side holds an equally good hand, a potential aggressor is likely to keep both hands on the table.*
>
> *Real peace will not come from some magic formula that will suddenly and once and for all be "discovered," like the promised land of the holy grail. Real peace is a process—a continuing process for managing and containing conflict between competing nations, competing systems, and competing international ambitions. Peace is not an end to conflict but rather a means of living with conflict, and once established it requires constant attention or it will not survive.*[2]

Analyzing what could happen if his own formula were not followed, Nixon later claimed:

> *President Carter had tried to practice détente without deterrence. The results were a disaster. The Soviets expanded their domination in the Arabian Peninsula, in Southern Asia, in Africa, and in Latin America. The lesson is clear. We can influence Soviet policies but only if we recognize that they will react to our policies. If we*

block their advances, they will choose restraint and negotiate. If we give an inch, they will take a thousand miles.[3]

The key to Nixon's policy of seeking détente based on a balance of power specifically hoped to combine U.S. deterrence, deriving from a weapons superiority or at least equality, with the will to use this force if necessary. He considered this policy confirmed when he ordered the bombing of Hanoi and Haiphong, shortly before proceeding to Moscow to meet with Brezhnev, North Vietnam's strongest ally. Brezhnev accepted the U.S. move without demur and the summit talks proceeded well. But Nixon was forced to realize subsequently that when Congress refused him the funds necessary to help South Vietnam against Hanoi's violations of the Paris cease-fire accords; and still more, when the president's hands were to a large extent tied by the War Powers Act, that he had been deprived by the legislature of the power to deter if détente were violated. He insisted:

Our policy must combine deterrence with détente. Détente without deterrence leads to appeasement, and deterrence without détente leads to unnecessary confrontation and saps the will of Western peoples to support the arms budgets deterrence requires. Together, they will lead to the containment of and peaceful competition with the Soviet Union.[4]

Other features of his fundamental policy were: U.S. propaganda must be strengthened and Radio Free Europe and Radio Liberty should intensify broadcasts to Europe, Asia, and the Third World; America's economic strength must be bolstered; and Washington must make it plain that it was not prepared to accept the existing status quo, East or West. All these factors required acute analysis by Washington and a display of will and determination.

NATO should spend 4 percent more per annum to beef up its conventional forces while consolidating economic power together with Europe and Japan. Meanwhile, the U.S. must arm itself to the limit permitted by the SALT agreements and restore a peacetime draft. Peace can only be produced by such "hard-headed" détente. "It can only be grounded on mutual respect for each other's strength."[5]

Hard-headed détente is a combination of détente with deterrence. It is not an entente, which is an agreement between powers with common interests, nor is it a synonym for appeasement. It does not mean that the United States and the Soviet Union agree. *Rather it means that we profoundly* disagree. *It provides a means of peacefully resolving those disagreements that can be resolved, and of living with those that cannot....*

Putting it simply, both sides want peace—the United States because we believe in peace, the Soviets because they need it.

The time is ripe for a deal.[6]

One striking and persistent aspect of Nixon's character was his determinattion to keep learning. In this way, despite little initial advantage, he turned himself into a successful public speaker at an early age. Although he was by nature reclusive, he forced himself to participate in outgoing aspects of life such as playing golf and poker (the latter more successfully than the former). But in this exercise of what Kissinger discerned as creating "a new personality," the primary effort was intellectual. From an early education as a lawyer he delved into far-removed aspects of learning not within the ken of the normal Whittier College or Duke University student, with a particular emphasis on international affairs and political science. Thus we can find him writing:

More than 2,000 years ago the ancient Chinese strategist Sun Tzu set forth this principle: Engage with the ch'eng*—the ordinary, direct force—but win with the* ch'i*—the extraordinary, indirect force. In his wisdom he saw that the two are mutually reinforcing and that the way to victory is by the simultaneous use of both.*

In our time we have no choice but to engage with the ch'eng*—to counterpose our military strength to that of the Soviet Union, to hold our alliances together and increase the combined strength of the West. This is the way to avoid defeat; this is the way to contain Soviet advance. It is an essential first step, just as the tide has to stop coming in before it goes out. The next step—to go on toward victory, to win with the* ch'i*—is at once more complex, more subtle, and more demanding. Yet here again the West has the greatest advantages, if only we can marshal and use them.*[7]

Nixon's main problem was his inability to perceive the trends of public and political opinion in the United States—and in time he thus proved unable to reverse unfavorable trends in time. He saw clearly what was needed to accomplish his foreign policy aims but proved incapable of reversing unfavorable currents at home. This was particularly true with respect to the Vietnam War, where his attempts to make the nation's position more powerful were actually counterproductive. He recognized rightly:

We should never negotiate from weakness. No further arms control talks, for example, should be held until the United States has firmly in place a credible program for restoring the military balance, vis-à-vis the Soviets, across the board. Otherwise, the Soviet leaders will be looking down our throats. At the conference table we can only negotiate on the basis of what we and they are definitely going to have in the arsenal.[8]

The position assumed by Nixon from the very start on China marked his most effective and most brilliant single step in diplomacy, one whose results redounded globally and are still a major factor in world balances. Nixon was thoroughly consistent on this policy.

Part of the process that Kissinger percipiently assessed as "making himself over" began to appear in Nixon once he reached the White House. On May 19, 1969, he received me there and I observed in my diary: "I felt that Nixon was a much-changed, much-improved man since his vice-presidential days. He looked me straight in the eye several times for considerable lengths of time; none of his former shifty gaze. His eyes are very dark and penetrating. He expressed himself well and without hesitation, never fumbling for a word...he exudes strength and self-confidence plus a very visible air of sincerity."

I had just been in Vietnam and remarked on the contrast between growing Vietnamese armed strength "and the U.S.A., where there is intellectual anarchy and disruption. I thought his primordial problem was to organize enough public support in time to carry out his objectives but I wondered if he had the time." On rereading my diaries I am surprised to find I was sufficiently perceptive to see the critical problem so much ahead of time, about four years before it skyrocketed and burst. I have no idea whether Nixon agreed with me then or not, as I have no record of his comment on my observation.

The next time I saw the president, on one of my occasional returns to the United States, was February 26, 1970 (again in the White House). I noted:

> He has a system, he is experienced, and he has no enormous delusions of grandeur. Moreover, he seems determined, as he says, to stick by his 'conceptual' view of both national and foreign affairs....
>
> Nixon shows many nice qualities and has a thoughtful approach to his responsibilities.... Yet, on the whole, I think that he is perhaps over-confident and not really either tough or strong, much as he would like to be thought so. He also leans heavily on Kissinger's well-organized, intelligent brain.
>
> Talking about his presidential job, he said he had learned from Eisenhower that it was silly to read through and amend every single document presented to him for signature.... One could not waste time on such things. On the other hand, he made it a point to carefully study important documents or contemplate important appointments.

And, as for press statements and speeches, "Anything I have to say or write I want to be said or written by me." He tried also to keep things in orderly patterns and logical relationship to each other.

What do you do? Do you worry about each one as it comes up? Do you worry about the colonels as against Constantine in Greece? Or do you try and see a broad future pattern for the area? And, if you can work that out, doesn't it become much easier to get a relatively quicker answer to each local aspect of the problem as it arises?

He said he wanted to look ahead and lay the groundwork for a period long after he himself would be out of office.... He thought his job was primarily "conceptual" and long range and that he had to think of our diplomatic as well as our strategic position. If our European or Asian allies suddenly realized we had become a second-class power instead of a power at least on a parity with the other top powers, they would fall off immediately. We would no longer have options of war and peace. We wouldn't even have decent options on such things as the SALT negotiations.

It is perhaps paradoxical that Nixon, the only president threatened with impeachment for broadly "moral" reasons and the first to lose his job, should have spoken so often and so sincerely (like the good Quaker he was brought up to be) of "moral" issues in governance. An example of this came on March 8, 1971, when he told me:

We cannot dodge our responsibilities. We are not bent on conquest or on threatening others but we do have a nuclear umbrella that can protect others, above all the states to which we are allied or in which we have great national interest. This is the moral *force behind our position. We could be a terrible threat to the world if we were to lose that restraint or if we were to sacrifice our own power and allow ourselves to become too weak to uphold the weak.*

On May 14, 1969, he said:

The real moral crisis in this country is a "leadership crisis." The trouble is that the leaders, not the country as a whole, are weak and divided. By the leaders I mean the leaders of industry, the bankers, the newspapers. They are irresolute and ununderstanding. The people as a whole can be led back to some kind of consensus if only the leaders can take hold of themselves.

This paragraph makes strange reading when placed in another context with the Watergate crisis in mind and the words that were very widely written about President Nixon and his own "leadership" crisis, involving the vice president and the president himself.

Nixon seemed to grope subconsciously around this problem, a problem that had not yet developed but one that was fated to destroy him personally, although not what he hoped his foreign policy could achieve. Two years later (March 8, 1971) he told me in Washington:

The big question to my mind is: Will our Establishment and our people meet their responsibilities? Frankly, I have far more confidence in our people than in the Establishment. The people seem to see the problem in simple terms: "By golly, we have to do the right thing."

But the real problem, what worries me most, is: Will our Establishment see it that way? I am not talking about my critics but about a basic, strange sickness that appears to have spread among those who usually, in this country, can be expected to see clearly ahead into the future.

The thought of "moral" acts, "moral" fiber, a "moral" policy enters into my notes on a long series of conversations with Nixon on many matters and over many years. Thus, on May 19, 1969, talking of the Vietnam War, he told me:

We can't fold. A great nation sometimes has to act in a great way. Otherwise it destroys its own moral *fiber.*

À propos of Vietnam he said:

A great power like ours sometimes has to meet challenges elsewhere in the world.

Some people talk of a pax Americana, *but we have to stay with it.... We would destroy ourselves if we pulled out in a way that really wasn't* honorable.... *And the reaction would be terrible. I hate to think of it. It would be destructive to our own* morale.

It is interesting to note Nixon received more impressive support for a tough policy from foreign statesmen than he did from American politicians. Harold Macmillan, as British prime mnister, cautioned him on his way to Moscow: "Alliances (NATO) are held together by fear, not by love." In 1979, five years after Nixon left the White House, Helmut Schmidt, the German chancellor, said: "For many years now I have regarded balance of power as the indispensable precondition for peace."

What its author called the Nixon Doctrine was simply a repetition of the original Truman Doctrine, which in itself was a continuation of Roosevelt's latter-day policy of lending threatened nations a hose to put out the fire. As Nixon described his theorem:

The Nixon Doctrine provided that the United States would supply arms and assistance to nations threatened by aggression if they were willing to assume the primary responsibility for providing the manpower necessary for their defense.

Nixon's addition was that threats of aggression could be "internal or external." He supplemented his "doctrine" by proposing that "trade with the Russians must be used as a weapon, not as a gift,"[9] thus intimating that misbehavior by Moscow might penalize it economically.

Nixon was also insistent on differentiating between authoritarian and totalitarian governments, allowing a loophole of comparative analysis to degrees of oppression. Thus he would describe Shah Reza Pahlevi's rule in Iran as "authoritarian" as compared with Castro's in Cuba as "totalitarian." This is certainly a fine distinction and subject to varying interpretations attuned to considerations of the moment. For example, there might be sharp arguments about Nixon's definition of the Greek colonels' rule as authoritarian, as well as Pinochet's in Chile, and Kadar's in Hungary as totalitarian.

Nixon warned that efforts to contain the Sviet Union without détente are dangerous and also foolish because "it prevents us from taking advantage of the difference between the U.S.S.R. and China,"[10] which is not a wholly logical assumption. But he cautioned wisely that one should never tell the Soviet leaders what one will *not* do, because they might think you would do more than you actually could or would.

His Soviet policy was always based on the Churchillian adage that there is nothing the Russians more admire than strength. And in a speech delivered in Los Angeles on March 6,

1986, he also considered with justifiable pride: "The most significant geopolitical event in the last forty years was the Sino-Soviet split in 1961, which was followed by the American-Chinese rapprochement in 1972." He was rightly proud of the most dramatic foreign policy achievement of his own presidency, the binding of new diplomatic ties with China.

And, in order to gird itself for a more effective foreign policy, the United States, Nixon urges, should tighten up its economy and also should accept a peacetime military draft rather than relying on a wartime draft during a possible conflict brought about by inadequate strength leading to war. A volunteer army, he argues, was inadequate.

There is a perceptible consistency in Nixon's foreign policy approaches, but the one big lacuna in his application of these ideas was the inability to perceive what Vietnam was doing to American public reactions and a total ineptness in handling the Watergate scandal. The use of wiretaps to listen to confidences of other Americans was illegal, although the strictness of that embargo had been violated by Roosevelt, Kennedy, and Johnson before him. I am certain that neither Roosevelt nor Kennedy would have faced serious trouble had there been political complaints about bugging. But then, after all, there was no Vietnam under Roosevelt and only a faint sprout under Kennedy. Lyndon Johnson would have suffered quite as badly as Nixon had he fostered a political burglary comparable to the Watergate break-in. The tapes revealed that Nixon wanted to quash any innuendo that the CIA had been involved in the break-in (although Howard Hunt, one of these caught, had been with the CIA) and erase such thoughts for reasons of "political" concern, denying this was the fact (and therefore not illegal) although the opposite was true. All this appeared on a tape handed over to the Watergate prosecution on demand, a piece of evidence that was lawless but also idiotic.

The public and congressional mood would have been far less vindictive when faced with a foolish peccadillo like Watergate had it not been for the Vietnam swamp and its spinoff effects. These included widespread hostility in American universities and colleges, underscored by the tragic Kent State affair. Nixon wrote, and it is obvious he was correct in his analysis:

The Vietnam war has grotesquely distorted the debate over American foreign policy. The willingness to use power to defend national interests is the foundation of any effective foreign policy, but our ineptness in Vietnam led many Americans to question the wisdom of using our power at all. . . .

Thus did our Vietnam defeat tarnish our ideals, weaken our spirit, cripple our will, and turn us into a military giant and a diplomatic dwarf in a world in which the steadfast exercise of American power was needed more than ever before.[11]

On August 1, 1974, Nixon decided he had to resign. On August 8 he told Gerald Ford of this decision and asked him to keep Kissinger on as "indispensable." On August 9 he resigned. The request about Kissinger was one more testimonial to the fact that Nixon's fundamental concern was foreign policy and his view of the position of the United States in the world.

His major accomplishments in this realm were the selection of Kissinger as his principal diplomatic agent; the brilliantly staged reversal of U.S.–China policy with its global repercussions; the saving of Israel from the threat of disaster in 1973 and the subsequent establishment of a long-enduring Middle East armistice that led to Carter's Camp David agreement; and, strangely enough, undterred by Watergate, the ability until the bitter end to deal sagely, shrewdly, and effectively with the Soviet Union, above all on arms negotiations, leading to the Brezhnev-Ford accords of Vladivostok in autumn 1974 and Carter-Brezhnev in Vienna in 1975.

This is no negligible record for a man who was constantly harried as a consequence of his own mistakes and his shortcomings in sizing up the political mood and exaggerating the public support of his countrymen. I can think of no finer tribute to him than that of Henry Kissinger, his remarkable right-hand man who shared the conception and execution of his foreign policy achievements. Kissinger wrote a sympathetic, understanding portrait of his boss after both of them had departed from public office. The former secretary of state said:

> He was a great patriot; he deeply believed in America's mission to protect the world's security and freedom. He did

not blame the Vietnam war on his Democratic predecessors as he might have; he thought he owed it to the families of servicemen killed in Vietnam to affirm that their cause had been just. And he did believe that the cause was just. With all his tough-guy pretensions, what Nixon really wanted to be remembered for was his idealism. On his first day as President he had called for Woodrow Wilson's desk and he used it while he was in the Oval Office; a portrait of Wilson graced the Cabinet room....

What extraordinary vehicles destiny selects to accomplish its design. This man, so lonely in his hour of triumph, so ungenerous in some of his motivations, had navigated our nation through one of the most anguishing periods in its history. Not by nature courageous, he had steeled himself to conspicuous acts of rare courage. Not normally outgoing, he had forced himself to rally his people to its challenge. He had striven for a revolution in American foreign policy so that it would overcome the disastrous oscillations between overcommitment and isolation....He was alone in his moment of triumph on a pinnacle, that was soon to turn into a precipice. And yet with all his insecurities and flaws he had brought us by a tremendous act of will to an extraordinary moment when dreams and possibilities conjoined.[12]

Notes

CHAPTER V. CHILE—WAITING FOR JEFFERSON

1. Kissinger, *Years of Upheaval*, 375.
2. Kissinger, *White House Years*, 653.
3. Ibid., 683.
4. Davis, *The Last Two Years of Salvador Allende*, 328.
5. Ibid.
6. Colby, *Honorable Men*, 305.
7. Nixon, *The Real War*, 35.
8. Colby, *Honorable Men*.
9. Ibid., 380.
10. Kissinger, *Years of Upheaval*, 413.
11. Nixon, *The Real War*, 35.

CHAPTER VI. CHINESE CHECKERS

1. Nixon, *The Real War*, 137.
2. Ibid., 134.
3. Ibid., 134.
4. Nixon, *R.N.*, 578.
5. Nixon, *The Real War*, 211.
6. Ibid., 302–3.
7. Ibid., 291.
8. Kissinger, *Years of Upheaval*, 687.
9. Ibid., 690.

CHAPTER VII. THIRD WORLD PROBLEMS

1. Kissinger, *Years of Upheaval*, 1112.
2. Ibid., 593.
3. Ibid., 599.
4. Ibid., 606.
5. Ibid., 853.
6. Nixon, *No More Vietnams*, 181.
7. Nixon, *The Real War*, 118.
8. Ibid., 116–17.
9. Nixon, *No More Vietnams*, 165.
10. Ibid., 166.
11. Ibid., 20.

CHAPTER VIII. THE WATERGATE WAR

1. Kissinger, *Years of Upheaval*, 328.
2. Ibid., 324.
3. Ibid., 369.
4. Nixon, *The Real War*, 114–19.
5. Nixon, *R.N.*, 889.
6. Nixon, *No More Vietnams*, 13–18.
7. Ibid., 181, 160.
8. Kissinger, *White House Years*, 1200.
9. Ibid., 1359.
10. Nixon, *R.N.*, 889.

CHAPTER IX. CLIMAXES

1. Nixon, *R.N.*, 888–89.
2. Ibid., 1012.
3. Ibid., 1013.
4. Ibid., 1016.
5. Ibid., 1017.
6. Ibid., 1018.
7. Ibid., 1034.
8. Ibid., 1036.
9. Ibid., 1047.

CHAPTER X. THE INFERNAL TRIANGLE

1. Kissinger, *Years of Upheaval*, 1189–92.

2. Ibid.
3. Nixon, *The Real War*, 186.
4. Nixon, *R.N.*, 1047.

CHAPTER XI. NIXON AND GAULLISM

1. Kissinger, *Years of Upheaval*, 432.
2. Barber, *The Presidential Character*, 436.
3. Ibid., 425.
4. Kissinger, *Years of Upheaval*, 1000.
5. Ibid., 425.
6. Nixon, *Six Crises*, xiv–xv.
7. Ibid., xvi.
8. Ibid., 69.
9. Ibid., 213, 235.
10. Ibid., 228–29.
11. Nixon, *Leaders*, 41.
12. Ibid., 51, 54.
13. Barber, *The Presidential Character*, 233.
14. Ibid., 431.
15. Ibid., 439.
16. Nixon, *Leaders*, 78–79.
17. Ibid., 51.

CHAPTER XII. WHITE HOUSE VERSUS STATE DEPARTMENT

1. Kissinger, *White House Years*, 11.
2. Ibid., 29.
3. Ibid., 28.
4. Kissinger, *Years of Upheaval*, 4.
5. Ibid., 54.
6. Ibid., 415.
7. Ibid., xix.
8. Ibid., 81.
9. Ibid., 82.
10. Ibid., 88.
11. Ibid., 127.
12. Ibid., 327.
13. Kissinger, *Washington Post*, April 9, 1985.
14. Kissinger, *Years of Upheaval*, 416.
15. Ibid., 415.

CHAPTER XIII. SUPERSUMMITS

1. Nixon, *R.N.*, 204.
2. Kissinger, *White House Years*, 572.
3. Ibid., 413.
4. Nixon, *R.N.*, 618.
5. Ibid., 619.
6. Ibid., 619–20.
7. Kissinger, *Years of Upheaval*, 287.
8. Ibid., 300.
9. Nixon, *R.N.*, 942.
10. Ibid., 937.
11. Ibid., 1026.
12. Kissinger, *Years of Upheaval*, 300.
13. Ibid.
14. Nixon, *R.N.*, 1029.
15. Ibid., 1033.
16. Ibid., 1034.
17. Ibid., 1036.
18. Ibid., 1039.
19. Kissinger, *Years of Upheaval*, 263.
20. Ibid., 246.

CHAPTER XIV. NO YEAR OF EUROPE

1. Kissinger, *Years of Upheaval*, 174.
2. Jobert, *L'Autre Regard*, 287–90, 352, 381.
3. Kissinger, *Years of Upheaval*, 183.
4. Ibid., 188.
5. Ibid., 190–91.
6. Ibid.
7. Ibid., 239
8. Ibid., 240.
9. Ibid., 242, 243.
10. Ibid., 245, 246.
11. Nixon, *Real Peace*, 29.

CHAPTER XV. SWAN SONG

1. Nixon, *R.N.*, 374.
2. Kissinger, *Years of Upheaval*, 155.
3. Ibid., 160.
4. Ibid., 162.
5. Ibid., 932.
6. Ibid., 707.
7. Ibid., 720.
8. Ibid., 726.
9. Ibid., 729.
10. Ibid., 731.
11. Ibid., 1152.
12. Ibid., 1162.

CHAPTER XVI. WHAT WATERGATE DID TO THE WORLD

1. Karnow, *Vietnam: A History*, 577.
2. Ibid., 9.
3. Kissinger, *Years of Upheaval*, 125.

CHAPTER XVII. SUMMING UP

1. Kissinger, *Years of Upheaval*, 1186.
2. Nixon, *Real Peace*, 3.
3. Ibid., 29.
4. Ibid., 95.
5. Ibid., 16.
6. Ibid., 22, 23.
7. Nixon, *The Real War*, 300.
8. Ibid., 294.
9. Ibid., 201.
10. Ibid., 286.
11. Nixon, *No More Vietnams*.
12. Kissinger, *Years of Upheaval*, 1183, 1184.

Bibliography

Barber, James David. *The Presidential Character: Predicting Performance in the White House.* Englewood Cliffs, N.J.: Prentice-Hall, 1972.

Callières, F. de. *On the Manner of Negotiating with Princes.* Notre Dame, Indiana: University of Notre Dame Press, 1963.

Colby, William E. *Honorable Men. My Life in the CIA.* New York: Simon & Schuster, 1978.

Davis, Nathaniel. *The Last Two Years of Salvador Allende.* Ithaca, N.Y.: Cornell University Press, 1985.

Jobert, Michel. *L'Autre Regard.* Paris: Bernard Grasset, 1976.

Karnow, Stanley. *Vietnam: A History.* New York: Viking, 1983.

Kissinger, Henry. *White House Years.* Boston: Little, Brown, 1979.

———. *Years of Upheaval.* Boston: Little, Brown, 1982.

Nixon, Richard. *Six Crises.* Garden City, N.Y.: Doubleday, 1962.

———. *R.N.—The Memoirs of Richard Nixon.* New York: Grosset & Dunlap, 1978.

———. *The Real War.* New York: Warner Books, 1980.

———. *Leaders.* New York: Warner Books, 1982.

———. *Real Peace: Strategy for the West.* New York: Little, Brown, 1984.

———. *No More Vietnams.* New York: Arbor House, 1985.

Sulzberger, C.L. *An Age of Mediocrity.* New York: Macmillan, 1973.

———. *Postscript with a Chinese Accent.* New York: Macmillan, 1974.

Index